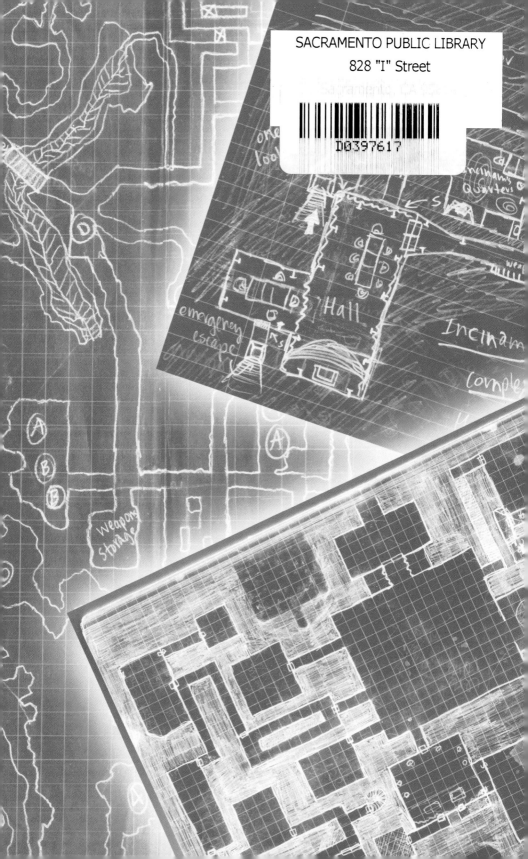

SACRAMENTO PUBLIC LIBRARY
828 "I" Street

D0397617

MORE ADVANCE PRAISE FOR *Fantasy Freaks and Gaming Geeks*

"This book—part memoir and part insider's guide—is both poignant and hilarious, baffling and informative, disturbing and entertaining. It is a must read for anyone whose idea of a good night involves dragons, spaceships, or one-eyed monsters dripping with slime."

—Jake Halpern, NPR Commentator
and author of *Fame Junkies*

"Ethan Gilsdorf's *Fantasy Freaks and Gaming Geeks* is alternately hilarious, surprising, poignant, and odd, but always utterly compelling. Beginning with his own teenage geekdom and addiction to Dungeons & Dragons, Gilsdorf transports us to the fantastical worlds of live-action role playing, Harry Potter tribute bands, creative anachronism, and *Lord of the Rings* tourism, reminding us that these substitute realities are not just amusements, but at times, life-savers. A must-read book for trolls, orcs, hobbits, or anyone interested in the quirky corners of popular culture."

—Dinty W. Moore, author of
The Accidental Buddhist and
Between Panic and Desire

"If you think fantasy culture is just a bunch of pimply-faced kids shouting about dragons in a finished basement, you haven't been paying attention. From wizard rock to chic French geeks, Gilsdorf catches you up on everything you need to know about the modern state of make-believe. And he does it with such humor, honesty, and, yes, cool, you'll almost wish you had an orc-slaying, princess-saving past of your own to suppress."

—Yael Goldstein Love,
author of *Overture:
A Novel* and *The Passion of Tasha Darsky*

"Intensely personal yet universally appealing, Gilsdorf's work speaks to the geek in all of us. *Fantasy Freaks and Gaming Geeks,* with its exploration of an emerging marginalized culture, rolls a natural 20."

—Larry D. Curtis, TheOneRing.net

"*Fantasy Freaks and Gaming Geeks* is a lively exploration of the fantasy realms into which boys and grown men retreat. Moms of teenage boys will find new insights about what makes these worlds so compelling as well as some encouraging stories about the friendships and communities they foster."

—Michelle Seaton, co-author of
*The Ways of Boys: Raising Healthy Boys in
a Challenging and Complex World*

"Unfortunately for the establishment, the geeks—like Frodo and Sam slipping into Mordor quietly and unobserved by the Dark Tower—have come out of the quiet and peace of the Shire, or the gaming dungeon, and merrily taken over a large portion of the world, as illustrated by this book. . . . Ethan Gilsdorf looks critically at gaming and fantasy and finds out how wonderful they can be for bringing people together across wage, ability, and ethnic divides, or from disparate places around the world, for developing imagination and creativity, and all in the name of fun! *Cogito Ergo Geek.*"

—Ian Collier, The Tolkien Society

"Vivid, moving, evocative, intriguing, engaging."

–Chris Castellani, author of
A Kiss from Maddalena and *The Saint of Lost Things*

FANTASY FREAKS AND GAMING GEEKS

AN EPIC QUEST FOR REALITY AMONG ROLE PLAYERS, ONLINE GAMERS, AND OTHER DWELLERS OF IMAGINARY REALMS

ETHAN GILSDORF

The Lyons Press
Guilford, Connecticut
An imprint of The Globe Pequot Press

To buy books in quantity for corporate use
or incentives, call **(800) 962–0973**
or e-mail **premiums@GlobePequot.com.**

Copyright © 2009 by Ethan Gilsdorf

ALL RIGHTS RESERVED. No part of this book may be reproduced or transmitted in any form by any means, electronic or mechanical, including photocopying and recording, or by any information storage and retrieval system, except as may be expressly permitted in writing from the publisher. Requests for permission should be addressed to The Globe Pequot Press, Attn: Rights and Permissions Department, P.O. Box 480, Guilford, CT 06437.

The Lyons Press is an imprint of The Globe Pequot Press.

Text designed by Sheryl P. Kober

Pages 310–311 are a continuation of the copyright page.

Library of Congress Cataloging-in-Publication Data
Gilsdorf, Ethan.
  Fantasy freaks and gaming geeks : epic quest for reality among role players, online gamers, and other dwellers of imaginary realms / Ethan Gilsdorf.
    p. cm.
  Includes index.
  ISBN 978-1-59921-480-1
  1. Internet games—Social aspects. 2. Fantasy games—Social aspects. 3. Virtual reality—Social aspects. 4. Online social networks. 5. Internet—Social aspects. I. Title.
  GV1469.15.G55 2008
  794.8'1—dc22
                    2009014047

Printed in the United States of America

10 9 8 7 6 5 4 3 2

Note: This book describes the author's participation in various events and reflects his opinions relating to those experiences. The people, activities, characters, avatars, and neuroses in this book are real. In some cases, names of people (and their characters or avatars) and other identifying details have been changed at the request of the individual—or because it seemed like the right thing to do.

For Sara Lynn Gilsdorf (1940–1997)
who could not escape

Contents

I am not now at all sure that the tendency to treat the whole thing as a kind of vast game is really good, cert. not for me, who find that kind of thing only too fatally attractive.

—J. R. R. Tolkien, writing to his publisher regarding his readers' requests for more background information on *The Lord of the Rings* (March 6, 1955)

[Dungeons & Dragons] is a game in which the continuing epic is the most meaningful portion. It becomes an entity in which at least some of the characters seem to be able to survive for an indefinite time, and the characters who have shorter spans of existence are linked one to the other by blood or purpose. These personae put up with the frustrations, the setbacks, and the tragedies because they aim for and can reasonably expect to achieve adventure, challenge, wealth, glory and more. If player characters are not of the same stamp as Conan, they also appreciate that they are in effect writing their own adventures and creating their own legends, not merely reliving those of someone else's creation. Yet because the player character is all-important, he or she must always—or nearly always—have a chance, no matter how small, a chance of somehow escaping what otherwise would be inevitable destruction. Many will not be able to do so, but the escapes of those who do are what the fabric of the game is created upon.

—*Advanced Dungeons & Dragons Dungeon Masters Guide* (1979)

The Momster

"Ethan! Eeeeeethan!"

I hear its screeching call. Its cry. Its need, booming off the peeled wallpaper, the woodstove, the sagging floorboards of the kitchen. What does it want this time?

"Eeeethan???"

Then, a door slam. It's escaped. It slides and scrapes from its lair. *Shhhh-thunk. Shhhh-thunk. Shhhh-thunk.* Right leg, then the left. Always that *thunk* of the left. I know it's coming, and I'm not ready. I'll never be ready.

It's the summer of 1979, I'm twelve, and my world is inhabited by monsters. A monster. My brother Adam, my sister Jess, and I, we call it—I mean, her—the Kitchen Dragon.

Whenever we enter the house, we must run the gauntlet. My secret trick is to find a way to get upstairs without her seeing me. Sensing me. I know it has tasks, requests, and questions. It's going to send me on an impossible quest: to do the dishes ("Don't break one or I'll dock your allowance!") or to the store, to buy more fire and smoke, more cigarettes. It's going to ask me about school, or *Playboy,* or blow jobs. Worse: it's going to wait till a friend gets here, and then it's going to quiz us, both of us, about all three.

Smoke trickles from her nose, seeking me out. She hobbles around like an extra in a horror movie: old hag, hunchback, trickster. Oblivious. Something there and not there. She lolls her head to the side. Her left arm is bent at the elbow, stuck fast at a right angle. Her hand is twisted, curled onto itself like a hook.

No one wants to face the Kitchen Dragon, this creature we've barely gotten accustomed to living with this past year. Mom.

My mother was thirty-eight when the Kitchen Dragon replaced her. Gone was the one who kept us clean, fed, and curious. The one who made us meatloaf, wheat-germ-and-yogurt smoothies, ratatouille. The one who taught me how to cross-country ski, plant pumpkins, develop black-and-white film in the dark, and swing a level baseball bat. Just like in a fairy tale, she is swapped. Spiteful goblins steal an unattended baby and switch it for a changeling of their own. Only this changeling, this doppelganger, is full-grown. My old mom disappeared a year ago. POOF! off to a hospital. Those sprites replaced her with the new mom, a stand-in bearing a nasty scar on the right side of her skull. Now she's out of the hospital and back home.

We also call her The Momster.

The Momster gets confused between the past, the future. The now is connected to both, or neither. What happened a decade ago—that happy, funny memory . . . say, the time as an infant

Sara Gilsdorf in 1974, as she appeared in her driver's license photo, four years before her aneurysm.

when I scaled a snowbank in my diapers and bare feet—is as accessible as yesterday. But the past of an hour ago—the toilet needing to be scrubbed or a cigarette needing to be lit—that's impossible to know for sure. She can't tell time. She doesn't even know the day of the week. Lucky if she knows the right year. Directions are meaningless. The left side—of her body, of the kitchen, of the world—has dropped off her map. Her brain got scrambled bad. Her seizures freak me out. She shouldn't even be drinking; when she does, booze messes with her meds and her speech slurs, she falls down, and has to be carried screaming out of restaurants. Only occasional glimmers of pre-illness Mom shine through.

Meanwhile, Adam, Jess, and I, we have to cut her food with a knife, help her into the bath, hike up her underpants.

DEFYING ALL RULES

Last night, the Momster threw buttered rolls during dinner. Not at anyone. Just at the television. Julia Child got a blob of butter right on her boob.

"Goddammit!" Mom screamed.

We couldn't decide whether to be horrified or find the episode hilarious.

"Har, har, har," she chimed in, her staccato laugh only half real. A forced cackle. We decided it was comic relief, and laughed, filing this little outburst under "Funny," or "J," as in "J for joke."

Mom poked at her food. Turned her head away. Then, with a cigarette wavering from the right corner of her mouth, its two-inch ash miraculously defying all rules of gravity, she rose, grabbed her cane in one claw, swung her left leg out before her like a boom on a ship, and walked away, oblivious, past the fireplace, the woodbox, and into the evening.

Shhhh-thunk. Shhhh-thunk. Shhhh-thunk.

I took a deep breath, someone wiped the butter off the TV, and we got back to dinner.

That night, the Kitchen Dragon stayed up late, as it often did, lying on its side in its lair, eyes Popeye-wide, stoned on television static, till 3:00 or 4:00 A.M., or later—way past *The Late Late Show*, beyond the badly dubbed movies and PBS mysteries and test patterns.

When she wakes the next morning at noon, her greasy black hair sticks up like a row of cornstalks. It's a Saturday. I'm home, unfortunately, but already trying to figure out an escape.

"Grmmmph," Mom says, looking up. "Can you help me?"

"Hey, Alfalfa," I say. One of our jokes. Har har.

Mom says, "Hey, smart-ass."

"That's a joke. 'J' for joke."

"I know," she ventures. Pause. "Gotcha." She pulls a cigarette out of her pocket. She's halfway up the stairs, good hand gripping the railing, and she's got the handle of her cane tucked in the back pocket of her brown corduroy pants. The hockey equipment attached to her left shin and ankle dangles halfway off. The Velcro straps of her sneakers aren't on tight. Still, mid-step, she manages to light the cigarette without falling over or tumbling down the stairs, and the morning coughing routine commences—a deep, black, guttural hacking that takes about ten minutes to work its way through her system. She looks up at me, mid-cough, and grimaces, then gets back to the business of climbing the stairs to the bathroom. Awful, rickety, wooden stairs in this shit-box, circa-1800s house my parents bought in 1966, the year I was born, that hasn't had an interior paint job since he left. Maybe longer.

Go ahead, fall, I find myself thinking.

"Be careful, Mom!" I say, my tone full of false concern, barely masking my annoyance.

Long pause. Always the long pause with her. The gears churning. The Rolodex flipping: names, words, faces. "OK . . . Adam."

"Mom, I'm Ethan."

"Right, Buster." And like a child still learning to climb a staircase, with slow, deliberate, drawn-out *Shhhh-thunks,* up the steps she ascends.

A KIND OF HALF-LIFE

My mother didn't fall—not then. Not till later. She didn't die. Not till later. But she didn't exactly live, either.

It was a kind of half-life that she endured after the brain aneurysm, or the "subarachnoid hemorrhage on the right," as her hospital record defined it. Right-brain damage caused crippling left-side paralysis, massive changes in behavior and personality, and dangerous bouts of epilepsy. The old Sara Gilsdorf—beautiful, vivacious, and fun—gone. No more athlete, artist, cook, photographer, teacher, doer. The free-spirited divorced mother who invited younger men home, read *The Joy of Sex,* hosted wild parties, pounded nails, and rallied our neighborhood for endless projects—international dinners, Bicentennial Parade floats, movie screenings on our front lawn—would never return. The center of my world had disappeared.

The new Mom: dead opposite. Shifty, sickly, needy, deformed, antisocial, frustrated, volatile, closed to the world. As if her dead left side—her useless left arm and half-useless left leg—absorbed all the good. Her aneurysm had become our aneurysm. She became the center of nothing I wanted.

The Gilsdorf family, after Sara's aneurysm, in front of their New Hampshire house. Left to right: Sara, Ethan, Jessica, and Adam.

I soon realized, The Momster was no damsel in distress. I couldn't save her. I couldn't tame her, either, not this beast. I longed for the goblins to swap this New Mom with the Old, to take back their spell, but the curse endured.

I want my mother back, I'd say to myself.

My wish wasn't granted. I was stuck with a mother I didn't know how to love.

Of course, even then, I knew none of this was her fault. Mom's friends and family all agreed what had befallen her was tragic, devastating, and plain lousy luck. As some doctor wrote in her medical file: "Unfortunate 38 year old ♀". But none of the condolences made it easier to remember or conjure up the old Mom, from that other, happier era. As we said now, "Before she got sick." Before our childhood went to shit.

SO MUCH I WANTED TO DO

Then, the summer before my eighth-grade year, the same year I was coming to understand the "new Mom," something wondrous happened. On a roiling June afternoon, I met JP, the new kid who'd moved across the street from me. JP showed me a clever trick—how to step away from my own body and mind, my family, and travel to places I'd never even seen. A way out.

"Ever play D&D?" JP asked, standing in my kitchen, eyes bright and magnified behind his extra-thick glasses. JP was a grade younger than me. He was quite short, frail-looking, but feisty and fast-talking. He wore a sling. He'd just broken his collarbone. Again.

"D&D? What's that—a board game?"

Rapid-fire, he explained the premise: "Dungeons & Dragons? It's not a normal board game. . . . Not like you've ever seen. . . . You play a character. . . . There's all these rules." He rummaged through his backpack and pulled out a pile of books. Then, he poured a sack of small, colorful objects onto the table. They looked like gemstones. "Check out these cool dice! . . . See, I'm the Dungeon Master. I create a scenario, an adventure, a world. I tell you about it. You tell me what your character wants to do."

"Character? What do you mean?" I asked. This kid was weird.

JP sighed. "OK, it goes like this." He thought for a moment. "Pretend you're in a dark woods. Up ahead on the path, you see a nasty-looking creature: seven feet tall, pointy ears, mouth full of black rotten teeth. It's wearing a ratty suit of chain mail and a helmet. 'Friend or foe?' it grumbles. Its fist tightens on the morning star in his hand, and it begins to heft it. Like this." JP looked around, and grabbed a frying pan off the stove. He swung it in the air. "What do you do?"

"What do I do?"

"It's an orc. What do you want to do?"

My crappy house faded around me. The peeling wallpaper, the mounds of dishes, the cigarette smoke, my mother's limp. All of it disappeared.

"Uh . . . " I stalled. I can do this, I thought. But I don't know what this game is. I don't even know what a morning star is. Or an orc.

"Uh, I'll attack? With my sword. Do I have a sword?"

JP rolled the dice. Squinting his eyes, he flipped through some books and papers and looked at a chart. "OK, your short sword strikes its shoulder. Black blood spurts out. It screams, 'Arrghhh!'" JP demonstrated, knocking himself backward against the wall. "You whack it for four hit points."

"Cool." I wanted to ask what a "hit point" was, but it didn't matter. I was hooked.

"Now the orc comes charging at you. He's really mad." JP bared his teeth and lumbered back and forth for effect. "*Now* what do you do?" he asked, a big grin spreading across his face.

What do I do?

There was so much I wanted to do.

Dungeons & Dragons is a fantastic, exciting and imaginative game of role playing for adults 12 years and up. Each player creates a character or characters who may be dwarves, elves, halflings or human fighting men, magic-users, pious clerics or wily thieves. The characters are then plunged into an adventure in a series of dungeons, tunnels, secret rooms and caverns run by another player: the referee, often called the Dungeon Master. The dungeons are filled with fearsome monsters, fabulous treasure and frightful perils. As the players engage in game after game their characters grow in power and ability: the magic users learn more magic spells, the thieves increase in cunning and ability, the fighting men, halflings, elves and dwarves, fight with more deadly accuracy and are harder to kill. Soon the adventurers are daring to go deeper and deeper into the dungeons on each game, battling more terrible monsters, and, of course, recovering bigger and more fabulous treasure! The game is limited only by the inventiveness and imagination of the players . . .

—From "Introduction" to the Dungeons & Dragons
Basic Set rule book (1977)

I Was a Teenage
Magic-User

I had other troubles beside my mother. For one, as an adolescent boy in small-town New Hampshire, I was mired in an anxious shadow land—bound on one border by a vague foreboding about an abnormal childhood, and on the other, as I left middle school, by President Reagan's menacing apocalyptic age of Evil Empires and nuclear Armageddon. Plus, the cruel hierarchies of Oyster River High School had stratified my classmates into layers as immutable as the Indian caste system. We had jocks; brains and nerds (often the sons and daughters of professors and professionals); untouchable grungies (the farm- and working-class kids); and the rest, unremarkable, invisible, and barely getting by. Me, I felt about as powerful as a three-foot hobbit on a basketball team.

But misfit boys need things to do together. I craved the camaraderie and fellowship that team sports denied me, minus the perils of a testosterone-charged locker room. Dungeons & Dragons was that collaborative refuge, outlet, and playing field. At that time, in the late seventies and early eighties, hobbies like reading swords-and-sorcery epics and playing these games were on the fringes of popular culture. Escapism—or, to be more accurate, fantasy escapism—was in its infancy, a scourge to Satan-fearing evangelists, but otherwise a minor fad, misunderstood and marginalized. For geeks only. That was me.

When people ask if I played sports in high school, I tell them I was on the varsity Dungeons & Dragons team, starting quarterback, four years in a row.* I can't speak for the other guys, but for me, RPGs (role-playing games) like D&D were empowering and exciting, and a clever antidote to the anonymity, monotony, and clique warfare of high school. In lieu of keg parties or soccer practice to vent our angst, we had D&D night. Who needs sports stardom when you can shoot fireballs from your fingertips?

I played every week, sometimes twice a week, from eighth grade to senior year. JP, my other neighborhood friend Mike, and I first played by ourselves, then found a peer group of other gamers: Bill K., Bill S., Bill C., Dean, Eric M., Eric H. and John. Some of us had endured plenty: Eric H.'s mom had died, John's dad had suffered a brain injury similar to my mom's, and JP was born with a disease that caused brittle bones, cataracts, and stunted growth. I think on some level we knew we didn't fit in. Perhaps we were weird. Girls were scarce commodities for us, and our group may have proved that tired cliché that outcasts, dweebs, and computer nerds couldn't handle reality, let alone get a date for the prom. But nothing stopped us from playing, and the popular kids didn't really care one way or the other. We were left alone to our own devices: maps, dice, rule books, and soda. It didn't take long before words like *halberd* and *basilisk* became part of my daily vocabulary. Like actors in a play, we role-played characters—human, Elvish, dwarven, halfling—who

---

* I was also president of the A/V club. And I memorized *Monty Python* sketches. And learned BASIC computer programming.

Part of the D&D gang, circa 1984. Left to right, top row: Ethan, John, Eric H., Bill S.; bottom row: Bill K., Eric M.

quickly became extensions of our better or more daring selves. We craved adventure and escape.

One of us would be the Dungeon Master (DM) for a few weeks or months. Games lasted that long. The DM was the theater director, the ref, the world-builder, the God. His preprepared maps and dungeons, stocked with monsters, riddles, and rewards, determined our path through dank tunnels and forbidding forests. Our real selves sat around a living room or basement table, scarfing down provisions like bowls of cheese doodles and generic-brand pizza. We outfitted our characters with broadswords, battle-axes, grappling hooks, and gold pieces. "In game," these characters memorized spells and collected treasure and magic items such as +2 long swords and Cloaks of Invisibility and Rods of Resurrection. Then, the adventure would begin. The DM would set the scene: often, we'd be a ragtag band of adventurers who'd met at the tavern and heard rumors of dungeons to explore and treasure to be had. Or some beast or sorcerer terrorizing the land needed to be slayed. Before too long, we'd enter some underground world. Our D&D sessions went something like this:

JP, as Dungeon Master (DM): The big stone door slams behind you. KA-BOOM! You're walking along a passageway, about a hundred feet long and ten feet wide. There is also a passageway going off to your left. Your torchlight is dim. It's quiet. You smell something foul. But about thirty feet ahead, straight ahead, there's a wider part, a cave. And you can see a small moving thing. A creature.

Ethan, as Elloron the human fighter: I go closer so I can see it. [He makes a map on a sheet of graph paper as the DM describes the space.]

John, as Malicus the half-elf magic-user: I do, too.

Bill K., as Virn the elf thief: I say, "Hello!"

DM: It's a little scaly creature with dark green skin. It picks up some rocks and starts throwing them. [DM rolls some dice.] A couple rocks bounce off your helmet, Malicus.

Malicus: "Ouch!" I yell, "Fuckhead. Who are you?"

Elloron: I ask, "Why are you throwing rocks at us?"

DM: It yells back, in the goblin tongue, "Foul enemy!" [The DM snarls for effect, doing his best impression of a goblin.]

Virn: Goblins!

DM: It starts to yell to something or someone behind it that you can't see, "Intruders! Quick! Get the bows!"

Virn: How fast could I get to the bastard? Is there a ledge? I'm a thief so I can climb. What do you think, Malicus? Elloron?

Malicus: Go for it, my good little thief! [John gets up from the table, and bows graciously.]

DM: There's no ledge. The wall is sheer. Besides, he sees you. You won't have surprise.

Elloron: Why don't you sneak down the side passage? Maybe it connects up. We can outflank it.

Virn: I'll sneak down the passage and be quiet about it.

DM: What's your dexterity?

Virn: Seventeen.

DM: OK. [He rolls some dice, hidden behind a screen.] OK, off you go. It doesn't look like he saw you. Do you have a torch?

Virn: Duh. I'm an elf. I have infravision.

DM: OK, OK. Meanwhile, more goblins appear in the cave and they're stringing their bows.

Malicus: How many are there?

DM: More than ten.

Virn: Virn readies his sling as he walks down the side passage. Where does it go? [Sometimes players speak in character, in first person, sometimes in third person.]

DM: The passage connects behind the goblins.

Virn: Cool. I'll sneak closer, then fire my sling.

Elloron: I fire my bow.

DM: Roll for initiative. [Everyone rolls dice; the DM asks what the players rolled.] OK, you strike first. Roll a d20 [pronounced "dee twenty"]. Both of you.

Elloron: Awesome! Eighteen!

5

Virn: I roll a four. Crap.

DM: Virn, you miss. Elloron, you hit. Roll d6 for damage.

Elloron: I get a six! [He jumps from his chair.] "Ha! Take that! [now in a French accent] You don't frighten us, you goblin pigdogs! I fart in your general direction!"

DM: Elloron, the one you hit screams and falls back, injured. Another goblin aims his bow and fires at Malicus. [DM rolls some dice.] He hits you in the arm.

Malicus: How bad?

DM: Four hit points. [Malicus scribbles with a pencil, subtracting four hit points from his character sheet.] How many hit points do you have left?

Malicus: Two. Crap.

DM: Malicus, you stumble to your knees. Then you all hear a rumble, and a blast of fire comes behind you. [DM rolls dice.]

Elloron: Wait—I thought the door was closed behind us!? What . . .

DM: Not anymore. It's open, and smoke and fire billow toward you. The fire just misses you, singeing your hair. Then a voice booms from behind you, "Who dares kill my henchmen?" [DM smiles.]

Malicus: Shit . . . We're surrounded. Uh, guys, what do we do?

Carry on this banter for six hours—the play-by-play melees, the stilted Monty Pythonesque dialogue, the DM's clunky narration—and you have some idea how I spent every Friday night from 5:00 P.M. until midnight, during my six-year diversion from, or into, a very curious adolescence. We solved puzzles, searched for secret doors, and found hidden passages. We parleyed with foes—goblins, trolls, harlots—and attacked only when necessary.

Or, wantonly, just to taste the imagined pleasure of a rough blade running through evil flesh. We racked up experience points. We test-drove a fiery life of pseudo-heroism, physical combat, and meaningful death. Whatever place the DM described, as far as we were concerned, it existed. Suspended jointly in our minds, it was all real. We were bards, jesters, and storytellers. We told each other riddles in the dark.

And each dungeon level would lead to the next one even deeper beneath the surface, full of more dangerous monsters, and even harder to leave.

AT LEAST THERE WAS A RULE BOOK

The joy in the game was not simply the anything-can-happen fantasy setting and the killing and pseudo-heroism, but also the rules. Hundreds of rules existed for every situation. Geeks and nerds love rules. D&D (and its sequel, AD&D, or Advanced Dungeons & Dragons) let us traffic in specialized knowledge found only in hardbound books with names like *Monster Manual* and *Dungeon Masters Guide*. As we played, we consulted charts, indices, tables, descriptions of attributes, lists of spells, causes and effects—like a school unto itself, filled with answers to questions about the rarity of magic items, crossing terrain, and how to survive poison. We loved to fight over the minutiae.* We could tell a mace from a morning star, a cudgel from a club, and we knew how to draw them. We knew a creature called a "wight" inflicted one to four hit points of damage when it attacked. Could we recharge wands? No. If I died, I could be resurrected, because, according to page 50 of the *Players Handbook,* a ninth-level cleric could raise a person who had been dead for no longer than nine days. "Note that the body of the

---

* Sample argument: Player: "What do you mean a gelatinous cube gets a plus on surprise?" DM: "It's invisible." Player: "But it's a ten foot cube of Jello! Let me see that . . ." Player grabs *Monster Manual* from DM. Twenty minute argument ensues.

person must be whole, or otherwise missing parts will still be missing when the person is brought back to life." All good stuff to know. The trolls and fireballs may be fanciful, but they have to behave according to a logical system.

Like in life, fantasy rules were affected by chance—the roll of the dice. And, as if they were jewels, we collected bags of them: plastic, polyhedral game dice, four-, six-, eight-, ten-, twelve-, and twenty-sided baubles that, like I Ching sticks or coins, foretold our fortunes when cast. A spinning die, such as the icosahedral "d20," could land on "20" ("A hit! You slice the lizard man's head off and green blood spurts everywhere!") as often as "1" ("Miss! Your sword swings wide and you stab yourself. Loser!").

The world my mother's illness left in its wake was unpredictable and emotionally unsafe. My parents had divorced six years before the aneurysm, and my father and stepmother, six hours away in Canada, couldn't offer much by way of daily guidance or supervision. My mother couldn't cook dinner or drive a car, so how could she possibly raise three teenagers? A good friend of my mother's named Alice agreed to move in with my family when my mom returned from the hospital. Over the years, a steady stream of my mother's other friends and Alice's relatives, coming and going, would pitch in to help. The role of "parent" was played by a cast of characters. But above all, Alice carried the weight. She ended up staying and caring for us, and my mother, until my siblings and I left for college. To cope with our home life, my sister chose class presidency, popularity, and sports. My brother found after-school work to keep him out of the house. I disappeared into my mind.

The lesson? Real life thus far had taught me that in the adult world, fate was chaotic and uncertain. Guidelines for success were arbitrary. But in the world of D&D, at least there was a rule book. We knew what we needed to roll to succeed or survive. The finer points of its rules and the possibility of predicting outcomes offered comfort. Make-believe as they were, the skirmishes and puzzle-solving endemic to D&D had immediate and palpable consequences. By role-playing, we were in control, and our characters—be they thieves, magic-users, paladins, or druids—wandered through places of danger, their destinies, ostensibly, within our grasp.

At the same time, we understood that our characters' failures and triumphs were decided by unknown forces, malevolent or kindly. Such was the double-edged quality of our fantasy life, where random cruelty or unexpected fortune ruled the day. The game was a risk-free milieu for doing adult things. It was also a relief to live life in another skin, and act out behind the safety of pumped-up attributes. D&D characters had statistics in six key areas: strength, intelligence, wisdom, dexterity, constitution, and charisma. These ranged from three to eighteen. Ethan the real boy's stats would have been all under 10; his fighter character Elloron's were all sixteens, seventeens, and eighteens.

Each DM had his world (and the DM was mostly a "he"; we had interest from a couple of itinerant girl players, but they never lasted long). As long as we agreed to keep playing in that DM's world and "campaign," his version of the law ruled. If I was the game master, I had ultimate power, even over chance. I loved DMing the most. I could overrule a bad die-roll, settle arguments, and dictate the fates of my friends. I got to make maps, draw dungeons, and design worlds. The universe seemed limitless.

When we mastered basic rules, we graduated to more advanced sets. When we disagreed with the rule books, we made up fresh ones: tweaks, amendments, entire combat systems, even inventing new games. When we got bored with standard monsters like the orc, goblin, and dragon, we invented more: the leem, the quizer, explosive larvae. Tired of role-playing characters in medieval-and-magic scenarios, we moved to outer space, then to the Wild West, or James Bondesque espionage land, or a post-nuclear-holocaust landscape haunted by mutant rabbits and

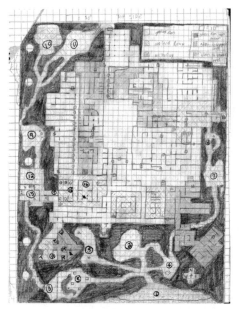

One of the author's D&D dungeons, drawn in pencil on the game's ubiquitous graph paper.

shards of past civilizations. In some ways, the worlds I created felt more genuine than the classroom, the mall, the Paris museums I learned about in French class.

It's no accident that the year I found D&D, or it found me, coincided with my mother's return from the hospital. It took courage for a teenage boy to deal with the Momster—more courage than I could usually muster. I couldn't face down the creature that plagued my own village and house. It was far easier to turn away—to think about imaginary battles than the real one waged within my family's four walls. To go underground.

Before I got into Dungeons & Dragons, I made Super 8mm animated shorts involving clay monsters that swallowed towns. I was a charter member of the *Star Wars* Fan Club. I shouted Bugs Bunny routines ("I will do it with my spear and magic helmet!"). I wanted to be a cartoonist for the *Boston Globe* and an animator for Disney. I wrote novels on an old typewriter. Already a storyteller, D&D was a logical imaginative leap.

I also jumped to reading J. R. R. Tolkien. D&D's swords-and-sorcery realm seemed as rich as Tolkien's Middle-earth, his elaborately mapped and populated setting for *The Hobbit* and *The Lord of the Rings,* and his various poems, legends, and lost tales. I didn't believe in God, or in heaven and hell. But Middle-earth's lands, or a D&D labyrinth, or a science fiction universe like *Star Wars*—those were places I could believe in, and visit as often as I liked. D&D's subterranean domain welcomed me; high school dances and locker rooms did not. Already the consummate dreamer, I was the perfect candidate for escape.

I LEFT THOSE DREAMY MEDIEVAL WORLDS BEHIND

Dungeons & Dragons began to die for me when, during my senior year in high school, 1983, I had my first kiss. My then-girlfriend's highly realistic look and feel banished those fantasy leather-clad, busty she-warriors for good. That first love was serious. With something else to do on Friday nights, and a female creature to do it with, I played D&D less and less often. High school led to other kingdoms, such as college, sex, beer, cars, jobs, travel, and heartbreak. The D&D gang dispersed from New Hampshire to Pennsylvania, New York, Chicago, and Alaska. I left those dreamy medieval worlds behind and mostly forgot about my role-playing years. They dissipated, and the netherworld released its grip, like a wizard dispelling a curse. I let my D&D obsession fade—not because my longing to role-play had ceased, but because, perhaps, I sensed I was through with childish things. I had gone on one adventure too many. If D&D was a rite of passage, then I had passed through the dungeon to become a young man.

Although I finally stopped playing D&D and other RPGs (role-playing games) just before college, over the years, I would check to see how my precious fantasy pastime had evolved. Secretly, without telling anyone, especially my girlfriends, I'd stalk gaming stores and peruse shelves of new rule books and games to see what had been published since I had last played. I'd handle packages of metal figurines. I'd loiter in video arcades. I'd study newfangled card games like Magic: The Gathering. As I entered my twenties and thirties, I noticed a fantasy entertainment industry that had gradually grown more massive and more socially acceptable than when I was part of it. Occasionally, I lamented over what I might be missing as the subculture moved on without me. I missed it. I shoved away something that had been important to me. Despite being tempted, I decided I would never seriously play D&D, or immerse myself in any fantasy environment, ever again.

As for my mother, I never got her back. She survived for nineteen years after her aneurysm, heroically, one might say, if somewhat oblivious to her condition. She lived in a nursing home for a decade, bored to death and suffering. I would visit her, sometimes regularly, sometimes not. On good days with her, when I'd let my guard down, I'd glimpse more of the old Mom. I'd try to shake the Momster role I'd put her in, and try to play not bitter caregiver, but normal son. After a long, slow decline, she passed away in 1997. She had lived though my high school years, and college, and early adulthood, until I was thirty-one. As the years passed after her death, my mother remained a presence—an unresolved foe, a spectral companion, a lost fortune. I often felt she had left me in the forest, alone on the cusp of an impossible quest. Like all wannabe heroes, I expected pat answers and satisfying victories. But none came. Dealing with Mom had been its own rite of passage, too, and I had rolled the dice and proceeded, somewhat stunned, through each level of adulthood.

Then, a "Huh?" moment. When Peter Jackson's *Lord of the Rings* movies came out in three successive years (*The Fellowship of the Ring* in 2001, *The Two Towers* in 2002, and *The Return of the King* in 2003), I got sucked in. I loved the films. I tracked gossip on popular fandom sites like TheOneRing.net and watched the online movie trailers repeatedly. *Rings* fever had spread everywhere, even to Paris, where I was living at the time. I visited French collectible shops whose windows were crammed with *Le Seigneur des Anneaux* (what the French call *The Lord of the Rings*) action figures. I had recurring dreams of visiting the filming locations in New Zealand, where I had never been, meeting Peter Jackson, and wearing an orc mask as an extra during the shooting of a battle scene.

This made no sense. Perhaps my fantasy obsession was more unresolved than I'd let myself admit. I found myself battling an uncontrollable urge to collect the entire set of *Anneaux* figurines, which came inside Kinder Surprise chocolate eggs. I purchased more than a dozen—a whole freaking fellowship of them—and cracked them open, hoping, as the TV ad says, to "collect them all!" Oddly, I had no qualms about being part of this worldwide pop-culture phenomenon. It

One of the many maps of worlds that the author created in the early 1980s.

was impulses like mine that merchandisers were preying upon, to the tune of millions of dollars. Of course, candy eggs are one thing; a $299.99 "Glamdring Foe-hammer" reproduction of the prop sword used by Gandalf in the movies was another. I would only let my collectibles phase go so far.

On my cluttered desk I had erected a shrine for my two-inch-high Fellowship. There was Sam Gamgee, Merry and Pippin, the ethereal Galadriel, and Frodo, who, despite my warnings—"No, Frodon (his French name), put it away!"—insisted on constantly brandishing his Ring of Power. Given to me by a friend, the most recent addition was the elf, Legolas. He stood with his quiver of arrows, guarding the telephone against the Nazgûl. My minor show of fealty gave me a sense of belonging. But also longing: I so wished for Gandalf, Gimli, and Aragorn to join the rest of this miniature, plastic band of heroes. And a tiny me had wanted to join them, too.

But I was a grown-up, right? I was over D&D and everything it represented. Picturing that imaginary self again, wandering through dungeons and hacking at goblins, didn't seem attractive. The image was pathetic. There was no way I was going to let anyone psychically scrawl GEEK on my forehead ever again. I was no longer a gawky, teenaged, introverted, antisocial, afraid-of-girls-and-drinking-games, role-playing, fantasy-realm-dwelling fanboy.

Right.

THE BLUE COOLER BEGINS TO SPEAK

Back in the day, Dungeons & Dragons was a pencil-and-paper game. Serious players amassed towers of books, papers, maps, and accessories. When I stopped playing, the various boxes and piles sat in my childhood bedroom closet in New Hampshire. After high school, even though I said I was done playing the game, the D&D gear came with me, eventually ending up in my first post-college apartment in western Massachusetts, which I shared with JP. I moved a lot in my early twenties and thirties. At some point, the D&D gear had disappeared.

One Christmas, after I'd moved back from France, I visited my father and stepmother in Ontario. I was looking in their basement for some of my things and BAM! there it was: my D&D gear, inside (of all places) a big blue Coleman camping cooler. I didn't remember storing it there. Perhaps someone else did it, some evil servant bent on reminding me of my hard-core days as a role-playing aficionado (or addict), or, as my sister still likes to say, affectionately, "freak." My trove of D&D paraphernalia had returned, unbidden.*

---

* Just like the scene in *The Lord of the Rings* where Gandalf the wizard explains to Frodo how the One Ring resurfaced: "The Ring is trying to get back to its master," he says. "It wants to be found." Much in real life has its *Rings* counterpart.

Crouching in the basement, I cracked the lid. I haphazardly pawed through its contents: a stack of sunken, mold-ridden game boxes, notebooks, and books. I sneezed—several times—then closed the lid. Without thinking what plot I might be setting into motion, I hefted the cooler—about twenty-five pounds—lugged it up the basement steps, loaded it into my rental car, and brought it back to Boston.

The cooler sat in my closet, a hard-plastic, thirty-six-quart Pandora's Box that by all rights should have been filled with cold beer, not the darkness of dungeons past. I found myself drawn to steal a glance at my gaming gear once more. I knew it was, in Gollum's words, *preccciousss* to me.

But I resisted the blue cooler. For a while.

The call to adventure signifies that destiny has summoned the hero and transferred his spiritual center of gravity from within the pale of this society to a zone unknown. This fateful region of both treasure and danger may be variously represented: as a distant land, a forest, a kingdom underground, beneath the waves or above the sky, a secret island, lofty mountaintop, or profound dream state; but it is always a place of strangely fluid and polymorphous beings, unimaginable torments, superhuman deeds, and impossible delights.

—Joseph Campbell, *The Hero with a Thousand Faces* (1949)

The Quest Begins

A year or so after rediscovering the blue cooler, I took stock of my so-called adulthood. The time had come.

One, I had a new love that was veering into the serious. But we both had doubts. Mine: Was I ready for commitment, cohabitation, and fatherhood? Hers: Who was this guy who seemed, at times, only half present? Half man, half boy. Were his mental wanderings—not to mention his hesitations about owning a car, getting a nine-to-five job, making good money, and siring children—all larger symptoms of some refusal to grow up?

I recall a watershed moment. My girlfriend and I, we're together. And I'm wearing chain mail. My +2 long sword is clanging at my side. I'm dashing through the underbrush, cape flapping behind me, horns and kettle drums punctuating my steps. DUM . . . DUH-DUH-DUM . . . DUH-DA-DA!

"Honey?" She raises an eyebrow. "Any luck?"

No time for questions! I draw my sword. "One does not simply walk into Mordor," I announce. "Its Black Gates are guarded by more than just orcs. There is evil there that does not sleep, and the Great Eye is ever watchful."

She rolls her eyes. "Ethan, please . . . Just find the car, OK?"

I march onward. I'm hunting orc. I'm hunting . . . Wait—I'm in the parking lot. I'm hunting . . . for her car. All in my mind. My reverie evaporates into asphalt, waves of heat, and rows of metallic beasts.

Then, about six months into our romance, I turned forty. I drank five too many tequila shots and spent the first night of middle age clutching my stomach and moaning in my girlfriend's parents' bathroom. The Middle Ages. Ha.

Forty was suddenly not sitting easy. The seeds of doubt had been planted in our relationship. She: Did Ethan live on Planet Adulthood? Me: Would I continue to escape? I realized I was now older than my mother was when the aneurysm cut her down. And then the blue cooler—I swear it was calling to me, until I couldn't ignore it any longer. It had appeared just as a midlife crisis started to hit. I had the sense that the D&D gear would somehow solve the riddle of who I was, where I had come from, and why I still needed imaginary realms. And maybe help me understand what I still had left to accomplish.

The contents of the blue cooler had saved me once. Could they save me again?

AT A DISTANCE FOR A REASON

I dragged the cooler from the closet. There it sat on the floor beside my desk. I took a breath, and popped open the lid.

Inside, a dragon's treasure. I rummaged through the piles. Hundreds of handwritten pages describing places, plots, and characters I'd created, named, and once knew quite well. Notebooks plastered with cartoons of dragons and warriors. Games whose flimsy cardboard boxes had half collapsed under weight and time.

Official D&D tables, charts, and other accessories. Rule books dutifully covered and protected, like all precious tomes, with brown-paper shopping bags. Pocket folders and three-ring binders, some filled with character sheets, some with typed drafts of my own *Lord of the Rings* rip-offs.* A gray felt bag of dice. And enough hand-drawn maps of far-away lands and dungeons to fill an atlas.

The author's D&D gear: dice, rule books and other papers, with the blue cooler in the background.

Before me, after all these long years, the backdrop for my heroic stories and imaginary derring-do: the Craggy Hills, the Untreaded Lands, the Lorsearch Plains. I looked closely at mountains called Ramen-Nashew that I'd painstakingly scribed, and Elfwood, the forest I had planted with my pencil tip. Here, an evil wizard's lair. There, an underground labyrinth guarded by traps and monsters, with rooms numbered from 1 to 37, which I had drawn on graph paper. And Elloron, my old friend, my old self, now just a sheet of gold paper. These game scenarios and imaginary lands were coming back to me. This D&D gear had once represented more than a teenaged pastime. It had been my world.

At first I only felt a wave of nostalgia for my old gaming days. I was pumped to revisit that time, even if I sensed a familiar *clunk* in my gut. A cocktail of feelings. The gear felt like a box of evidence

---

* Actual sample text: "It was a time of despair in the land of Rothian. The townsfolk were uprising [sic] and the men from Drean were invading from the north, in the Forgotten Land. . . ."

at my own trial. I had found not simply a road map to my adolescent wanderings, circa 1978 through 1984; this was a personal archive of escape. The scribbled sheets revealed an insecure adolescent trying to prognosticate something better. A desperate kid. The more I reflected, the more I worried about the residual damage. How healthy was it to have devoted so much mental energy to a world that didn't exist? Had we checked out of real life? What were the long-term effects? Did fantasy escapism explain why the person I'd become at forty now felt unsatisfying, and unsatisfied?

When I tell the story of my life, I often say (in what feels like a rehearsed speech) that D&D taught me vocabulary and verbal skills, math, statistics, and how to read maps; it developed my interest in history, flexed my imagination, and schooled me in team-building, personal expression, and interaction with others. I would always say, "Yes, I was a geek, but on balance, D&D was a good thing." And, I told myself, I wouldn't be ashamed to teach my own kids (if I ever had any) how to play. But did I really believe that? The game and other Tolkienesque fantasy worlds had bewitched me in moments of weakness. They had consumed my teenage years. My friends and I were obsessed by the drama and sucked in by the power. Poring over the contents of the blue cooler raised further fears. If the adult me was so "over it," why did I still want to reread *The Hobbit* and *The Chronicles of Narnia*? Why had I recently enrolled in a "world-building" workshop, given by a local science fiction writer? Why, when a video game called *Lord of the Rings: Conquest* promised to let me "play out all [my] darkest fantasies" in Middle-earth—allowing me to assume the form of a fearsome Balrog wielding a fire sword, sack The Shire, and destroy Rivendell—was I so eager to play? I was assailed with self-doubt. The interest still lingered. What was wrong with me?

I knew that since my teenage years, I had kept role-playing games and similar activities at a distance for a reason. I just didn't quite know what that reason was.

Those Kinder Surprise miniatures were the first warning shot. They had tempted me to throw myself wholeheartedly back into fantasy. But I kept that desire at bay by worries: that I'd enjoy the loss of self and responsibility too much; that the unreal would become more engaging than the real; and that my dormant freakishness—expressed as giddy, unselfconscious geekspeak about light sabers or hit dice—could bubble to the surface and erupt at any time—at a job interview, at a party, or on a date. Perhaps I couldn't admit to myself that I still needed the escapist crutch of a fantasy life to hobble through the real world. Or possibly, that I would allow RPGs to consume my life again, intentionally or subconsciously in an unspoken act of self-sabotage, so that no time or energy or mental space would remain to solve my real-life problems. Or was it simply some nameless dread about being stuck in Geekland forever?

Whatever the explanation, flipping through my old *Dungeon Masters Guide*—its charts and tables for "Thief Abilities," "Turning Undead," and "Morale Failure"—suddenly felt not only dangerous, but filled with a sense of foreboding. Here I was, more than two decades after quitting D&D and becoming a man, but susceptible to the fantasy bug. Not immune.

Too many questions remained, so I began looking for answers. A quest was a-brewin'.

21ST CENTURY GEEKDOM

I knew that the perception of fantasy hobbies had changed since I was a card-carrying member of the D&D tribe. Today, *geek* is no longer a four-letter word. Fantasy subcultures have shifted from the fringe to pockets of cool, and their associated terminology and cultural references—Gandalf, leveling up, griefing—have been absorbed into the mainstream. Playing fantasy games, reading fantasy books, and watching fantasy movies are infinitely more permissible now than when I was exploring dungeons in rural New Hampshire. Eleven and a half million (and counting) subscribers to World of Warcraft (WoW), and their spouses, attest to that, as does the international literary phenomenon called *Harry Potter.* Adult men and women own Xbox and PlayStation consoles, and arrange Yoda and R2-D2 Pez dispensers on their computer monitors. Online worlds like Second Life have made role-playing second nature and a widely acceptable behavior. Even Muggles understand it.

Sigh of relief. At least I'm in good company. Millions now turn away from the "real" world to inhabit others. But just because it seemed like everyone was headed to a Renaissance fair or was hooked on Nintendo Wii or Warhammer didn't mean all these neo-medieval or magical-themed options were necessarily *good* for you. Fantasy as a cultural phenomenon felt vaguely unsettling to me. I wondered if pervasive escapism had infantilized an entire generation. Was fantasy in all its forms fundamentally good or evil? Were some subcultures more doomed than others? Deep thoughts.

Perhaps nobody else spent time pondering these matters. Or maybe I just wanted to reassure myself that I wasn't any more of a freak than they were.

Whatever the reason, as a recovering D&Der playing the role of a so-called "grown-up" arts and travel writer for national newspapers and magazines, I started to take on any assignment I could find that would let me write professionally about Tolkien, gaming, or fantasy. I embarked on a nonlinear, noncontiguous odyssey of self-reflection, cultural analysis, and free mead. I needed to put myself face-to-face with these escapist pursuits. Before, as a kid, my D&D obsession was a haphazard consequence, a symptom of being lost. I was oblivious. This time, I would get lost on purpose. I wouldn't be escaping again; I would be excavating. Examining the unexamined in an effort to find out what fantasy meant to me, to all of us. Could I make the trip as a cool observer? Did I *want* to be a cool observer? My journey would become this book.

My plan evolved. I would crisscross the country, the world, and other worlds, from Somerville, Massachusetts, to Lake Geneva, Wisconsin; from France to New Zealand; from Planet Earth to the realm of Aggramar. I would ask gaming and fantasy geeks how they found balance between their escapist urges and the kingdom of adulthood. I would question Tolkien scholars and medievalists. I would speak to grown men who built hobbit holes and learned to speak Quenya and Sindarin, and to grown women who assumed digital personae to explore Warcraft and EverQuest. I would seek out those who dreamt of elves, long swords, and heroic deeds, and mentally inhabited faraway magical lands. Old, young, male, female, able-bodied and disabled—I wanted to hear, in their own words, what lured them in, and for what reasons, whether healthy, unhealthy, or in between. And, given the precariousness of my own romantic life, I had already become curious to know if any hot single gamers lurked out there, in the shadows, waiting for me.

Now that I'd opened that blue cooler, slowly and possibly insidiously, I vowed to become a more active participant in the subculture. Simultaneously fascinated and repelled, I would watch fantasy movies and read books. Tentatively, I would play games again. When massively multiplayer online games (MMOs) like D&D Online and *The Lord of the Rings* Online: Shadows of Angmar debuted, I would write articles about them. This, of course, meant taking the games out for a test spin, for "research purposes." I schemed to play WoW for several weeks. I planned to travel to pilgrimage sites: Tolkien's hometown, movie locations, castles, and archives. I decided to hang out with Harry Potter tribute bands. At a LARP (live-action role-playing game), I would dress as a pacifist monk for a weekend. I would attend fan conventions and gaming tournaments. I would camp with medieval reenactors for a week—12,000 of them. I would sew my own tunic. I was even determined to play D&D again.

Geek Threat Level: High.

SPEAK, FRIEND, AND ENTER

I was steeled to explore my fantasy past. But before I began these adventures, I had to 'fess up to my friends. If I couldn't admit I was a geek to those who knew me (or thought they knew me), I would be just a fake freak. Time to go public. To test my mettle, I threw a party. A "Geek Weekend" to launch me on my IRL (in real life) quest. What would my friends think of me now?

I covered the windows in my apartment with thick blankets to block out the light. I transformed my hallway into an Elvish forest, with tree branches, twinkling lights, and pumped-in ethereal soundtrack music by Howard Shore. I made a cardboard Doors of Durin, that magical portal to the Mines of Moria, and painted on the archway the words, in Elvish, for "Speak, friend, and enter." On a winter's morning, a fellowship of my friends and family members humored me, one by one entering the gate to embark on my "Geek Weekend" trek through the land of hobbits, wizards, Rings of Power, and pipeweed. Once in Middle-earth, we gathered for a hobbit "elevenses" (the meal that comes right after "second breakfast"), which was a brunch of eggs, sausages, and Elvish *lembas*. We drank artisanal beer with medieval-looking labels. We discussed the high school strata of freaks and geeks and jocks, and reminisced about our awkward adolescences. I dragged out the blue cooler and showed my friends my D&D dice and rule books. Then, we watched Peter Jackson's twelve-hour film trilogy, *The Lord of the Rings*. At about 1:00 A.M., an hour into the third film, *The Return of the King,* our merry band of adventurers conked out. And dreamed of that other, possibly better world, that we'd like to tramp across, with our hairy little feet.

Too late to turn back: the magic doorway had swung wide open. And I, an avowed, out-of-the-closet geek, stepped through. I wasn't sure what I would discover, and I wasn't sure how far I wanted to fall back into geekdom. I formulated tests in my mind that I would have to pass—or intentionally fail. Would I need to grow a ponytail, or bone up on *Battlestar Galactica* trivia? Would I run away in horror, or fall for gaming all over again? I didn't even know if I'd fit in anymore.

I did know this: The blue cooler had opened a world again—a world that had multiplied exponentially since I'd been a young escape artist. The ways to lose ourselves have since become myriad. An entire universe of fantasy exists, with many lands to travel. On my globe-trotting, dungeon-crawling search for fellow fantasy companions, my people, my kin, they'd have the answers I sought. At least I hoped they would.

The first stop on my quest felt obvious: England. What better place to explore these escapist urges than the home of the father of modern fantasy, J. R. R. Tolkien, aka "The Professor"? I hoped to find out what it meant to be a latter-day Tolkien freak. Plus, I wanted to meet others like me—people who bridged the abyss between the imaginary and the real, and, like me, occasionally fell in. So, with my +2 long sword back at my side, eyes trained on my foe, and cape flapping behind me, I took that path into the forest and into the deep and dark places of the world once more. And other worlds.

I have claimed that Escape is one of the main functions of fairy-stories, and since I do not disapprove of them, it is plain that I do not accept the tone of scorn or pity with which 'Escape' is now so often used: a tone for which the uses of the word outside literary criticism give no warrant at all. In what the misusers of Escape are fond of calling Real Life, Escape is evidently as a rule very practical, and may even be heroic. . . . Why should a man be scorned, if, finding himself in prison, he tries to get out and go home? Or if, when he cannot do so, he thinks and talks about other topics than jailers and prison-walls? The world outside has not become less real because the prisoner can't see it. In using Escape in this way the critics . . . are confusing, not only by sincere error, the Escape of the Prisoner with the Flight of the Deserter. Just so a Party-spokesman might have labelled departure from the misery of the Führer's or any other Reich and even criticism of it as treachery.

—J. R. R. Tolkien, "On Fairy-Stories" (1964)

On the Tolkien Trail

"I can guarantee this young lady here has walked the forests of Middle-earth," Mark Egginton told me, gesturing with his chin toward a woman in a long velvet gown. "I've been to Middle-earth. It's everywhere."

On his right hand, Egginton wore a gold Ring of Power. In his other hand, he gripped a pint of beer. Shooting an eye in my direction, Egginton continued. "I go into that world very often." Then he caught himself, adding, "But I'm not devoid of reality. My feet are planted firmly in the real world."

A retired British infantryman and former tailor from Fleetwood, Lancashire, Egginton stocked shelves for ASDA, a supermarket chain owned by Wal-Mart. He had been a member of the Tolkien Society (TS) on and off since 1980. The TS is an officially sanctioned, quasi-scholarly organization that celebrates all things Tolkien. It sponsors conferences, publishes a newsletter, and holds yearly events like its Annual General Meeting. The year I met Egginton, the AGM was held in Chester, a small city near Liverpool with a Roman, medieval, and Tudor pedigree and gobs of really old buildings. The meeting was packed. Minutes were read, officers elected, and an award was given out—that year, to actor Sir Ian Holm, for his portrayal of Bilbo Baggins in the *Rings* trilogy (Holm wasn't able to make it, but sent a letter of thanks). Overall, it was a fairly staid affair.*

The pub crawl was about as madcap as the AGM got. I had joined Egginton and a small group earlier that afternoon. We shuffled from one watering hole to the next, drinking at each stop and intermittently admiring the views from Chester's medieval walls, until the tour fizzled out in a dim tavern. The discussion turned to Tolkien—thankfully, not a tired retread of the old "Do Balrogs have wings?" debate. Someone brought up the Istari, the powerful order of magicians that included Gandalf. Who were they really, and why had Tolkien included so few? In all of Middle-earth, how many actually existed?

"Two," muttered someone at the bar. "Gandalf, Saruman."

"No, three," a half-drunk semiprofessional scholar replied. "You're forgetting Radagast the Brown."

"Right. Radagast. What ever happened to him?"

"I heard there were originally five," another offered. A lively debate ensued, one that included words like Maiar, Valar, Alatar, and Pallando, an entirely foreign tongue to a mere journeyman Tolkienite like myself. Middle-earth's intricately described "legendarium," as Tolkien called it, meant serious fans, just like D&Ders, could be fanatical about the facts. The conversation moved to grumbling about new converts whose arrival in Middle-earth was not via old-school channels—the books—but via the films. Hardcore Tolkien purists fretted about the denizens of fandom drawn by shallow elements such as the swordplay of Viggo Mortensen (the hunky, bad-boy ranger who becomes King Aragorn) rather than Tolkien's creative genius.

---

* More outlandish costumed revelry—fans donning elf ears, hobbit dancing, that sort of thing—was reserved for events like Oxonmoot, which the TS ran each September in Tolkien's hometown of Oxford. Egginton told me he attended Oxonmoot every year.

I wanted to contribute. Really, I did. But I was sleepy from the train ride and the half-dozen beers, so I bowed out and went back to the hotel. I took a nap and woke in time for the banquet that evening. I strolled into the hall, where I rejoined Egginton. The meal was set, the assembled all toasted "The Professor," and we quickly returned to talking Tolkien.

"Escapism is an essential part of life," Egginton said, picking up a thread from the conversation that afternoon. He kicked back another pint and let his head drift to the side. "If you are stuck within a realm of reality that is unpleasant, you will escape to the world within."

After the food was cleared away, Egginton turned to me and kept talking. "What I find is that having read Tolkien for the past thirty years, I can quite easily descend, or ascend, depending on how you look at it, into Middle-earth," he said. "Within the world as we stride it, there is the world that Tolkien created." In his mind, he conceptualized Tolkien's world as "mirrored" by the real one we all know and live in.

Right on, brother.

Egginton was the first person I had ever had a serious discussion with about Tolkien, or about any of this stuff—escapism, fantasy, and why it's so appealing. He seemed to be gazing into that mirror as we spoke.

TALKING THE TOLKIEN TALK

I had come to England in the fall of 2003 at the height of *Rings* fandom, just before the release of *The Return of the King,* the third film in Peter Jackson's trilogy. I had gotten a newspaper assignment to explore Tolkien's enduring and universal popularity, and reflect on the reasons why Tolkien believed society needed modern myths. I figured the Tolkien Society AGM in Chester, as well as Oxford, Tolkien's hometown, would be fertile sites for my inquiry. But beyond the assignment, I wanted to make a personal pilgrimage to his houses and haunts where he wrote *The*

Hobbit and *The Lord of the Rings.* Tolkien was the master. I felt like a lost clan member visiting my chieftain's homeland, looking for my ancestry. Nonetheless, I had mixed feelings. On my trip, I wanted to test myself to see if I was still a member of this tribe. Could I talk the Tolkien talk? Walk the Gollum walk? And why would I want to keep doing either? I had hoped my trip to Oxford and Chester would clarify these issues.

For any fantasy spell to work, you need a believable setting. For his novels, Tolkien conjured one of literature's most intricate: Middle-earth, a world autonomous and detached from our own, far from familiar racial and social problems, yet infused with archetypical, high fantasy themes of good, evil, honor, and justice. Tolkien devised his own races of people and creatures; created languages for them to speak; gave them histories, poems, songs, beliefs, and family trees; created lands, maps, geographies, and calendars; and invented a detailed backstory and consistent nomenclature to bind it all together. Because this world was not specific to a single culture or religion, readers found it applicable to all. Estimates suggest his books have sold some 200 million copies worldwide, making him one of the best-selling authors of all time. *Rings* also periodically tops "greatest book of the century" polls. Given their complexity and detail, Tolkien's writings invite participation unlike any other literary work before them—with the possible exception of religious texts like the Bible.

"You have to believe that it's possible without believing that it's real," Egginton had told me. Those people who really believe that they're living in Middle-earth, he added, "are mad. They've got a screw loose."

I wondered about the curious mismatch of desires he seemed to be expressing—both nostalgia for a lost world he had never seen, and a melancholy toward the real, modern world he inhabited. Where did this guy actually go when he "escaped"? Was he a bit cracked himself?

I would have thought that Egginton, as an army veteran, would have had no reason to play D&D or other games he liked, such as World of Warcraft. Egginton fought in the Gulf War. He also used to stand guard at Buckingham Palace and the Tower of London. Stuff of bravery and valor. What did he need fantasy for?

"I was somewhat to the rear," Egginton told me. "I didn't feel heroic at all. Servicemen have always been treated with indifference until we're saving the country's ass." Besides, society celebrated "cheap tacky celebrity" more than real heroism, he lamented. "When a sportsman earning millions can be called a hero and a policeman, fireman, or nurse gets paid peanuts for being ten times more worthy of praise, then the world stands on its head."

Growing up, Egginton didn't have English schoolboy dreams of scoring the winning goal at Wembley Stadium. All he ever wanted to do was explore the mountains, wander the forests, and look for elves. What attracted Egginton to Tolkien was imagining himself on a quest in a realm far removed from the twenty-first century. To attack an enemy, to speak an ancient language, to immerse himself in history; to create his own existence unrestricted by modern-day life, where it still might be possible to achieve greatness.

But only freaks would truly be influenced by Tolkien—the ones without a life. I had no need for these Tolkienesque reveries, I told myself. I wasn't into these fantasies—not anymore. Meeting Egginton made me feel superior—even normal. I had moved on.

Then a funny thing happened. Spending time with Tolkienites like Egginton 24/7, I was reminded how easy it might be to fall for Tolkien. The more I kept talking to him, the more I found his articulate take on his own obsession comforting. Egginton was a model of conformity: fully formed, grown-up, and mature. His hair was well groomed, he spoke thoughtfully, and he made appropriate eye contact. While he did call himself a "karaoke dwarf"—he had that stout, burly, bearded look—he appeared to have a firm grip on reality. Not only that, but Egginton was also refreshingly unapologetic about the draw of Middle-earth. He found great meaning in the deeds of its heroes. He studied its Elvish languages and appendices. Other forms of escape existed, but none quite did what the fantasy genre did for him. An escapist activity like television, Egginton said, was the "eye of Sauron, telling me what to buy, what to do." Taking action, even vicariously in the imagination—identifying with the protagonist, like what happens when reading a Tolkien or Harry Potter novel—was preferable to passive consumerism.

As I dove deeper into Tolkieniana and talked to fans that weekend, it became clear that Tolkien's readers aren't only adolescent males and computer geeks. Tolkien isn't just for children. His readers are a surprisingly diverse cross section of gender, age, and walks of life.* "There are as many left-wing dolphin-saving liberal peacenik *Rings* fans as there are gun-toting Bible-bashing parochial ones," Erica Challis, one of the founders of the fan site TheOneRing.net, told me. "Plus every shade of religious, cultural, and political opinion in between. It's a very diverse community, and generally pretty intelligent, funny, well-read, and entertaining." At the height of movie-driven fandom, her site received some 1,100,000 unique hits each month.

For sheer commerciality, *Rings* has arguably become the most profitable and influential fictional work of all time. Every hobbit cake decoration, Balrog votive candleholder, or Aragorn shot glass attests to that. The film trilogy's worldwide success as all-time box-office champs in such countries as Denmark, Russia, and Turkey also helped legitimize the fantasy genre. But even before the movies, Tolkien's legacy had fueled a boom in science fiction and fantasy that's now 10 percent of the total book-trade business. J. K. Rowling's phenomenal success is due, in part, to the appetite for fantasy that Tolkien whetted.

---

* The Tolkien Society says their membership is 57 percent male and 43 percent female; the average age is late twenties to early thirties, with members as old as eighty and as young as eight.

Once marginalized as unworthy of the label "literature," Tolkien is now taught in classrooms. The field of Tolkien studies produces doctoral dissertations, fan clubs from Poland to Argentina, and, at last count, translations of *The Hobbit* and *Rings* into thirty-eight languages. At the annual meeting of the International Congress on Medieval Studies, held each year at Western Michigan University in Kalamazoo, Michigan, many panels are devoted to Tolkien and "Neo-medievalism." From that conference has sprung The Medieval Electronic Multimedia Organization, which studies "film, television, electronic games and other electronic media that portray or rewrite the Middle Ages." My friend Elly, whose Harvard PhD is on medieval automata (Dark Ages robots—cool!), alerted me to papers such as "Orc Bodies, Orc Selves: Medieval and Modern Monstrosity in Middle-Earth" and even one in the field of gender studies titled "Knights, Dykes, Damsels, and Fags."

WE'D BE WORSHIPPING GANDALF

Egginton and I kept drinking. He told me that he began reading the Narnia series at age eight. "Got any more of these?" he asked his local librarian at the time. She gave him *The Hobbit* to read. He read the King Arthur legends. He was fifteen when he tackled *Rings.* He read other authors of fantasy like Terry Brooks, David Eddings, and Stephen R. Donaldson, but he said "they don't have the same depth" as Tolkien. So he kept returning to Middle-earth, reading *Rings* and *The Silmarillion* (Tolkien's creation-myth "prequel" to *Rings*) every other year since he was a teenager.

It was hard not to question the wisdom of Egginton's devotion to a Middle-earth, a world that didn't exist. As I said, I figured he was sane. But was he, on some core level, detached from Planet Earth? Or perhaps that was the effect of the many pints of porter. I certainly knew exactly what Egginton meant by straddling two worlds mirrored in each other. Lots of people seemed to do it. My friend JP (the one who taught me D&D) juggled it rather seamlessly, from my perspective. I knew he was as warped by fantasy as I was, but he managed to snag a wife and be a father to two kids. What about me?

Had I been set up for a lifelong dissatisfaction with reality? I often dreamt up parallel lives for myself—fantasy girlfriend, fantasy job, fantasy Pulitzer Prize. My creative undertakings— tree forts to build, comic books to draw, novels to write, films to make, poems to compose—often let me down. When I tried to translate the creative spark into irrevocable form and substance, I'd mess it up. The made thing would become real, but inert, a vast compromise, and inexorably flawed. I came to prefer that other Middle-earth-like place, in my own head, where my creations hang like untouched jewels, perfectly realized.

An hour later, perhaps longer, Egginton's chatter was still going strong. It was late. "Who's to say Tolkien was any different than Moses?" he said. "Tolkien's world is more credible than Moses'. The Bible is full of inconsistencies. Tolkien could go back and revise. Moses never did that." Tolkien was "the sub-creator"— beneath God, but also creating life. Egginton said Tolkien told the same stories we have been hearing forever, "retelling a myth in a new form." Just like Christianity. Middle-earth is a belief system. "Maybe two thousand years ago Tolkien would have created a new religion . . . We'd be worshipping Gandalf. . . . We wouldn't be reading the Bible today, but *The Silmarillion.*"

Egginton was convincing, and I was ready to convert to the Church of Middle-earth. I imagined Tolkien leading humans and hobbits to the Promised Land. Egginton certainly had the accoutrements to lead his cult. He told me that at home, his converted cellar, or "orc cave," was filled with Tolkienalia: 61 copies of *Rings;* 43 copies of *The Hobbit;* over 180 other Tolkien-related books; more than two dozen helmets, shields, wizard staffs, daggers, dwarven axes, and swords (with names like Narsil, Andúril, and Hadhafang); 20 board and computer games of Middle-earth;

and more than 100 painted figures. "If I told you that I spend seventy-five percent of my spare time down there I wouldn't be far wrong," he said. "I live in a world surrounded by Tolkien." Too bad I couldn't see it for myself.

He paused, took a sip, and spoke again. "It's hard not to see Tolkien's beauty . . . It's like a dream, a sleeping dream."

That dream. I thought I had moved on, but the Tolkien spell still lingered in me. I was suddenly happy to be heading to Oxford, Tolkien's home for fifty years, and excited to pay homage to fantasy's patriarch.

IN WHICH THE AUTHOR STRAYS FROM THE PATH

John Ronald Reuel Tolkien (1892–1973) didn't live long enough to witness video games, or play Dungeons & Dragons, or even to see his works turned into movies. But as his books became underground hits in the 1960s, Middle-earth mania arrived. FRODO LIVES and GANDALF FOR PRESIDENT slogans began to appear on bumper stickers, T-shirts, and buttons. Fan clubs sprang up. As readers began writing him, pestering him for details, noting discrepancies in his universe, and wondering when he'd write the next installment, he began to see how fans could get sucked into his world. While Tolkien was said to be secretly pleased by how devoted his audience had become, the attention also made him uneasy. He named his readership "my deplorable cultus." He knew fantasy could be dangerous—a "vast game," he once wrote to his publisher about his writings, which could be "fatally attractive." Even to himself.

The reclusive British scholar, lexicographer, and Oxford don was, in a way, the original geek. He specialized in the rather mundane field of philology (the history of languages). Most authors of the early twentieth century were busy smashing Victorian conventions and reassembling the pieces into irony-laden Modernism. Not Tolkien. An amateur writer, he didn't even read contemporary fiction. He eschewed the modern world. He had founded literary clubs with archaic names: the TCBS (Tea Club and Barrovian Society), the Kolbitars society (so named because they sat so close to the fire they virtually bit the coals), and the Inklings. C. S. Lewis, author of the Narnia series, was also an Inklings member. Tolkien hung out with these fellow egghead, Middle Ages–minded pals in pubs, where they drank ale, smoked pipes, and made up stories by firelight.

To Tolkien the medievalist, Icelandic sagas and

J. R. R. Tolkien, the father of modern fantasy.

thousand-year-old poems like *Beowulf* were the finest literature ever written. Domineering dragons and world-weary wizards seemed perfectly legitimate characters for twentieth-century fiction. Tolkien didn't worry whether his novels were seen as high art or bedtime story; in fact, he was doubtful his creations would have any appeal beyond his children and Oxford colleagues like C. S. "Jack" Lewis. Surrounded by those who didn't get it, Tolkien was ridiculed. "How is your hobbit?" his colleagues mocked. Despite peer pressure, Tolkien remained undaunted. The Professor felt compelled to invent legends because, he believed, Britain lacked its own, true, homegrown mythology. With *The Hobbit* (published in 1937) and *Rings* (1954–55), Tolkien's goal was to "open the door on Other Time" and "stand . . . outside time itself."

Because the fantasy genre is well established today, Tolkien's neo-medieval quest stories can seem somewhat clichéd. But he wrote them when few others did. They were epic in length and told in a lofty language. Their plots unfolded over a span of many years and often put ordinary characters—like Bilbo and Frodo—in extraordinary circumstances that involved magic, battles, strange creatures, and evil forces. Their quests restored some primal balance to the world. Of course, Tolkien did not invent the genre. But, reviving its rules, he was the right author at the right time, and he hit the jackpot. No one could have predicted how well his heroic, romantic, high fantasy would catch on.

FLY, YOU FOOLS!

After the Tolkien Society AGM in Chester, I took the train to Oxford. I had come to see the murky pubs where Tolkien drank up inspiration and to visit the homes where he'd scribbled drafts of *Rings.* I vowed to sneak into the Gothic-trimmed courtyards where he lived and studied, to wander beside the shadow of Tolkien, and listen. And what better time for this journey than at the height of the movie trilogy frenzy.

But Oxford University, where Tolkien taught medieval languages and literature from 1925 to 1959, did not celebrate their literary hero. In fact, they practically ignored his entire legacy. Only the faintest trace of Tolkien's time here remained etched in the silhouettes of the eight Oxford homes and four colleges he haunted. Here, my quest was to recover and record Tolkien's mark as I stumbled along. He may have avoided the spotlight, but I believed Tolkien—master mapmaker and quest-taker—would have approved. And I felt I owed him. I remembered the words of Gandalf to Bilbo Baggins and the dwarves in *The Hobbit,* before they enter the forests of Mirkwood: "Don't stray from the path!" But here, the Tolkien trail was shrouded in rumor and false steps. There was no path. Oxford would be a solo Choose Your Own Adventure.

I had a few days in Oxford by myself. Charged with a mission high and mighty, I set off on my pilgrimage. Alone. In a foreign city, I hardly expected to run into anyone I knew. But walking down George Street five minutes after my train screeched into the railway station, I saw a familiar face.

"David?"

"Ethan!"

We stared at each other, flabbergasted.

"What are you doing here?" we more or less blurted simultaneously.

As a longtime friend of my father and stepmother's, and a personal mentor, David had known me since my Dungeons & Dragons days. He lives in Ontario, when not flitting off to the Sudan or Bangladesh doing humanitarian good deeds, a real-world hero. He told me that he was in town for an Oxfam meeting, and I quickly summarized my reason for being in Oxford. Our stays overlapped for only one day, so we made a hasty plan to meet that evening at one of Tolkien's regular drinking spots. I took David's presence as an omen, and wondered if a fellowship was enigmatically gathering for my Oxford quest.

At seven o'clock, I met David outside The Eagle and Child, the seventeenth-century pub where The Inklings used to meet to discuss their writings on Tuesday mornings, from 1939 to 1962. I looked up at the pub's sign: a raptor flying away with an infant. Seeing it flapping in the wind, I wondered if the image had inspired a famous scene from *The Hobbit:* Bilbo and company's rescue by giant eagles. (That's chapter six, for those of you following along at home.)

With its modern beer signs, a computer at the bar, and a plaque proclaiming THE INKLINGS WERE HERE, the pub came as a disappointment. We relocated to another literary hangout just down the street, The White Horse. Ah, this was more like it: a low-ceilinged lair with rough wooden tables and a rougher clientele. Here, in the 1940s, Tolkien received feedback on drafts of *Rings* from his erudite beer aficionados. I ordered a pint and David got a brandy. We raised our glasses.

"To the Professor," I said.

I was glad David was with me; I was eager to share with him my nascent ideas about fantasy, gaming, and the legacy of Tolkien. I told him about my encounter with Egginton. I said that people who read Tolkien often went on to play D&D. And I explained to David how D&D was low-tech, almost anachronistic, compared to games like World of Warcraft. Audiences accustomed to today's computer-generated eye candy would find it difficult to imagine the fanatical draw of a fantasy world played with pencils, paper, and metal figurines—tools as crude as bones and clubs. When I had played D&D, computer graphics were boxy, primary-colored, shaky. No photo-realistic textures, no twenty-four-bit sound cards. Nothing terribly immersive. The experience had been largely in our heads, relying on our own private imagery.

"It's not like what kids play today," I grumbled.

A generation older than me, David talked about his relationship to fantasy. He said he had read a cheap paperback edition of *Rings* as a 1960s Canadian college kid, but not since. It had not grabbed him.

"Why not?"

"It just wasn't my thing."

"I've been thinking," I said, a bit emboldened by the alcohol. "This whole Tolkien thing, this fantasy of fellowship among men, elves, hobbits, and dwarves—it's kind of important to me." But I was only beginning to form my theories about fantasy escapism. I had been reading a biography of Tolkien on the train ride from Chester. "You know, he had been traumatized. Tolkien and many of his male friends, like C. S. Lewis, they had barely escaped the Battle of the Somme in World War I. They had seen their friends die." I also noted that both Tolkien and Lewis suffered the loss of their parents at a young age.

"Maybe that's what drove them to recoil from the world," David suggested.

"Yeah, and another thing," I added. "Neither Tolkien nor Lewis had a car. They wouldn't drive. Both pretty much ignored politics and the news." I didn't have a car either, and identified with *Rings'* pseudo-environmental message that lamented the advance of technology. Perhaps sorrow over his past and a retreat from modernity gave Tolkien nowhere to go but into his own imagination and its anachronistic tales, all the more groundbreaking as this was long before science fiction and fantasy became the established genres they are today.

We had another round, then bid farewell as we headed to our separate hotels. The Fellowship, such as it was, had been broken.

I walked to my guesthouse, marveling at the fortress-like block walls and iron gates of each of Oxford's colleges. Semisloshed before sleep, I speculated whether the University's jagged skyline of church spires had stirred Tolkien's visions of cities like Minas Tirith. Or if the reproduction Venetian Bridge of Sighs inspired the Bridge of Khazad-dûm, spanning the void that Gandalf, Frodo, Aragorn, Sam, Pippin, Merry, Legolas, Boromir, and Gimli cross while chased by orcs through the Mines of Moria.

In my room, I read the corresponding passage from *The Fellowship of the Ring,* one of my favorites. Tolkien describes Khazad-dûm as a "slender bridge of stone, without kerb or rail, that spanned the chasm with one curving spring of fifty feet." On this bridge, Gandalf the wizard strikes down the foul Balrog.

I paused in my reading, and remembered the first time I had read those words, probably eighth grade, when my friend Mike and I were racing simultaneously to see who would finish the trilogy first. (He won.) Being here in Oxford, my conversation with David had made me reflect on all of the reasons why people would be attracted to Tolkien, or anything fantasy-related. Being a list maker, I sat up in bed, and on a scrap of paper, I started scribbling:

Why fantasy?

1. Blatant escapism (from problems: emotional, marital, societal—terrorism, economic)
2. Feelings of powerlessness (related to 1)
3. Desire to not feel ordinary, to feel "heroic"; to feel part of larger narrative (immortality?)
4. Too much leisure time (compared to peasant/farmer life—Monty Python "autonomous collective"?)
5. Urge (genetic?) to play-act primal human struggles—betrayal, revenge, and overcoming great odds
6. Safe way to express needs, fears, and wishes
7. Fantasy = good vs. evil. Reality = too gray. Need simplistic worldview.
8. Connect with nature/magic—lost Eden? Preindustrial time?
9. Reality overwhelming. News saturation.
10. Regress to childhood / relive childhood.

This last one I crossed out.

10. ~~Regress to childhood / relive childhood.~~
10. Play cops and robbers / cowboys and Indians again.

Then I added:

11. FYI, this is not me.

I went back to reading *Fellowship,* where Gandalf and the Balrog had been waiting for me on the bridge, locked in combat: "But even as it fell it swung its whip, and the thongs lashed and curled around the wizard's knees, dragging him to the brink. He staggered and fell, grasped vainly at the stone, and slid into the abyss. 'Fly, you fools!' he cried, and was gone."

I slid off into sleep.

ASHAMED TO ADMIT ITS TOLKIEN LEGACY

Morning two of my quest, I reviewed my provisions. Map (of the tattered tourist variety)? Check. Umbrella (also worse for wear)? Check. *Lembas*—Elvish "waybread," like hardtack, for sustenance on the trail (technically, scones, but whatever)? Check. Hangover (woozy, mild headache)? Check. Off, then, into the mists.

I assumed that a chronology of the many residences housing J. R. R., his wife Edith, and their four children would lead me to insight. But as I walked from home to home, I learned that, well, Tolkien was restless. His homes seemed fairly ordinary to me, if not dreary. I wondered if by staying put in Oxford, his wanderlust was sated only by uprooting every few years. Or by daydreaming.

He began writing Middle-earth's backstory in the trenches of World War I, but he began his novels in the house at 20 Northmoor Road. I stood outside the modest, gray stucco house. While grading exams, during a reverie, he scribbled the first lines for *The Hobbit*—"In a hole in the ground there lived a hobbit"—on the back of one of his student's examination blue books. I pictured the author in his study, staring into the fire with pipe in hand, his family asleep, then dipping his pen to write, in longhand, a line of Gandalf's dialogue or invent a few words for an Elvish song. Was Middle-earth his ultimate form of armchair travel? I pictured Jack Lewis saying, "I daresay, with the wife and kids and all the examinations to mark, of course a little fantasy is justified, old chap!" I didn't linger long, figuring the current residents were wishing they could pry off that blue plaque declaring

J. R. R. TOLKIEN, AUTHOR OF THE LORD OF THE RINGS, LIVED HERE 1930–1947. I'm sure the homeowners didn't appreciate Tolkienites lurking in the bushes and snapping pictures.

Back in town, Oxford the institution hardly remembered him. Other than conferring an honorary Doctorate of Letters upon him a year before his death in 1973, and installing a bronze bust of Tolkien's likeness, sculpted by his daughter-in-law, Faith Tolkien, in the English Faculty Library, Oxford had turned its back on Tolkien, and his legacy.

I realized conjuring up and communing with my literary hero would require more imagination, but as dusk drew its cloak over Oxford, I had little time for reflection. I took a bus to Wolvercote Cemetery. Little brown signs led me past characterless tombstones to Tolkien's final stop. With a thick headstone and a stone border framing a rectangle of rosemary, pansies, and roses, J. R. R. and Edith's grave resembled a bed. Some fans had left offerings: a candle, a wooden rosary, a jeweled barrette. In raised black letters on the flecked granite tomb, the inscription read:

EDITH MARY TOLKIEN

LUTHIEN

1889–1971

JOHN RONALD

REUEL TOLKIEN

BEREN

1892–1973

"Luthien" and "Beren"? They are heroes of a 1917 fairy-story Tolkien wrote about a mortal man who falls for an immortal elven maiden. This theme bloomed later, in *The Lord of the Rings,* between the characters Arwen and Aragorn. In death, the Professor had managed to turn himself into myth. Who wouldn't want that?

Tolkien and his wife Edith's grave in Wolvercote Cemetery, Oxford.

I thought back to what Mark Egginton had said about escapism being an essential part of life, while keeping one's feet planted firmly in the real world. Egginton had given me permission to admit my own obsessions. I was also reminded of conversations I'd had with fans during the Tolkien Society pub crawl. The appeal of high fantasy was not simply pretending to be an uber-powerful hero type endowed with studly strengths and magical abilities. With Tolkien, the central protagonists—the humble hobbits—have no special prowess whatsoever . . . just like the average Tolkien fan. And yet it is the hobbit, Tolkien's real invention, not wizards and warriors, who end up saving the world.

When you read the books or watch the movies (and even play the games), you sense that if a mere hobbit can withstand evil, why not you? If the little guy can enter Mordor and destroy the One Ring in the fires of Mount Doom, then perhaps we can take on our own problems. I wasn't sure what knotty personal issues Egginton faced, but a certain Ethan action figure knew he had a mountain to climb.

Tolkien's world sprang from a book—one facet of this many-sided fantasy d20. What about games; could they offer anything but mindless diversion for an adult? I wasn't anywhere near out of the woods yet. I didn't have all the answers. And my own vast game still awaited.

Gelatinous Cube

Frequency: Uncommon
No. Appearing: 1
Armor Class: 8
Move: 6"
Hit Dice: 4
% IN LAIR: Nil . . .

The gelatinous cube is one of the scavengers not uncommon in dungeons. Its cubic form is ideal for cleaning all living organisms, as well as carrion, from the floor and walls of underground passageways. . . .

If a gelatinous cube touches (hits) an opponent, a saving throw versus paralyzation must be made, or the creature touched is anesthetized for 5–20 melee rounds. The cube then surrounds the victim, secretes digestive fluids, and digests a meal. Damage caused to opponents is due to the digestive secretions.

—From *Advanced Dungeons & Dragons Monster Manual,*
4th Edition (1979)

Into the Dungeon Again

You must forsake the sun. For surface dwellers, it may be an idyllic day. Never mind. You have your own battles. Even in summer's 90-degree heat, approach the door, speak "friend," and enter.

Cool in here. You pass the rows of tomes, the authors both hallowed and new, the velvet bags of gems, the creatures loitering about. Do they mean you harm?

You walk quickly, descend the steps, turn left, then left again. Poorly lit. Dank. Messages from those who have been here before pinned to the wall.

"Adventurers!" "Are you ready?" A rogue's gallery of heroes and demigods. Maps, battlefields, ruined castles. Row upon row of foot soldiers, still as statues, waiting for war.

Snickering in the corner of the tavern. Friends or potential foes? Men with long hair, beards, and portly build, many in black, baggy attire. Clothing emblazoned with heraldry of a sort: dragons, werewolves. Leather boots. Piercings. Tattoos. A fashion not seen in these parts for some time. Womenfolk are few.

Strange locals in this tavern. Fidgety. Fast-talking. No one looks you in the eye.

Still, you eavesdrop: They've heard tell of kidnapped children. A haunted crypt. Sorcerers and undead guarding treasure. Do they need your thieving ways, your healing spells, your skill with an ax or blade?

"Um, hey guys," you meekly offer. A few heads turn to you. "Can I play?"

They make room. Most still won't look you in the eye.

A voice from on high, some God, begins to narrate the tale you will soon inhabit, and help to tell:

Two young boys have gone from their home in the middle of the night, and their father, a silversmith named Quinn Stasi, has come to you for help. Though he does not know who has abducted his sons, or the reasons why, thanks to a ritual casting procured from the local temple of Erathis, he knows the boys are alive, in the area, and that their current location is in the direction of the Shadowhaunt Mausoleum, an ancient tomb of some long forgotten line of warlords avoided by the locals and believed to be haunted.

"Want a Starburst?" says Evon of Pelor, a human cleric.

"Thanks." You reach for the candy, unwrap it, pop it into your mouth.

You're in. You're playing again. You fool.

I GET MY ROLE-PLAYING MOJO BACK

"I haven't played D&D in seventeen years," said a guy about my age, playing a character named Desand Quickfoot, a half-elf rogue. He brought his old bag of dice to the game and tossed his d20 to see if he'd hit his foe. "And my first roll is a 1!" Big swing and a miss. He smiled an "it's OK" smile, but he was clearly disappointed about his less-than-triumphant return.

Yet I was gladdened by this guy, bravely returning to the dungeon once more. When his Desand tried what he called a *"Lord of the Rings* elf move" and leapt over a sarcophagus and through a raging fire, taking 18 points of damage in the process, I knew he was a kindred spirit, and a crazy bastard to boot.

I was in my local game shop, Pandemonium Books and Games, in Cambridge, Massachusetts. By "games" I don't mean Monopoly and Scattergories. None of that here. We're talking war games, fantasy games, miniatures, and SF/fantasy novels and accessories such as felt dice bags. I had met my girlfriend at a party not far from this game shop. Never in a hundred years would I have admitted to her that I was hanging out here, yet the demands of my quest trumped full disclosure. My mission: to play D&D again, to see what I remembered and what had changed, and if I could or even wanted to get my role-playing mojo back. To dance with dice again.

Despite the popularity of online role-playing games—including D&D's own massively multiplayer online game, or MMO—D&D parent company Wizards of the Coast estimates that four million people still play the game the way I used to, in person, sitting at a dining room table or on a basement floor strewn with bags and bottles of junk food and hoards of polyhedral dice.

It was June 21, 2008, the day Wizards of the Coast (WotC) released its much-anticipated fourth edition of D&D. WotC had cleverly launched the new rule books to coincide with a "Worldwide Dungeons & Dragons Game Day." Anyone could wander in off the street and, like joining random strangers for pickup basketball, give the game a spin. Thousands of gaming and hobby shops worldwide were running a four-hour mini-adventure called "Into the Shadowhaunt" about the kidnapped boys and the fifty-gold-piece reward to investigate the mausoleum, plus an extra fifty gold piece if the boys were found. It was the teaser to get us hooked so we'd shell out $34.95 for each of the hardbound rule books, or $104.95 for the slip-cased set of all three. Fantasy, she is not cheap.

I met the DM, a guy named Matt, looked at the premade character sheets, and selected a dwarf fighter named Durgen Darksteel.* The sheet's stats looked familiar: Strength: sixteen; Constitution: fifteen; Charisma: ten. But other attributes boggled me: "Healing surge"? "Will Defense"? "Reaping Strike"? I attempted to introduce myself to the other gamers, mostly in their twenties and thirties. Little response. No time for pleasantries, it seemed. Quickly the game was afoot. Matt the DM rattled off the backstory about the kidnapped kids. I tried to get into the swing of things. We focused on the task, entered the crypt, rolled dice, and killed hobgoblins and undead skeletons. Not much "role" in the role-playing, other than the Starburst-offering guy, whose cleric character occasionally shouted, "In the name of Pelor I will smite you!"

I felt . . . excited—and disdainful. Was this a step back, or a step down? I hadn't played since 1985. Then I noticed that the four other gaming tables, where the same scenario was being run by four other DMs, seemed to be having more fun. Even in the depths of geekdom, I wasn't with the cool group.

IN WHICH WE DEFINE GAMER, NERD, AND GEEK

Jocks vs. nerds, brawn vs. brain, hunks vs. dweebs; America has a conflicted relationship with the smart, studious, or anyone who has not taken the hunter-gatherer macho path. As David Anderegg notes in *Nerds: Who They Are and Why We Need More of Them,* there's a divide in our culture between "Men of Action" and "Men of Reflection." Superman embodies the polar extremes.

---

* Another character choice, a female Eladrin wizard named "Althaea Gild-leaf," was too creepily similar to my own name for me to role-play her with a straight face. Names of characters I would play on this quest would come to haunt me. It was bad enough that people I met thought "Ethan Gilsdorf" sounded Elvish.

Clark Kent represents the private, introverted, nerdy side. But it's the public, muscle-bound he-man from Krypton the culture celebrates. Our society purportedly encourages high achievement in math and science, but also crucifies brains for being smart. Yes, we do want our kids to do well in school—just as long as the passions they relish, the knowledge they acquire, and the pursuits they master have relevance to the real world. In other words, being an astrophysicist better make them a bunch of money. Too smart, you're declared a freak, thus ostracized, and picked last for the kickball team at recess. It's a mixed message.

Terminology time: the words *geek* and *nerd* are often used interchangeably. "Geek" once stood for "General Electrical Engineering Knowledge," a leftover scrap of U.S. military lingo. A geek was also a circus performer who ate the heads off animals. Hence the science-math-freakazoid association. In its common usage, *nerd* is synonymous with computers and poor social skills. You know—the smart kid who lacks confidence, is physically awkward, and unaware of appropriate cues like eye contact and the normal give-and-take of conversation. But the term *geek* has recently come to mean anyone who pursues a skill or exhibits devotion to a subject matter that seems a bit extreme: movie geeks, comic-book geeks, theater geeks, history geeks, music geeks, art geeks, philosophy geeks, literature geeks. Both geek and nerd might identify someone who expresses passion for a hobby in an uninhibited monologue. As for the word *gamer,* it refers to serious players of board games, role-playing games, war games, and video games. Intricate plots and complex rule systems tend to excite those obsessed with "the way things work," so games often appeal to geeky minds. But gamers aren't necessarily stereotypical geeks or nerds; I met plenty who were armed forces veterans. Keep in mind, before pigeonholing anyone, these terms are just general parameters.

Since the days I played D&D as a teen, it's become cool and even fashionable to declare your geek pedigree. When I announced my quest to explore my fantasy past, friends suddenly admitted to playing D&D in middle school, or being a Harry Potter fan, or once having had a boyfriend "who was really into Ultima Online." Mike Myers, Robin Williams, and Stephen Colbert all supposedly used to play D&D; apparently Vin Diesel still does. But it's not simply that activities like gaming and science fiction / fantasy have become more generally acceptable. Adult gamers themselves aren't ashamed anymore. Yes, some may be oblivious to snickers about their collections of Warhammer miniatures. But just be careful whose back you snicker behind: Some of the gamers at Pandemonium Books and Games looked like members of Motörhead. Or Hells Angels.

I spoke with a woman who worked at Pandemonium. She wore a lime-green knit cap and a DIE ORC T-shirt. Taking a drag on her cigarette, she said she knew what she was, and she wasn't ashamed to admit it. "'Geek' works for me," she said. Some of her best customers of science fiction and fantasy books and games were high-powered CEOs, doctors, lawyers, and contractors. "Geeks are not in the closet anymore. People are proud to wear their geekdom."

Why didn't I feel the same?

A SENSE OF BELONGING

As I met more and more gamers, particularly those my age, a pattern began to emerge. They'd tell me that after years of playing only online, they had returned to in-person paper-and-pencil games. "Soloing" on adventures in WoW and other MMOs made them lonely. They missed the face-to-face-ness of low-tech, tangible, tabletop gaming. I knew I had missed D&D's weekly ritual of camaraderie and fellowship.

A couple weeks before my D&D re-indoctrination, I met Pete Nelson on a Wednesday night at Pandemonium. I had come down to the basement to snoop around. At one table, a group huddled over the wildly popular strategy game Settlers of Catan. In another corner of the basement, two guys played a game called Blood Bowl. Imagine forming a team of humans, goblins, dwarves, orcs, and trolls and playing a fantasy hybrid of football, rugby, and Rollerball.

"Take your stinking paws off me, you damn dirty ape!" one of them yelled, waving a miniature. A rapid-fire *Planet of the Apes*-meets-the-NFL patter ensued. Looked like a hoot.

In another nook, Nelson and a guy named Max hunched over a table, playing a different game with miniatures on a glossy, full-color map. I walked over.

"Hey. We're playing D&D Minis," Nelson said. "I'm here every Wednesday to teach people. Want to learn?" The two men were articulate, well dressed, clean shaven; both wore wedding rings. Unfathomably normal. Why not?

"Uh, sure," I said.

Dungeons & Dragons Miniatures was launched in 2003. The game is played with small cards covered with attributes. Each card corresponds to a painted plastic miniature figurine. The minis fight on premade paper "battlemaps" marked off in grids. Nelson told me players start with the same number of points to outfit their "warband" of monsters and humanoids. By creating Minis, WotC was clearly trying to compete with Warhammer, a popular fantasy tabletop skirmish game set in a fictional universe of magic, guns, and armies of different creatures. With its fast-paced, simplified combat system, D&D Minis was also bridging the gap between war games and role-playing games to attract battle-addicted MMO players. Or perhaps it aimed to draw in nostalgic gamers like me who couldn't justify playing D&D for days anymore but could play Minis a couple hours a week. The game used D&D combat terms like "Armor Class" and "Hit Points" and

A close-up of figurines for the D&D Miniatures game.

trotted out monsters from the old D&D universe, like the Mind Flayer, Umber Hulk, and Shambling Mound that even I recognized. Plus, the figurines were fun toys to play with.

Sincere and soft-spoken, Nelson was a slight thirty-six-year-old with glasses who lived in Cambridge and worked as a software salesman. He told me that about two years ago, after he'd gotten married and changed jobs, he suddenly had lots of free time. He had already "taken video games as far as they'd go" and wanted to socialize again. "You don't get that with electronic games." He didn't even know if old-school D&D, which he had played as a teen, existed anymore; in any case, he had "trashed all that stuff" years ago. Because he worked from home, getting out, he said, was "a necessity." So he did; he found a gaming group and began playing and DMing RPGs again. Then he stumbled into D&D Minis, and bought a starter set. "The next thing I knew," he said, as we sat down to play, "I was amassing a collection."

D&D Minis has no role-playing, but like D&D, it's stats-heavy, borrows D&D's combat system, and involves constant dice rolling. At its highest competitive levels, the game focuses on individual player rankings, much like a professional sport such as tennis. Nelson got into the tournament scene a year ago and floated around 80th to 120th out of about 920 tournament players worldwide. Nelson hoped to compete at the game's Wimbledon, the championships at Gen Con, one of the world's biggest gaming conventions held each year in Indianapolis. He competed in local tournaments and needed to be in the top 100 by June 30, 2008, to compete at Gen Con in August. He'd go online every day to talk on miniature gaming forums like hordelings. com, where haggling over the intricacies—"Can a creature teleport from a teleporter square occupied by an ally, to an unoccupied teleporter square, even if it has no remaining movement left before teleporting?"—seemed half the point.

During the summer, Nelson's ranking went up and down. In early June, after reaching 62nd, he slid down to 98th. Then he dropped to 105th. Later in the month, Nelson played the number-four player in the world, a guy named Pat Lynch, whose win-loss record was about 600-100 in tournament games. The "turning point of the game was round 2," Nelson posted, sports-news-highlights style, on hordelings.com after the game. "Lynch charges into the chokepoint at the base of the tower and kills a stranded Hag with the horse and Wulfgar. . . . I need a 19 or better to hit Wulfgar, and I roll . . . wait for it . . . natural 20!" Nelson's Wulfgar killed Pat's Wulfgar, and he used his Hag and Eternal Blade to finish off his opponent's warhorse. Nelson went on to win two games to Lynch's goose egg. "Well," Nelson later wrote to the world of D&D Minis, "I feel a little like the '86 Mets must have felt after the ball went through Buckner's legs . . . really happy to be so lucky, and get a win!"

His rating should have risen to about 80th—enough to qualify. Then, a "dramatic update in my journey to the D&D minis championships," Nelson e-mailed me. "That tournament that I went 2-0 in on 6/24 was not processed in time to be counted, so right now I am not in the championships." Other players experienced glitches. His only hope to qualify was to do well at one of two open tournaments, or "grinders," at Gen Con that same summer. "They will take the top four finishers from each, so there are still eight spots available. It won't be easy, but I have as good of a shot as anyone."

When Gen Con rolled around later that summer, Nelson drove to Indianapolis to play D&D Minis eight hours a day, but the highest he finished in the grinders was seventh. "I didn't become champion of the world," he told me a few months later. WotC later announced they would no longer be supporting D&D Minis tournament play. The genial guy had been playing for more than a year, training every week, mastering the rules, and rising in the rankings. He was still feeling positive the last time I saw him at Pandemonium, looking forward to playing Minis for fun again since losing at Gen Con. Nice silver-lining attitude, but I'm sure he was disappointed. "I'm looking at it as a chance to reevaluate how to use my time," he said. Regular D&D still tempted him, but so did practicing piano and guitar.

Still, Nelson said his wife approved of him playing the game and coming down to Pandemonium and the other game shops where he competes. "She likes me socializing and making friends." But preferred he keep his "game life" separate from his home life. His wife was concerned about the stigma. Welcome to the club.

"'Isn't that geeky or nerdy?'" Nelson said, repeating his wife's initial reaction. "Yes," he'd told her, "it is geeky and nerdy. But it is also fun."

RELEASED FROM CAGES OF IDENTITY

Geeks are a tolerant people. They take in "the other," the misfit toys, and not simply because no one else would sit with them at the cafeteria table. They have felt the sting of not being included. They know what it is like to not feel cool. Thus, it didn't surprise me to learn during my quest that gamers and costumers—particularly LARPers or medieval reenactment groups like the Society for Creative Anachronism (SCA)—accept gays, lesbians, cross-dressers, and transgendered folk without hesitation.

Populated with cross-bred elves and dwarves, fantasy realms make people feel not quite so freakish, releasing them from their cages of identity. Playing half- or non-human characters can be an exploration of their freak side, a new door into themselves.* Loners also connect via gaming; hence, the reason so much geek activity is centered around conventions and groups. At last, they think—other like-minded people who dig costume making, fairy festivals, *The Hitchhiker's Guide to the Galaxy,* and live performances of video game theme music.

Of course, sustained deprivation of normal, intimate human contact can take its toll. I didn't kiss my first girl till I was a senior in high school. Did that make me a freak? Perhaps. Certainly, geeks and nerds don't have a monopoly on odd behavior, nor are they the most egregious offenders, but it's they who get picked on for their version of being "antisocial." Misunderstanding leads to widespread dismissal. Not fair. I once saw a T-shirt that addressed this double standard: I'M NOT ANTISOCIAL; I'M JUST NOT USER-FRIENDLY.

As for the male-only geek stereotype, I observed that fantasy attracts plenty of women, in large part because of more-inclusive, less-violent subcultures such as LARPs, theater- and music-based "cosplay" (costume-based fandom events), and "filk" (folk music with SF- or fantasy-themed lyrics). Boys want to save the world and kill the dragon. Girls want to make a nest

---

* A real organization, the Otherkin Resource Center (ORC), attracts people who truly believe they are not human, but "Otherkin": faeries, elves, vampires, and unicorns.

and befriend the dragon. LARPs and the SCA have goals other than combat and death. Who wants to fight when there's heraldry, calligraphy, cooking, singing, instruments, storytelling, and poetry to learn?

That said, many *do* want to slay that dragon, including the womenfolk. And given a preference for long hair drawn into a ponytail or braids, and facial hair in the form of a goatee or bushy beards (on the menfolk, that is), it would not be in poor taste to suggest that many a gamer could step in as an extra for a remake of *Camelot* at the drop of a helmet. But we're straying into stereotypes again. For every anachronistically coiffed or pear-shaped body, there is a plain-dressed lord or lady that could easily be mistaken for a stockbroker or customer service associate. Geeks come in all shapes and sizes.

Despite the evidence that geeks are ubiquitous, married, and successful, some members of the fandom community told me that they still find themselves struggling against prevailing stereotypes—mainly, that their hobby is juvenile, frivolous, or a waste of time. But the modern geek has an answer to this critique. On more than one occasion I found fantasy fans eager to draw comparisons between their imaginary worlds and the worlds of other passions. Sure, society shuns the Tolkien or calculus fanatic, I was told, but it tolerates and even encourages the oddball who is seriously into model trains, fantasy football, or fly-tying. Somehow, the terms *freak* or *geek* are not attached to such pursuits, which are called "hobbies." Another gamer told me, "People memorize baseball player stats the way some people memorize *Lord of the Rings* lineages." Any number of interest groups—gardeners, dog breeders, Francophiles—have their own geek-driven lexicons and specialized knowledge. It's deemed acceptable to know these things. Yet it's not OK to discuss, in public, the myriad ways a night elf hunter was more fun to play than a human druid in World of Warcraft.

Where most people draw the line is at "dress-up." Poker night is fine for adults to play; Grand Theft Auto, too; and even D&D has become passable in some circles. But unless required to because of one's profession—soldier, police officer, fast food restaurant minion, theme park character, superhero—anyone over sixteen who wears a costume is engaged in *verboten* "make-believe." No more playing cowboys and Indians. No more raiding Mom's closet for goofy clothes or her vanity for her makeup. At Halloween and Carnival time, costumes are fine. Otherwise, put them away.

The irony is that we all engage in some form of minor dress-up and role-playing. At a wedding or cocktail party, on a first date or during a job interview, or when home for the holidays, we all dress the part and adopt another character: Witty or Well-Adjusted, Stockbroker or Salesman, Happy or Perfect. Unless you're not willing to play along and put on a mask, friends will say, "You're not yourself. What's wrong?" Who, indeed, are you, if you're not you?

A TWITCHY KID WITH FEW FRIENDS

In a deep dungeon chamber, toward the end of the adventure starring my dwarf Durgen Darksteel, the other players and I faced an evil wizard and his skeletal henchmen. After a long melee, we managed to finish them off. Suddenly, one previously quiet player leapt to his feet, almost knocking over his Diet Coke.

"We are the heroes!" Jumpy shouted. "We are the heroes of the battle!" He did a little dance, akin to how a football player might celebrate after scoring the winning touchdown. A broad grin broke across his face. The outburst startled us, but no one said a thing. I wasn't expecting his victory high-five, either. I paused. Then I slapped Jumpy back, smiling. "Well done, man."

Gamers gathered in the basement at Pandemonium because the space was a refuge, just like JP's bedroom had been for me and my D&D pals. Earlier that afternoon, Jumpy had quite casually told everyone that he had ADD—"not Advanced Dungeons and Dragons, but Attention Deficit Disorder." (Nice joke for a humorless guy.) Hence, his proclivity during the game to hop up, pace, and fidget. Here was a twitchy kid who probably had very few friends. At Pandemonium, he could drop in and play a game, no questions asked. Games fostered a sense of belonging. For adult geeks who have difficulty expressing their real emotions, games help them vent with no fear of judgment. No more feeling like an outcast. Instant fellowship.

Back on the surface, out of the dungeon and into the broad sunshine, the prejudices against gamers quickly struck me about the head and shoulders. When I ran into a friend on the street, I told her I was dabbling in D&D and tabletop gaming again, and that I'd planned on participating in a LARP and SCA event. "Oh, those people!" she exclaimed. "They used to dress up in the park near my house and whack each other with swords every weekend. What a bunch of losers." Another day, a married woman I know told me she was OK with her husband playing poker with the guys. But him playing D&D? "I would have a problem with that." A week later, I mentioned my research to a friend of a friend who I had just met. "Oh you mean Renaissance fairs?" the person blurted, Tourette's-like. "They're so gay!"

Losers. Problem. Gay.

It was still early in my quest, my toes only just wet. But the comments stung. Those were my people being slighted. My compatriots. My race. My class. It didn't feel so cool for me to put down my fellow gamers anymore.

You're in the dungeon again.

It's dark, but your elf eyes can see. (Duh! you have infravision.)

You sense . . . something unexpected. Safety. Nothing can hurt you here. Fear not.

You sense kinship again. Your people.

But you exit, climb the steps, enter the world once more. You go home, and add your war booty—a Troglodyte Bonecrusher, a Dwarf Warlord, a Boneshard Skeleton—to that shrine of miniatures, vigilant and loyal, guarding your desk.

You are ready, my disciple, for the next level.

[D&D] is actually nothing more than a game. The "magic spells" are all make-believe, [they] don't work. They, along with the demons, devils, dragons, swords, thieves, gold and gems—the whole kit and caboodle—are fictitious. Imaginary things are not evil nor harmful. As to "occult," how can a game played by millions be "hidden," "secret" and the like? Complete nonsense. As to being dangerous to the minds of players, there is no basis for such assertions either. The vast majority of qualified mental health experts have no such concerns in regards [to] normal persons. That a group playing a fantasy RPG will lose touch with reality, or become "mind-controlled," is completely fatuous. This is obvious to any observer of or participant in RPG activity. Those who claim such an effect is possible are the ones who have lost touch with reality.

—Gary Gygax, in interview on TheOneRing.net
responding to accusations that D&D might be a "gateway"
to Satanic practices (2000)

The Fount Whence Fantasy Games Flowed

With a four-hour Dungeons & Dragons refresher under my belt, the time had drawn nigh for a more powerful dose. No watered-down role-playing game experience would do. No tarted-up, overhyped new edition would cut it. I knew I wanted to play old-school D&D. I knew I wanted to play with E. Gary Gygax, the game's co-creator, the source. If I dared to play at all.

For this leg of my quest, I had questions. I had bailed on D&D after adolescence. I had said to myself, *It served its purpose.* But Gygax and his contemporaries kept on playing and designing games through the 1980s, 1990s, and 2000s. These guys were in their fifties and sixties now. I wanted to find out what kept them going. Weren't they embarrassed to be playing kids' games? Why had they never outgrown the hobby? And how could primitive tabletop games, played with obsolete objects such as wooden pencils, cardboard counters, and plastic dice, compete with all the online eye candy?

Besides, from a pure and geeky fanboy perspective, I was fired up to meet Gygax. And why not? If you loved basketball, you'd want to travel back in time to pester the sport's founder, Dr. James Naismith. Gygax was the missing link between *The Lord of the Rings* and modern fantasy role-playing games. If Tolkien had opened the gates, then it was Gygax who led the first participatory sorties into its depths, rallying kids like me with that battle cry, "Adventurers, take up your swords and follow me!"

Re-geek me, I thought. That which does not kill me—a Dungeon Master's traps, for example—makes me stronger.

I knew just the place to find Gygax: in Lake Geneva, Wisconsin, an unassuming lakeside resort town about an hour southwest of Milwaukee. Here, Ernest Gary Gygax founded the company called Tactical Studies Rules in 1973. This became TSR Hobbies, Inc., which Gygax built into a role-playing game empire. The company thrived here through the 1980s, churning out the original blue-and-white D&D boxed set that JP taught me to play. To my adolescent mind, TSR had been a mysterious entity and Lake Geneva an unimaginable land, both as distant from New Hampshire as Middle-earth. I had always wanted to see Gygax's house, walk the streets of his town, and see the old storefronts that once housed TSR. Though the company had long since left Lake Geneva and ousted Gygax, for me, the place remained the fount whence fantasy games flowed, a holy site long on my list of pilgrimages.

Gen Con, an annual gaming convention, or "con," had its etymological roots in Lake Geneva.* Over the decades, the

---

* In 1967, several years before D&D had even been dreamed up, Gygax organized his first war-gaming gathering, a twenty-person event called "Gen Con." Its name was a spoof on the Geneva Convention rules for warfare. It was held in his basement.

event outgrew Lake Geneva to become a chaotic, ultra-corporate gaming maelstrom held in Indianapolis each August, attracting approximately 25,000 gamers. I wasn't up for Gen Con. Too much, too fast. The temptations might overwhelm me. Besides, Gygax was no longer associated with it.

But a newer, smaller, three-day con, called the Lake Geneva Gaming Convention (LGGC), had been quietly coexisting with Gen Con since 2005. Staged in the original town, it seemed more my speed. Gygax would be there to meet fans, run D&D adventures, and play other games. And LGGC IV, with its theme of "Walking Amidst Giants," would be the ideal place to hang with players and game designers from the halcyon days before computers and the Internet knocked the industry upside its head.

I was psyched. I would finally meet the creator, the deity, and master of the realm where I dwelled for many a year. If I couldn't meet Tolkien, who died in 1973 (interestingly, a year before D&D debuted), at least I'd get to hobnob with Gygax, the other hero in my pantheon. Both loomed as distant and abstract father-figures, as my therapist might add. In the absence of my own male rule-maker and storyteller, I had let these two creators of worlds into my world, where they helped fill the void.*

But on March 4, 2008, about three months before the convention, E. Gary Gygax, age sixty-nine, died. Like my mom, Gygax was vanquished by that ticking time bomb of blood and hemorrhage and heartbreak—an aneurysm.

---

* In high school, in an effort to try to explain to my dad what D&D was, I once pulled out maps of a land I had designed. "This is the Withering Wood," I said. "And this is where the orcs come from. And this . . ." He never judged the game or made me feel like it was a waste of time, but I don't think he ever understood it, or saw me play.

E. Gary Gygax at Gen Con in Indianapolis in 2007, one year before he died.

GARY WANTED PEOPLE TO GAME

As I drove into Lake Geneva, nerdster music parodist extraordinaire "Weird Al" Yankovic was the in-studio guest at a local radio station. "White & Nerdy," his spoof of rapper Chamillionaire's "Ridin' Dirty," thudded from my rental car stereo as I cruised through town, trying to find my motel. The lyrics enumerate the qualities of an archetypal geek: chess club membership, enrollment at MIT, prowess at D&D, penchant for memorizing Monty Python routines and attending Renaissance (Ren) fairs, expressing a distinct preference for Captain Kirk or Captain Picard. Yes, I, too, once knew my beloved Python by heart. I, too, was president of a certain high school club.

I pulled into the motel parking lot just as the song petered out. The Weird Al parody proved nerd culture had hit the mainstream. I took the song, and coincidence, as an omen of good, not evil. That Weird Al song also flashed me back to my unwieldy adolescence. I had not quit D&D from disinterest—I loved playing. I stopped because I'd wanted to be cool. Was a dormant "Uninhibited Gamer Guy" my true identity? I hoped, and feared, to find out.

I checked into my motel and studied my map of the place (all ex-D&Ders love their precious maps) to pinpoint the precise location of the pre-con gathering on Thursday night. Normally, this party would have been held on Gary and his wife Gail Gygax's front porch. For obvious reasons, not this year. A man named Steve Chenault told me to meet him at the Lake Geneva American Legion Hall for the party—a poignant choice, as that was an early venue for Gygax's conventions. Chenault ran a Little Rock–based gaming company, Troll Lord Games. After Gygax was ousted from TSR in 1985 (a long story), he eventually hooked up with Troll Lord. Chenault and Gygax had collaborated on the creation of an RPG system similar to D&D, called the Castles & Crusades. Troll Lord owned and ran Lake Geneva Con. With about 150 players, the event tried to recapture the original spirit of gaming conventions.*

"All cons are very structured. We don't do any of that," Chenault told me on the phone a couple of weeks before I arrived. "You walk in the door, there's a chair and table, and you sit down and game." No flashy product launches or presentations by industry executives. Lake Geneva Con, he reminded me, was a small event. "Like coming home to dinner," he chuckled in his Arkansas drawl. "Then you go to the bars afterwards." He told me about a local watering hole called the Fat Cat, and promised a high-level night of beer consumption.

Gaming and drinking? Beer = cool. If brew had been involved when I was a teen, maybe I would have stuck with D&D. But how much of a hootenanny the weekend would become was up in the air. This was the first LGGC since Gygax had died, Chenault warned me. The mood might be somber.

When Gygax died, geeks crept from the woodwork like ear seekers, those beloved D&D creatures who burrowed out of wooden dungeon doors and into the heads of adventurers (laying d8 + 8 eggs, which hatched 4d6 hours later). The media had been flooded with testimonials, homages, and eulogies. Blogs and op-

---

* By the end of 2008, Gygax's heirs would withdraw all Gygax product licenses from Troll Lord.

eds praised Gygax's genius. People posted D&D-themed art shows, YouTube videos, and songs. Troll Lord's Web site had some 200,000 page views and 2,000 comments posted on their message boards. In the game EVE Online, players bought a spaceship, named it *Gary Gygax,* and "gave it a nice Viking-style funeral" by blasting it into oblivion. Close to my home, Massachusetts Institute of Technology students displayed a giant fabric twenty-sided die on campus. Even friends who I never knew were gamers suddenly 'fessed up. Nostalgia for the game outweighed any shame.

I walked the half-hour from Lake Geneva's Main Street to the Legion Hall. This town was no Tolkien's Oxford. No moody Gothic stone redolent of great deeds. Gygax's imagination worked harder to wrest swords-and-sorcery from this classic slice of Americana. In fact, Gygax said he'd never liked Tolkien all that much. His true literary loves were more hack-n-slash authors like Robert E. Howard (*Conan*) and Fritz Leiber (*Tales of Fafhrd and the Gray Mouser*). Adventure, yes; high and noble fantasy, not so much.

I was one of the first to arrive at the Legion Hall. One older guy—baseball cap, gray ponytail, considerable girth—stood in the empty hall and reminisced about the good old days. "Nineteen seventy-eight, seventy-nine . . . that would have been thirty years ago. I remember playing games near the window." Eventually, around fifty early-bird gamers arrived; they had flown in or driven from as far away as Arizona, Texas, and Florida. They, like me, had made their pilgrimages. One D&Der from the Chicago area, who played as a college kid in the 1970s, had recently started up again. "I'm making up for twenty-four years of missed gaming," he said. He had taught his teenage daughter to play. "It was my dream to meet Gary Gygax," another gamer from New Hampshire told me. The game "literally changed the course of my life." He had met Gygax the year before. Lucky.

I found Steve Chenault in the bar area, where he held court, telling stories. I liked this guy: genial, wise-cracking, and a bit wild. He pointed out some of the hotshots from the old TSR days, including Frank Mentzer, fifty-eight, a former TSR employee and game designer best known for revising D&D's rules in the early 1980s. Founder of the Role-Playing Games Association (RPGA), Mentzer was a game expert and owned hundreds of board games. Within five minutes of meeting him, Mentzer spun for me a history of the hobby: ancient times to the Civil War, Milton Bradley and Parker Brothers, the birth of the "roll two dice and move" game mechanics. "It established the American climate for the family game," he said. But D&D was never considered "fun for the whole family." D&D typically appealed to that single misfit who'd find other misfits to play with, not Mom and Dad and the other sibs.

Gygax's memorial service had been held a few weeks earlier, so there were no speeches at the Legion Hall, just chatting over $2 beers, $2.50 gin and tonics, and a potluck dinner. When I had asked Chenault if there might be some tribute, he said, "Gary didn't like that stuff. He wanted people to game." Indeed, that's what happened. When folks in the Legion Hall ran out of talk, out came the games. Perhaps games were another way of communicating. I downed another cheap G&T, and half in the bag, sat back to watch.

I'd missed Gygax. Why did he have to die? He wasn't here to answer my questions, like how D&D began, or what he thought of the hobby since the old days. Plus, I had wanted to game with him, toss some d20s and have him as DM throw some bad-ass monsters at me. To help me find this arc I was trying to trace— adolescence to so-called adulthood—and connect it full circle. To commune with the savior of my youth.

I saw a kid, probably ten or twelve, with his dad, hunched over a gaming table, eating fried chicken and drinking Coke. The kid chucked dice, hooting when the roll went his way. A second-generation gamer. Like father, like son.

Here we were in Middle America, not Middle-earth, in an

American Legion hall devoted to the memory of war heroes. And there we sat, playing games that reenacted hero-worthy conflicts—future, past, but mostly just made-up.

AN EXTREMELY BRIEF HISTORY OF D&D

Some call the British writer H. G. Wells the "Father of Miniature War-Gaming." In 1913, he wrote the book *Little Wars: A Game for Boys From Twelve Years of Age to One Hundred and Fifty and for That More Intelligent Sort of Girl Who Likes Boys' Games and Books.* The book described the first rules for combat with toy soldiers. The games that followed tended to favor Napoleonic, Civil War, and World War II scenarios. They weren't for everyone, yet they had their basement-dwelling subcultures. Companies like Avalon Hill sold over 200,000 war games in 1962 alone.

The face of gaming began changing after unauthorized paperback editions of the book *The Lord of the Rings*—cheap bootlegs a U.S. publisher issued to attract college-aged readers—hit campuses in the 1960s. Tolkien became a cult figure. Around this same time, gamers began making variant rules for medieval and Roman-era war games, detailing individual effects of small units and actions of a single soldier. Gygax was a huge war-gamer, and founded a group called the Castle & Crusade Society, which had a particular interest in medieval miniature war gaming. With Jeff Perrin in 1971, Gygax created rules for a medieval combat game called Chainmail. He then added a twist that made the battles loads more fun: fantasy elements, like a dragon that had a fire-breath weapon, a hero that was worth four normal warriors, and a wizard who could cast fireballs. Players loved the innovation.*

---

* Gygax converted a plastic stegosaurus "into a pretty fair dragon, as there were no models of them around in those days," Gygax said in a 2001 interview. "A 70mm Elastolin Viking figure, with doll's hair glued to its head, and a club made from a kitchen match and auto-body putty, and painted in shades of blue for skin color, made a fearsome giant figure."

Gygax and a new collaborator, Dave Arneson, took the game a step further. Arneson had created a fantasy world called Blackmoor based on individual adventurers, not armies. Tolkien's fantasy novels had already pioneered the group quest "fellowship" premise of mixed race "parties"—dwarves, humans, elves, hobbits—who adventured together. Each member had traits and skills, such as fighting, spell-casting, or picking locks, that came in handy. Gygax and Arneson adapted this idea, shifting Chainmail's game-play focus from "you are a general commanding hundreds of soldiers" to "you are a hobbit thief stabbing an orc in the back." Players could role-play a single character. Rules were expanded to replicate that Mines of Moria experience of exploring dungeons populated by monsters. In 1974, these rules became an entirely new game: Dungeons & Dragons. Dice with various numbers of sides—four, six, eight, twelve, and twenty—were used to determine combat and random events. Frank Mentzer told me the game became known in the industry as "that game with the dice."

First called "The Fantasy Game," D&D got turned down by several orthodox game companies. The collaborative (rather than competitive) game play and the Dungeon Master referee concepts were too radical. "There's no win? There's gotta be a win," Mentzer quipped. Gygax's company published the game itself, figuring to sell a couple hundred. The hand-assembled print run of 1,000 games sold out in the first year and caught on as the first-ever, first-person fantasy game that let the players be the heroes.

But D&D's history was interlaced with controversy from the start. While today, its play violence seems tame, in its heyday as a new and strange pop-culture phenom, D&D was accused of causing disappearances, murders, and suicides. Rumors of D&D luring susceptible kids to the dark side added to its geek creep factor, forever linking the game to deviant and antisocial behavior. But that reputation did pay off in sales. Word spread even further. Kids like me got hooked. The game taught the concept of role-playing to millions. It was a groundbreaking step for immersive escapism entertainment. D&D influenced artists, filmmakers, and game designers. The dungeon-crawling, monster-killing, and booty-raiding routine became a mainstay in the fantasy genre. Some would say the entire video and computer game and MMO industry exists today thanks to Gygax's game. Certainly World of Warcraft would not exist without D&D.

"Certainly they played games before Gary. But they didn't play games like they do now, whether it's role-playing games or video games, with the magic and all the strange concepts. . . . Anything that's got elves and dwarves and fighters, that's Gary's legacy," Chenault said. "It's part of the cultural fabric now . . . part of the fabric of what we do."

IN WHICH THE AUTHOR HAS HIS FIRST ADULT GEEK MOMENT

If there was a point most removed from the monied hubbub of weekenders who'd come from Chicago and Milwaukee to speed their boats on Lake Geneva, the Lakeshore Room of the Cove, LGGC's "resort hotel" HQ for the weekend, was it. The generic, turquoise-accented conference room was located in the wing farthest from the lakeshore. The gaming convention was listed neither on the hotel's events board nor the town's Chamber of Commerce events schedule. The omission felt like a further stab, driving home the lowly status of gamers in the cultural pecking order.

Undeterred, the next morning, I proudly marched into D&D's storied history. I compared hangover notes with Chenault as several dozen gamers milled about the two dozen gaming tables. Others perused the racks of Troll Lord product: magazines, hardcover rule books, posters of she-warriors in skintight leather. If gamers weren't in on a game, they were watching a game, or waiting for the next game, or sitting in the corner snarfing down burgers and sodas.

"The demons weren't so bad," I overheard one guy say.

"This guy has killed three giants," another gamer said.

"Wait—you had how many hit points left?" said a third. He wore a purple pointy wizard hat and a Led Zeppelin concert T-shirt.

I took it all in. Outside, an immaculate blue June morning of tourists strolling town and boarding lake cruises spilled through the windows. Inside: fluorescent lights, junk food, and guys (with a few scattered gals) debating the merits of game systems. Oh boy.

And then . . . I saw it. My skin tingled. Like a four-year-old who sprints down the sidewalk as a fire truck passes, I almost yelped. I was experiencing my first geek flashback in decades.

Chainmail.

I approached a group of men huddled around an eight-by-ten-foot game spread out on several tables. Twenty two-by-two-foot Masonite panels made up a landscaped battlefield. A foam and wooden pull-apart castle sat at one end. Mountains ringed the border of the playing field, and trees made from tufts of lichen dotted the faux grass. The massive spread looked like the HO-scale train layout my brother and I once made, but about quadruple in size. Upon this 3-D land swarmed rows and rows of armies—cavalry, foot soldiers, catapults, trebuchets, the occasional dragon or troll. Most were painted in white and black, to better tell the good guys from the bad guys.

This was it: Chainmail, the missing link that connected old tank battles and Napoleonic wars to D&D. This obsolete game still existed. I could not contain my smile.

The man behind reviving Chainmail was Paul Stormberg, who had driven up from Omaha with his game boards and almost 7,000 figurines. An archaeologist and mapmaker by training, Stormberg was otherwise a stay-at-home dad who occasionally ran auctions selling classic gaming paraphernalia. He had invested "an exorbitant amount, more than my wife knows," in Chainmail. It didn't sound like he was ever going to tell her.

Stormberg—could a more perfect war-gamer name exist?—first brought Chainmail to LGGC in 2006 for a reunion of older gamers. They hadn't played in decades. "My main focus in the whole thing was to get Gary to reconnect with his past," Stormberg said. Gygax's first love was war games; after his death, the gathering became especially poignant. "The pictures of the [old gamers] arm in arm," Stormberg said, "is the reason I did it." He kept bringing Chainmail to Lake Geneva to keep the past alive.

A twelve-year-old kid helped set up the first skirmish. His name was Alex Clark, and his father Chris, forty-six, was "probably the most prolific game designer you have never heard of," according to the Troll Lord Games Web site. They were the father-son duo I had seen the night before. Founder of Inner City Games, the elder Clark had 100 published games to his name, games like Fuzzy Heroes (tactical combat for stuffed animals and toys). He was, in short, a lifer, and it looked like his son might become one as well.

I stood and watched the action of the first battle unfold. This was the opposite of real-time, online strategy war games like Warcraft III or *Lord of the Rings:* Conquest, where players furiously punch keyboards and manipulate mice, armies move fast, and outcomes are calculated rapid-fire by the computer. In Chainmail, battles evolved incrementally. Moves were carefully considered, chess-speed. How low-tech was it? The game used a wooden stick with marks on it to determine the range of missile fire and distance each unit may move. A D&D Minis skirmish maybe lasted a half an hour; a Chainmail scenario like the one I watched, "Battle for the Moathouse," took several hours to play itself out.

"The idea is to kick your friend's ass in four hours over beer and pretzels," Stormberg explained as he dug into the bins and pulled out more armies. "I certainly know way too much about this stuff."

And he did. He knew the minutiae of every rule book. Stormberg was forty-one, my age. A vision flew overhead of me, in my basement, surrounded by thousands of 25mm miniatures. *Yeah!* I quickly dispelled it.

THE WORLD DEMANDS YOU GROW UP

What happens to gamers when they grow up? They become grognards.

Grognard, French for "old soldier," used to be slang for "wargamers." But the term has come to mean any gamer who ignores new editions of a game. The grognards of Lake Geneva were not interested in D&D 4th Edition. They were not interested in D&D 3rd Edition, either. Even though the game had since spawned dozens of movies, novels, computer games, and even a computer role-playing game called Dungeons & Dragons Online, for them, D&D's evolution stopped around 1987. They lived in a gaming time warp. Most only played AD&D (Advanced Dungeons & Dragons), the edition of the rules that I had played twenty-five years ago. These grognards were not teens, college kids, or twenty-somethings slumped at gaming tables drinking Diet Coke and eating Doritos. They were guys in their forties, fifties, and sixties, slumped at gaming tables drinking Diet Coke and eating Doritos.

At LGGC, the eldest grognards hailed from TSR's golden years. Many had been Gygax's colleagues. Some were shortish, stocky with potbellies. They had gray ponytails, white beards, and heavy eyeglasses. Some wore baseball caps and fishing hats. They hobbled more than walked or strolled. They had cackling laughs and glints in their eyes, like a herd of Santa Clauses cross-bred with battle-ready dwarves. They moved from table to table, chatting with fans and signing autographs. To my eyes, they looked like wizards, mages, and mystics. These guys loved to game, they knew the history of games, they designed games. They had come, I think, to pay tribute to Gygax, and to make sure these games would never die.

There was Frank Mentzer, wearing a nametag that said MASTER OF THE TEMPLE. He talked about running an ongoing AD&D game that he began in 1976. "I was the best DM in the Philly area, they said," he boasted. He once made his career at TSR. Some

75

gamers had struck it rich like Gygax had done, when TSR was a multimillion-dollar company. But most relegated game design to hobby status. "You don't write games for a living." Mentzer had recently sold his bakery in northern Wisconsin and harbored dreams of becoming a full-time writer and game designer once again. He arrived at LGGC with huge boxes of cookies and brownies to sell.

There was Tom Wham, dressed in his signature blue-striped overalls and a railroad engineer's cap. His nametag: GAME LAIRD. The Navy and TSR veteran was an artist and game designer, best known for Snit's Revenge and The Awful Green Things from Outer Space. At Lake Geneva, he patiently explained how to play his new inventions, games like Missing Mining Moon and Dragon Lairds. I was thrilled to learn he had done work on Divine Right, a fantasy war game that resembles Risk, set in the world of Minaria. The game was a personal fave that JP and I had played to take a break from D&D.*

And there was Jim Ward, another of my idols, a fact I hadn't realized until I met him. A former TSR employee, novelist, and game designer, Ward had written my favorite D&D spin-off game, Gamma World, a mutation of his Metamorphosis Alpha, the first-ever science fiction RPG. No longer in print, Gamma World was a similar RPG, but set in a postapocalyptic world full of mutant humanoids, messianic cults, and irradiated ruins. A dark but ideal antidote to the Reagan-era arms-race dread I had experienced as a teenager.

"That gamers are portrayed as nerds drives me nuts," Ward offered me without any prompting. "It irritates me when people do that to my hobby."

---

* Wham later e-mailed me: "Over the last few years of his life, I became closer to Gary than I did way back in 1977 and the early days." Many from the old guard came close to tearing up when speaking of Gygax.

Ward, fifty-seven, looked like a big boy. He had Philip Seymour Hoffman's same pudgy face and unflappable personality. Ward was having a hard time making ends meet in an industry that was veering away from tabletop gaming and toward an unholy alliance with the computer. "All these computer companies want to make a billion a year," he bemoaned. I could sense that Ward, like the other old-timers, missed the old TSR days. He missed Gygax. "Gary was first. He made a new entertainment genre." Ward had been playing these games since the age of twenty-three, and had met Gygax right after he graduated college. Gygax taught Ward how to Dungeon Master, how to play games, how to have fun. "[Gary has] always been my idol," Ward said. "He was good at making other people do well. He was good at mentoring."

Gygax also left behind "tons of projects that were half done," Ward mentioned. I got the impression Ward would love to help finish them. He wanted to keep making games, keep writing books, keep dreaming big. But reality always threatened. "There's a stigma attached to gaming. We used to say, 'We have them [gamers] until they find girls and go to college.'" He looked away. "The world demands you grow up."

I'LL MAKE SURE YOU DIE SPLENDIFEROUSLY

The cry of an umber hulk being slaughtered. The group cheer after a successful battle. The laughter after an elf stabs a kobold with a broken arrow. This gaming banter could actually be funny, and I realized I'd missed it. I wanted to channel that twelve-year-old brain again.

On Saturday, I decided it was time to let my guard down and play. I wanted an un-ironic, unselfconscious good time. Frank Mentzer was running an AD&D game in one of the hotel's remote basement meeting rooms. I wasn't going to get to game with Gygax, but this was the next best thing: an old-school game, refereed by one of the original Dungeon Masters.

Mentzer arrived at 6:00 P.M. with hundreds of dice in a clear plastic briefcase. "If you can't go past 10:00 P.M., I'll make sure you die splendiferously," Mentzer promised, his bushy eyebrows fluttering as he spoke. He pulled out his maps and notes, scrawled in ballpoint pen and dating from the 1970s. He was no draftsman, but their handmade quality was endearing. This reminded me why I loved D&D—its anyone-can-be-God, DIY, homespun soul.

A few players made a last-minute McDonald's run. A woman tried to get her two-year-old son settled in his stroller. I borrowed some dice. We began.

"Your characters are average Joes," Mentzer declared to the eight assembled players. "You guys are the essence of mediocre." With his fingers, Mentzer sharpened his gray goatee into a point. Then he set the scene.

Our party of adventurers had come upon a castle. Rumor had it the keep was abandoned. I played Ethora, a third-level, half-elf, half-human thief. We approached the fortress and attracted the attention of six hobgoblins. After a skirmish, we broke into the castle. Walking though a passageway, we survived an attack by a carrion crawler (a worm-like scavenger whose tentacles cause paralysis). Our dwarf got stung. We surprised giant lizards basking in a fountain. We killed more stuff.

In a courtyard, a giant scorpion jumped from a doorway and began to kick our butts. A couple of the characters were close to death.

"Half-elf thief," Mentzer asked me, raising an eyebrow. "What do you do?"

I thought back to a conversation I'd had earlier that day. "It's just the same as cowboys and Indians," Troll Lord pressman Mark Sandy had told me, taking a cigarette break. "Instead of running around and getting hot, we're inside in air conditioning, eating our Doritos." Like guys at a poker or football night, gamers just want to have fun. Yet even now, I resisted letting myself go. Like my response to Mark Egginton at the Tolkien Society meeting, I had latent prejudices—even against myself. These gamers were beneath me.

My hesitation wasn't because I didn't know how to let loose and enjoy myself. I could drink, dance, and barf with the worst of them—even at age forty-plus. My D&D superiority complex wasn't about gamers; it was about me. The memory of not having "cool" friends, not drinking beer, not having girlfriends. D&D was inextricably linked to the self-loathing "Ethan the Geek" I had tried to shake—inarticulate, invisible, meek. Graduating from high school and D&D, I remade myself as Ethan Not Geek. I remember playing one last time in college, with strangers in my freshman-year dorm, and immediately deciding, *I have outgrown this. These are not my people.* I vowed I would become a bold lover of women and booze, an artist with hip friends who did artsy things. A different Ethan, not needing games. But at the same time, that new persona I had forged for myself was a betrayal of my past. My geeky gang of brothers had helped me survive high school, and life. They were my friends; I was still close to some, like JP. How could I turn on them? I had been torn all these years and never knew it.

"Ethora, you're up. What's the thief going to do?" Mentzer asked me, impatient now. "The scorpion has poisoned the two in your party."

I thought about how different I was now. How I should behave. It didn't matter anymore. Hero time. "I'm going to run and leap on its back," I said.

"All right!" someone yelled. "Go for it!"

Mentzer told me to roll some dice. I rolled.

"Twenty!" I said. Natural 20; a perfect roll. Like winning the lottery.

"You're on its back. You're riding the thing!" Mentzer and the other eight players cheered.

"Way to go!" someone congratulated me.

Way to go.

BEAUTIFUL PEOPLE DOING EXTRAORDINARY THINGS

Despite D&D thriving at this mini con, the game's imaginative foundation felt under threat. Several gamers I spoke with lamented that "kids these days," they weren't playing tabletop games that encouraged creative thinking. Nor were kids running around outside, play-acting cops and knights and Luke Skywalkers. The age of World of Warcraft had arrived. Chenault worried kids didn't know how to interact around a table, face-to-face. They didn't know how to be a referee, or tell a story. Their imaginations were spoon-fed. To turn these various tides, he was teaching kids in his Little Rock neighborhood the glories of role-playing games like D&D and Castles & Crusades. "I love running games, telling stories," Chenault said. "It's like a good movie: beautiful people doing extraordinary things." He hoped to hook youngsters on that imaginative play of being extraordinary.

On the last day of the convention, I spoke with Kerry Bourgoigne, a thirty-five-year-old, part-time game designer from New York City. All weekend long, Bourgoigne had been trying to generate buzz for his company, Shadowcircle Press, and their "dungeon-crawl card game" called Adventurer. Like D&D, the game existed partly on playing cards, but mostly in the imagination.

"Gary was into this game," Bourgoigne told me as he taught me to play. He was hoping his game would help lay the foundation for a new generation of role players. "It gets them into the idea of 'kill the monster, get treasure, get more powerful, kill the baddy.'" As World of Warcraft continued to surge in popularity, I was heartened that low-tech games like Adventurer still existed. While some grognards had adapted (Mentzer ran D&D online games, via e-mail or Skype), others stuck with their cardboard maps and plastic figurines. As primitive as rocks, paper, scissors—and swords.

The ultimate tribute to Gygax was this convention—the people he affected. D&D players weren't misfits. They went on to become creative, successful, and socially savvy. Some were writers, poets, and filmmakers. Normal, it seemed to me. Now grown-up (like me) and married with children and grandchildren (not like me), gamers felt unafraid to declare their geekhood (like the new me?). Grognards, they had a healthy, who-cares, F-you attitude. We game, we're grown-up, get used to it. So what if some were a little overweight, or liked labyrinthine rules? D&D had turned them into problem solvers and creative thinkers, because the rules required them to figure things out as they went along. To use their minds to imagine a different world. Gary helped make that happen. He showed us how to be bards again, how to entertain each other as we once did.

During some downtime, I wandered the game tables and sat down to play an old-fashioned world-conquest antique from 1940 called Empires with Frank Mentzer, Tom Wham, and Jim Ward. I cleaned their clocks.

PLAYING WITH THE BIG BOYS

Back at the Chainmail table on Sunday, the convention's last day, I caught up with twelve-year-old Alex Clark. A dragon had joined the skirmish, and it was not fighting for Alex's side. But the tidings looked good. Alex was beaming.

I felt like one of those sports reporters swarming the field post–Super Bowl, poised to jam a microphone in his face: "So, Alex, how did the game go?"

"I killed the dragon with my hero archer!" he said. Still high from the final battle, he recounted his final moves against the dragon. "Some say the heart is in the neck. Others say it's in the belly." He had had to roll boxcars—a "six" on two dice. He did. He found the chink in the dragon's scales, and the dragon had come crashing down.

With his blond buzz cut, utterly all-American-looking Alex had been playing games "since as long as I can remember." But he didn't play with kids his age. His family had recently moved and he hadn't made any friends at school. His dad's friends came over to his house once a week, so he played with them. I asked him about playing Chainmail versus WoW and other online games, where monsters and violence were a palpable, visual feast of action and graphics. Chainmail's fantasy world was elusive: obsolete, motionless plastic figures stood in for dragons and men. I suspected a kid like Alex would find it boring. Quite the opposite: "very interactive" was how he described the miniatures game. "You have to imagine what it would be like to be this person at this exact moment," he said. "I can get a pretty good time from Chainmail."

Alex held up the dragon. "It was pretty slim chances," he said. "I thought, 'Wow, we're kinda outnumbered.' But, I'd seen a bunch of battles, lots of blood." Like a war veteran, he became reflective. "I'm a big chance kind of person, and it usually turns out I come out lucky. My mom said I'm lucky."

Looking at the wide grin on the boy's face, there was no point in asking further questions. Alex had played with the big boys— the big boys with little toys. I knew exactly what he felt: victory. Alex was still a kid, the same age I was when I'd gotten hooked on D&D. Perhaps I was just seeking validation—a chance to feel good about the countless hours I'd spent lurking in Gygax's evil forests and dungeons—but this kid gave me hope. And he supported my wish that measuring the arrow-range of a squadron of miniature Elvish archers with a wooden stick could be at least as entertaining and immersive as playing World of Warcraft shackled to a PC.

I was hungry, so I walked to one of the fast-food joints within eyeshot of the hotel. I saw Jim Ward sitting on the grass by the roadside. He said he lived a few towns over, and he and his wife had recently downsized to one car to save money. "Sometimes I bike, but this was too far," he said. He was waiting for his wife to come and pick him up.

Ward reminded me of a pre-driver's-license teenager, hanging out after some after-school event, at the whim of adult schedules and transportation and responsibilities. Lost in thought, Ward sat patiently. He looked not exactly bored, but something bubbled under the surface. Dissatisfaction, or perhaps disappointment, or helplessness against a world that had let him down. I saw in him a younger me, stuck in a real and too-serious civilization that clearly needed more monsters, more robots, more adventure. More fun.

The night before, in Frank Mentzer's D&D game, my character Ethora had jumped on the giant scorpion. He attacked. I rolled again. "Seventeen."

"Hit!" Mentzer cried. I had managed to lodge a dagger into its back. "The scorpion squeals. He's been hit pretty hard."

Other characters pelted it with arrows. In the end, we lost a fighter, but I rode that beast into the arms of the reaper. Then it was 11:00 P.M. and we ran out of time. The mom roused her toddler. The gamers packed up their things. Some of us stuck around to hobnob with Mentzer.

"That was fun," he said to me, snapping his briefcase of dice shut.

"Yes, it was."

I had not found Gary Gygax. I had not found absolution. But I had found fun, and in the process, a piece of me.*

---

* Gary Con I, a new, free gaming convention named in Gygax's honor and organized in part by the Gygax family, debuted at the American Legion Hall in Lake Geneva on March 7, 2009. According to www.garycon.com, over 150 gamers attended. D&D co-creator Dave Arneson died a month later, at age 61.

The Forest of Doors is a mysterious frontier that lies somewhere between all the worlds. Its animals, magic, and environment are at once familiar and alien. It is a place that still awaits exploration and explanation.

Dark Mountains: *A sunless land ruled over by evil Dark Lords who use vile magics and force to keep their peasants in thrall . . .*

Desert of Brass: *A great expanse of desert inhabited by merchants, scholars, sages, and the mysterious Djinn . . .*

Empire of Perfect Unity: *A rigorous, bureaucratic society protected by a great wall . . .*

The Enchanted Glade: *Home to playful fairies, each as curious as they are innocent . . .*

The Goblin City: *Buried deep underground, teems with uncountable numbers of green, pointed-eared Goblins . . .*

The Realm of Castles: *A land of nobility, ruled over by women whose leadership is supported by virtuous knights of the Realm . . .*

The Rock of Storms: *A terrible blasted archipelago sitting in the middle of a stormy sea that sees no rest and offers no respite . . .*

Undersea: *A strange underwater world inhabited by the Apsara, a race of water-breathing people . . .*

—from the Forest of Doors live-action role-playing game Web site
(www.forestofdoors.com)

The Monk Went Down to Georgia

On a Saturday night, I was drinking in the tavern, listening to a Viking describe how he attacked a troll in the forest earlier in the day. "And then, I took my broken arrow and stabbed the troll in the eye!" the dude bellowed. "Har har har!"

He and two others, dressed in animal skins and what looked like togas, staggered as they approached my table. I looked up from my plate of roasted meat and potatoes. "I'm Leif Thorsson," the storyteller said.

"I'm Ulrich," said the guy next to him.

"And I'm Skylar," said the third.

"And together, we are the Thorsson Brothers!" they shouted in unison, banging their swords—*clank, clank, clank!*—on the table. "Huhh!" My tavern mates erupted in laughter.

Leif told me he was from the Rock of Storms, a stormy, sea-faring realm of hardy, ice-worn warrior people. "And who are you, my friend?" Leif asked.

"Me?" Who was I? I was out of practice at this sort of thing. "Friend?"

"I'm Ethor," I muttered, "uh, a humble monk from the Realm of . . . Castles."

I explained to Leif that I was learned and studious, a man of the cloth. I avoided violence; I was not a warrior like him. I was also tired, and not exactly excited about engaging with this half-drunk Viking. It was the month of March. I had left a cold and dreary Boston behind, and boarded a flight for Atlanta that morning, traveled some more, and wandered into this tavern—*a tavern that served no alcohol.* Leif's drunkenness was an act.

A few months into my quest, I wasn't all that surprised. After exploring England, Lake Geneva, and my own past, I had come to appreciate the potency of fantasy. And after playing the bane of my obsession years, D&D, and feeling quite proud of "Ethora, Arthropod Smiter," I concluded that it was time for my next step, deeper into the dungeon. But was I ready for LARPing—live-action role-playing?*

---

* A few things you need to know about LARPs:

- LARP is a noun (the game itself); it's also a verb ("I LARPed last weekend"). Hence, "Am I LARPing?" "You're a good LARPer!" and "I really like a good LARP."
- Each LARP group differs in its philosophy toward rules, costumes, combat, role-playing, participation, and genre.
- LARP settings can be high fantasy, science fiction, Goth, espionage, or cross-genre like steampunk (Victorian era meets SF).
- LARPs can involve as few as a dozen participants playing over the course of an afternoon, or hundreds of participants in a game lasting several days.
- LARPs can be divided into two general categories: boffer LARPs (games using physical combat with padded weapons or airsoft guns that shoot pellets) and those that use symbolic contact (rolling dice, playing rock-paper-scissors, etc.).
- Another way to classify LARPs: boffer (combat being the focus) vs. salon- or theater-style (where the main focus is improvisational interaction between characters).
- Although the swords may be made of foam, PVC pipe, and duct tape, get smacked and it could sting.
- No, LARPing is not the same as "playing make-believe." It's not a good idea to make fun of LARPers. They are often armed.

Apparently, I had no choice. You see, I had walked through a magic portal and ended up here, in the Forest of Doors. Like a tunic-wearing Dorothy in Oz, I didn't know how to get home. If I survived this weekend, I would have successfully completed this leg of my quest.

I needed a *real* drink.

OCCASIONALLY YOU BEAT THE CRAP OUT OF THEM

Being a D&D veteran, I didn't find LARPing entirely foreign. But a LARP differs from D&D in one essential way. In a tabletop RPG like D&D, the world exists largely in the imagination. You have maps and dice, but actions are described verbally: "I will strike the evil zombie priestess bitch with my +2 long sword." A D&D game tends to be combat-heavy and role-play light. Players might pantomime picking a pocket, or a DM might writhe like a purple worm, but otherwise, as we have seen, people tend to stay seated, in their street clothes. LARPs are all about 24/7 immersive role-play. They take the fantasy a step beyond. You create a character, invent a backstory, put on makeup, dress the part, and physically wander around a real setting, interacting with other players and making up the banter as you go along. And occasionally you beat the crap out of them.

In the LARP I attended, if you wanted to attack a "terror-beak" (an "extra" actor wearing a bird mask and black clothes), you unsheathed your "boffer" weapon and whacked away until it keeled over with a shriek and "died." Both players and non-player monsters kept track of how and where they'd been hit and knew what it took to die; strict adherence to the honor system was expected.

Like in D&D, behind-the-scenes game masters dream up the LARP's adventures, puzzles, and foes that players will encounter. They're also like theater directors and set designers, adding props and wearing costumes to make the illusions more convincing. But these games don't have Disney-quality sets or Industrial

Light and Magic–level special effects. So LARPs get inventive. A cheap trinket is a magical gem. Some black plastic sheets strung between a few trees might be a dungeon. A monster is a fellow player whose face is smudged with green war paint. You have to suspend your disbelief.

Live-action role-playing games are an offshoot of the D&D movement. Some claim the first LARP group dates back to 1977; the first theater-style LARP group was the Society for Interactive Literature (SIL), founded in 1981 at Harvard University. In the 1980s, the New England Role-playing Organization (NERO) became a widespread franchise of boffer LARP groups. But no matter what the LARP genre—espionage, historical reenactment, science fiction, swords-and-sorcery—the concept is the same. The directors set the story in motion, but there is no script. The better an improv actor you are, the more fun you'll have.

I hoped playing in a LARP would help untangle a paradox I sensed was at work amid the fantasy experiences I had been thinking about. Gaming and fantasy geeks were increasingly choosing online games and special effects–laden movies. Technology had made these ultrarealistic fantasies believable. While no longer at the center of the subculture, Renaissance fairs, old-school paper-and-pencil D&D, and LARPs were still alive and well. I wondered if low-tech games were a backlash movement within fantasy escapism for those fed up with the digital age. I was also curious to role-play in costume, if my mortification didn't kill me first.

In LARPs, like in RPGs, outcomes and actions are based on a system of rules. But the playing field is much larger than a dining room table. Theater LARPs can be self-contained in a hotel meeting room, but boffer LARPs need more space. The Holiday Inn doesn't take kindly to costumed patrons running the halls screaming "Die, foul beast!" LARP groups often rent campsites in state parks, complete with bunkhouses or cabins and a kitchen, and acres of fields and woods to use as battlefields.

By now, I had come to expect that gamers would defend their turf. LARPers I spoke with claimed not to care what others thought of their hobby. If prodded, they'd insist that what they did one or two weekends a month wasn't escapist. It was a sport (sans ball or racket, but with just as much gear). It was improv theater. And, they'd say, if you had the guts and could forget your inhibitions, you'd love it.

NO ONE WANTS TO FIGHT EVIL IN THE RAIN

The largest LARPs, such as England's Lorien Trust, draw as many as four thousand players. In the U.S., the biggies attract a thousand or more participants, and tend to be combat-heavy. I had searched around for a LARP that was smallish and welcoming to beginners. I found Forest of Doors (both the name of the LARP and the world where it is set). Population: fifty or so players. I registered for the weekend event, booked my flight to Atlanta, and immediately felt that familiar tug in my stomach. Compared to D&D, this was a deeper step into the dungeon. *Costumes? Weapons? Ethan, why are you doing this?*

Like many live-action role-playing games, Forest of Doors (FoD) was organized and administered on the Internet; once the game began, it took place in the brick-and-mortar real world. My contact was Christopher Tang, the group's cofounder and ringleader, a thirty-year-old real estate lawyer from the Atlanta suburbs. Tang's group rented a campsite at Indian Springs State Park, in a small town called Flovilla, about an hour southeast of Atlanta. When we spoke on the phone, he agreed to let me tag along and take notes. But he also admonished me to play—to take it seriously. "If you want to have a good time at LARPs," Tang said the week before my arrival, "you need a little self-direction. This isn't dinner theater." I made arrangements for Tang to pick me up in Atlanta the Friday afternoon before the game began. We'd ride to the site together and have a chance to talk.

I hadn't decided on what character I would play, but I figured I could wing it once I got there. Before I'd left Boston, Tang advised me to haunt my local thrift shop to find some kind of medievalesque costume. "A dirty LARPer's secret: Don't be afraid to look in the women's section," he said. Sheepishly riffling through the racks, I found a white puffy smock, some black yoga pants, and a deep purple shirt my mother might have worn to a Fleetwood Mac concert.

Compared to the Northeast, Atlanta was hot. Tang, stocky and dark-haired, pulled up in a pickup truck that was crammed with bins of props and costumes, boxes of food, and a pile of what looked like lumber. On the drive to Flovilla, amid other errands—picking up a costume at the dry cleaners, loading into the truck a huge HERE AND THERE signpost—he recounted the local gaming history. In Atlanta, each LARP was a "subculture within a subculture." Tang knew of some 300 people involved in LARPs in the Atlanta area; FoD was actually a splinter group of another game. "Each LARP has its own reputation," he said. Tang and his fellow game masters started their own LARP because "we wanted to improve on things." Like all world-builders, game masters loved to invent their own rule books. He described FoD's milieu as more than simply Tolkien-inspired elves-and-dwarves fare, but a fantasy hybrid, "more *Narnia* meets *Lost*."

As we drove past signs for boiled peanuts, pit BBQ, and fresh peaches, I asked Tang to explain what drew players to LARPing. Though Tang did call the combat side "an elaborate pillow fight," he said LARPers weren't just into the padded-weapon combat. I had talked to men and women who played these games—students, waitresses, salesmen, lab researchers—and they confirmed Tang's assessment. The primary allure was found in the ephemeral heroism, random interaction with each other, and fantasy violence on a sprawling, amorphous stage. "There's an acting element, there's a fighting element, the physicality," Tang told me as we drove. "There's the arts and crafts element, people making things. There's also a camping element, running around in the woods."

And as with camping, the last thing you want is crappy weather. "No one wants to fight evil in the rain." Fortunately, our weekend weather looked good.

What was remarkable about LARPs, I soon understood, was that beyond spreading a few rumors and periodically setting up ambushes of monsters, the game masters pretty much sat back and reacted to the action unfolding. Character interaction drove the game. Players did stuff the moment the game began: solved puzzles, killed monsters, chatted and argued, and all of this complete with individual motivations and petty differences. Even if players ran out of "in-game" time, they could tell the game master what their character was doing between games, and communicated via e-mail to advance the plot. Rather than micromanage, game masters improvised. If my character decided he wanted to explore a haunted forest, the game masters did their best to round up some ghosts.

"We can't entertain people," Tang said. "People entertain each other." He compared being the game master to "throwing a party for three days—you can't be the host and be everywhere all the time."

We arrived at the campground, a cluster of park-brown cabins and mown grass fields at the edge of a pine forest. Tang ran off to set up "monster camp," a cabin at the forest's edge, the backstage area where the extras ("non-player characters," or NPCs) would gather and Tang and his minions would plan the next encounter. He left me alone.

I stood uncomfortably, watching players check in at a makeshift desk, still in street clothes and out of character. I waited on the sidelines, thinking about what persona I'd be playing, and observing the giddy excitement. Skinny or with paunches, ponytails or clean-cut, glasses or not; except for their fairy wings and chain-mail shirts, my fellow players looked like typical D&D

players. Although I was shouldering my large backpack (with the purple shirt burning a hole through it), the weight of my hesitation felt even heavier.

Like that first moment at summer camp when my parents drove away, a wave of *I want to go home* washed through me. But I couldn't. Home was far away. No Mom to get me. Besides, before long, I wasn't even going to *be* me.

SOMEONE HANDED ME A MACE

I dumped my pack in the bunkhouse and sat on my bed. Several minutes passed. I had a couple of hours before the game began at 9:00 P.M. Time to mingle. Sucking up my courage, I walked back to the check-in area, approached some players, and asked for advice about rules and building a character. Learning I was a newbie (and a journalist), players swarmed me. The premise of Forest of Doors, I learned, was that people and creatures from eight Homeworlds— places such as the Dark Mountains, the Empire of Perfect Unity, and the Enchanted Glade—had passed through magical doors to appear in this "place of infinite secrets." (These were colored prop doors—the "lumber" that Tang had brought with him. He positioned them in various locales around the park.)

According to the game's backstory, the folks who had wandered through the doors didn't know how to get back, so they were left trying to figure out this new world, how to form some kind of society and structure, and how to return home someday. A bit like *Lord of the Flies* with better costuming (but worse British accents).

Kyle Christian, a big twenty-three-year-old guy wearing black clothes and carrying a foam-and-duct-tape pole arm called a halberd in his hand, saw me taking it all in. He understood how strange this all must have seemed. "You get dressed up and hit people in the woods?" said the real-life college student, recounting his initial skepticism before playing his first LARP. "You must be in real culture shock," he offered sympathetically. A string of bear claws dangled from his neck.

I needed to pick a character. The official, 239-page rule book for FoD had promised, "You may forge a new destiny for yourself." Hence the appeal of the game—the freedom to be someone else. Who did I want to be? And was that character man or woman enough to wear purple? I settled on the monk.

As the afternoon progressed, the rest of the players arrived in cars. More and more costumed characters appeared at the "tavern" (the campground dining hall). Their weapons were checked for any hard edges; archers were instructed how to safely fire their

Aerie (Erin Praeter), a fairy, listens at one of the "doors" at Forest of Doors.

foam-tipped arrows. I worked on playing Ethor, the humble monk, and began fleshing out my character. I chose my main traits and skills, such as "agile," "perceptive," "scholarship," and "diplomacy." My backstory was that I hailed from the Realm of Castles, my Homeworld, and that as a monk, I was sent here to observe, ask questions, and be a scribe and record facts about the people and deeds of this world. Good cover for a freelance journalist/author.

OK, Ethor, costume time. I riffled through my pack and weighed my options. The puffy smock turned out to be a maternity shirt. I decided to nix the Stevie Nicks purple blouse as well. I slipped on the yoga pants and a blue tunic Tang had mercifully lent me. Instant monk. Before long, I was surrounded by about forty bantering barbarians, snickering goblins, giggling fairies, and nodding sages.

As the hour of 10:00 P.M. approached, Tang gave a talk to the assembled players, urging us all to stay in character for the full two and a half days. "You will," he warned us, "be attacked in your sleep." Then, new players were initiated into the game by embarking on a "newbie module" to teach game-play basics. The short scenario in the woods involved a dark cabin, hallways wrapped in black plastic, and bands of giant rats and night stalkers. These creatures attacked from the roadside.

Someone handed me a mace. My monk Ethor was a pacifist, but given the monsters in the Forest of Doors, I was going to need a weapon.

A FORM OF SECULAR RITUALISM

"We understand these things aren't real—but that is the value in it. We are part of this shared ritual, but we don't carry it into real life," said Charles Kelley, twenty-seven. A self-described visual artist, writer, and "creative unemployed guy," Kelley was one of four game directors for Forest of Doors. That first night, when I felt the most out of place, Kelley drew me into the game. Somewhat stout, he had long brown hair and a beard. Bespectacled with black-rimmed, hipster throwback glasses, he looked more Ginsberg-Beatnik than geek-nerd. He smiled and laughed as he explained the rules. I liked him immediately.

Some players I met had seemed defensive, almost apologetic, about their interest in LARPs, saying the game was no worse than the escapism of a movie or a book. Kelley was refreshingly unselfconscious and up-front. He had a great sense of humor about the entire enterprise, which he admitted could look ludicrous to most bystanders. He compared LARPs to "D&D on crack."

I asked Kelley about his introduction to gaming. He had lived in Texas as a teenager where a friend had invited him to play "a lame D&D clone." Still, the fantasy game fired his imagination. "I've never been addicted to any substances, but I can imagine it feels something like how I did during that time in my life," Kelley said. He got into LARPing via Vampire: The Masquerade, a game set in a Goth-punk world. Playing it gave him an excuse to "be seen in our Gothed-up and glammed-out costumes" in a small Texas town. When he moved to Atlanta, he tried to get back into LARPing, but the vampire salon-style game no longer interested him. He found the "constant retreading of the same tired tropes" of fantasy novels a bore. Other gamers, whose creative vision "extends no further than their Dungeon Master's Guide," also became tedious. He gave up the genre altogether, until a friend dragged him to a boffer LARP. The experience, he said, "literally changed me."

"This was a far more primal role-playing experience," he said. "There was a physical reality to it all. When a monster bore down on you, it was literally bearing down on you, and in real time. There was no possible way I could return to throwing rock/paper/scissors." Compared to a tabletop RPG like D&D, he loved the LARP's physicality. The arc of a sword was real. The dark energy of a corrupt wizard's spell was represented by a material thing that hits players, who fell to the ground and pretended to be paralyzed (until the spell was broken, anyway). Real things happened.

That FoD replicated the experience of a small band of strangers in an uninhabited forest made it all the easier to fall under its spell. Other games he played, "almost all of them mediocre beyond measure," failed because the game masters set them in "vast kingdoms and bustling economic metropoli," difficult illusions to pull off. It turned out Kelley didn't enjoy playing games as much as he liked running them. "I cannot abide ceding any measure of creative freedom to another game master," he told me. "Having tasted the forbidden fruit of total creative dominance, I have no desire to return." (When he did play, he tended to play antiestablishment characters.)

Though FoD was a relatively new LARP (the first game debuted in July of 2006), personality conflicts had already arisen. Kelley said he struggled with the styles of the other three game masters. But once the game began, squabbles fell aside. "When I am running a game, I am engaged from the moment the game begins until it ends. When one person resolves an action, the next speaks up and I deal with them. It is constant, unending creative arbitration. It's a little like pure bliss." He liked how an obstacle he invented and described—say a wall, or a troll—became a real entity in the players' minds that they had to acknowledge. "They will have to devise a means of defeating this challenge," he said. He liked seeing how they interacted with the challenge, and how he could make it more plausible for next time.

Gaming was central to his life. Each week, Kelley ran a tabletop RPG (four hours). He played in a weekly D&D game (four hours). He attended weekly Forest of Doors meetings "to organize and write story" (five hours). His hour tally could be skewed higher by his "habit of going off into the woods to game for an entire weekend." Some months, he spent upward of 150 hours on gaming. He was also working on his own fantasy novel: "It has more to do with existentialism and Eastern European surrealism than it does with *The Beastmaster* and *Willow*."

Writing stories. Telling stories. The human being's essential need for theater. LARPs provided a way to manufacture this drama. For me as a kid, even self-told stories of evil wizards were better than contemplating my family doom. Kelley compared LARPs to a form of "secular ritualism," like native cultures using masks to inhabit gods. "It's like the guy in the mask. You live in the hut across the street [from the guy in the mask], but you say 'I know you were a god.'" In other words, you only bought into it as much as you wanted, for the reasons you wanted. "We stretch the imagination a lot, but there's a point where it becomes silly."

"Role-playing stimulates something primal in me. I can't explain it other than to say it is a deep compulsion that is both out of my control and fully under my control." He foresaw himself running Forest of Doors for another eight years at least. "Most people who are role-playing lifestylers couldn't leave the hobby if their lives depended on it."

SELL TAX SOFTWARE OR SLAY BANDITS AND BOINK ROYALTY?

Wander the Forest of Doors, like Ethor did, and it doesn't take long to run into Wolf.

Dressed in armor, a furry white cape, and an imposing, wolf-like headdress, the warrior Wolf was a crude and outspoken character itching for battle. He tried to convince other players to join him in vanquishing the bands of marauders threatening their town. "Bandits are definitely on my list of things to do today," he exclaimed. Wolf liked to spout obnoxious and provocative things. In response to a princess, he said, "Royalty are beneath me—where all royalty should be while I am above them, doing my business."

Wolf was played by Nick Perretta, a twenty-nine-year-old tax software salesman, husband, and father with a black beard and stringy hair that hung past his ears. Wolf strutted around. Meanwhile, Perretta's wife's character quietly ran the tavern, "the in-play place to get food and drinks," he said, "so no one passes out from dehydration." Before he came to LARPing, Perretta played RPGs, but found them lacking. "When you play a paper-and-pencil game," Perretta said, "it is hard to get into the action of swinging your sword without looking like a mental patient."

His approach to playing Wolf was curious: He told me he doesn't play characters so much as write a story with a main character. "Using that, I begin to adopt his ways of looking at things and how he acts." Wolf's backstory involves a woman that he loved (though Wolf would never admit that). The woman was killed. Wolf believes he could have saved her. Enter guilt-ridden, doomed, loner-type melodrama. "I thought about what would happen to a person who actually had that happen to them. They close down. They move away from even kind of caring about other people and they create a shell for themselves." That was Perretta's planned starting point for Wolf. The emotional journey would be Wolf slowly letting people in and having Wolf slowly find family again.

But a funny thing happened when Wolf strolled through the magic portal. "I found that he was growing and doing it fast," Perretta said. "In the very first game, I became a voice of reason on why we *shouldn't* kill all of the other people even though they were very different from us." The character that he thought he controlled surprised him. Wolf had a mind and a heart of his own.

Perretta once played a real slimeball named Tassidar. "Just once I wanted to play the bad guy," he said. "I played that character for around a year and a half, and honestly, when he finally got killed off, I wasn't sorry to see him go." But Tassidar helped Perretta work through a gloomy period in his life. "I needed a Tassidar so that I could express negative things to get rid of the negativity I was feeling at the time. But I did it through a character that was smiling to your face and then working behind the scenes to stab you in the back. This is very close to what I was going through at that time." He'd also played characters that slinked in the shadows and went unnoticed. It all depended on his mood. He saw his present character as serving a different purpose. "Wolf is a way to shape the world around me rather than shape myself around the world."

LARPs could be cathartic, psychoanalytic, or accidental therapy. Perretta worried that it all sounded horribly egomaniacal. "But really, this is the only way I would ever express these things. I live, what I hope is, a good life. But sometimes it is just fun to really get into the idea of being the center of the universe. Gaming can let you do that."

It seemed to me that he had a healthy attitude about his habit. Gaming let him express emotions, be physical, be what he'd never be in real life. It also gave him the chance to socialize. He wouldn't have seen friends for months, and "when we get together it is like we just saw each other the other day and you just pick up the conversations right where they left off." So what if he looked like a polar bearskin rug?

A FIDGETY BALL OF INARTICULATE ENERGY

"Game on!" And the game was afoot. Players introduced themselves, picked up the storyline from the last game a month ago, and began discussing the threats to their town. When partici-pants began playing—fighting, talking, eating—immersion was nearly total. When a garbage truck roared into camp, the players took it in stride. "It's a stone monster!" someone said. "Look, a dragon!" "No. If it was a dragon we'd all be dead now." I even added a quip of my own: "But is it a god-fearing creature?"

They played not only an amalgam of characters influenced by the many fantasy movies, books, and games featuring heroes, wizards, and fairies they'd absorbed throughout popular culture; they were also playing themselves. But because LARPs are a form of collective storytelling, they're highly affecting expe-riences, even transformative, like good literature. I can recall scenes from D&D games I played two-plus decades ago; they seem to me as memorable as "real" experiences. Other gamers have told me much the same.

Leif Thorsson, the drunk Viking, was played by Chris Jones, thirty-three, who worked in Internet advertising. Jones was aver-age height, average build, with brown hair and a gift for gab. He was also an erstwhile seminary student pursuing a dual theologi-cal / clinical counseling degree. Before that, he served in the Air Force for seven and a half years, both in Afghanistan and Iraq. Jones credited his wife, Rachel, twenty-seven, for drawing him into LARPing. "She's the reason I do this," he said later. "She wanted to be a fairy. She wanted to wear ears and glitter and the costume. Myself, I didn't care. I didn't want to dress up and run around in costume."

When they moved to Atlanta after they got married, they had never heard of boffer LARPing. At Dragon*Con, a fantasy conven-tion, they talked to Chris Tang, who explained the FoD concept. The clincher: fairies. "She was grabbing my arm like a little kid and said 'They have fairies, they have fairies, they have wings!'" Rachel created a character named Tyrsia. Chris agreed to try it out. "I made up a character. It took me about an hour. It wasn't exactly what I thought it was going to be." But then he got into it. He spent two or three nights at home in costume, making a backstory for his character. "I crafted the whole tale right up until he stepped through the door." That character was Magnus Tigersblood, not Leif Thorsson. He started playing, and he was hooked.

Jones told me about his gaming past. He recalled running around his Florida neighborhood as a child and battling other kids, using palm fronds as swords. He would make up characters and go out and act them out. "It was like boffer LARPing." He read *Narnia* and *Rings*. He and his friends were into strategy games, RPGs, paintball, video games, and chess; when they grew older, it was camping and partying. "We were the kind of group who went out and did things," Jones said. "It's a little embarrassing how old I am and how long I've been doing this."

Jones could recount in intricate detail the events of his first FoD battle, as if reliving it all again. He peppered the story with snippets of dialogue. People yelled "Charge!" He was "swinging wildly in berserker mode." Over forty-five minutes, he discussed fight strategy with me: tactics, scouting, and flanking maneuvers. "My ax got tangled up in vines," he said. "Not very heroic. Not what you hear about in the stories. . . . They beat me like a baby seal." Magnus and his group had lost badly. "I tend to remember the battles. You tend to remember the dramatic things in life. Whether you succeed or fail, you remember them."

Jones's characters seemed to flow from facets of himself. Other LARPers were attracted to cool effects and combat mechanics. One college student I talked to post-game, fresh out of his goblin costume, was new to FoD but already smitten. "I like the ability to cast fireballs," he said, his eyes wild. Fireballs being just cloth packets of birdseed that are tossed, like water balloons, in combat. The fireballs only exploded in his mind. All good. As long as he didn't start concocting Molotov cocktails back in his dorm room. Fireballs were probably cathartic, like Perretta suggested. I didn't really worry that LARPs encouraged aberrant behavior. Quite the contrary: I suspected that for introverted players, a LARP might quietly teach leadership and social skills. Within the first hour of play at Forest of Doors, I watched a young man who seemed to prove the point.

He was a first-time player, pacing back and forth, a fidgety ball of inarticulate, hand-rubbing energy. He had a hard time engaging other people in conversation. He was a spaz. Yet once the game began and he had donned his chain mail and slung his great shield over his shoulder, he blossomed. He became Sir Talon, a chivalrous knight with a not-bad English accent, pumped to defend a woman's honor and lead a sortie of fighters into the woods to combat some unknown, menacing force.

"I'm going to go see what's going on out there," he commanded, pushing his glasses up his nose. "Who will join me?" Then he strode off into the darkened fields to kick some ass.

WHAT THE HECK—I WAS ON A QUEST, TOO

The morning of day two, I pulled myself out of bed and headed to the tavern, grumbling, *The Forest of Doors better have coffee.*

I had not slept well. My role-playing brain maxed out, I had turned in early, the first to bed in my cabin. I assumed Sir Talon and his merry men would rid the darkness of nasties. As I had headed to the dormitory, the half-moon rose like a Viking ship on a sea of clouds. I was alone in the cabin. When a black-shrouded spirit wandered past my bunk sometime in the night, wielding a white sword, I almost had a seizure. I decided it wasn't real and went back to sleep.

But I was safe in the daylight. On the tavern porch, a player in a Robin Hood–like outfit, feather in his cap, recounted an adventure from the night before: "There were rat-wolf things and a cave of extreme foulness and I hated it." Folks shared war stories. We began to bond. But true adventure had still eluded me. I mean, Ethor. Until, that is, an armored knight clanked and stumbled by.

"I seek people of wit!" he cried.

"What do you mean, good sir?" I asked, sipping my coffee. I tried to get the knight to explain further. "What is your name?"

A skirmish in the woods of Indian Springs State Park, Flovilla, Georgia, at the Forest of Doors LARP.

He was evasive. "I have a quest," he said. "I seek . . . the most beautiful thing."

I tried to get the knight to explain further. "What is this . . . *thing* you seek?" We sounded like a *Holy Grail* outtake. He kept repeating himself. There was something odd about him. But, oh, what the heck—I was on a quest, too. One that kept slipping between my fingers. Right now, it seemed to be whether I could commit to this game.

I left the relative safety of the tavern and tagged along with a hastily assembled fellowship: a fighter, a healer, and me. The knight said we had to go back into the forest. Perhaps it was the caffeine rush, but I felt a thrill as we hurried down the path. Adventure! Anything could happen . . .

After a short walk, we came to a dungeon (a cabin, that is) whose door was bound by four different-colored ribbons: red, yellow, black, and white. A note was taped to the door frame. It read:

SOUGHT BY THOSE

OF WICKED ARTS,

HIDDEN WITHIN

LOATHSOME HEARTS

A riddle. Or a magical trap. The Monty Python knight suggested the answer might be one of the four colors. But pull the wrong ribbon and . . . BOOM!

"Don't kill me," said Ramavadi, an Apsara spell caster from "a race of water-breathing people who live within an endless whirlpool." He was a mystic, a learned man—a lover, not a fighter. Like me. "I can bring people back to life," he said.

Right. Don't kill off the healer. He'd come in handy.

We guessed "black" and yanked the corresponding ribbon. No explosion or curse or cloud of doom. The door opened and we entered the cave unscathed. Ahead stood a statue, frozen in the gloom. If we didn't answer the puzzles in the cave correctly, it would probably attack. We guessed right for all three riddles, each written on a slip of paper, and brought back the booty: something called the Idol of Forbidden Knowledge.

By now, it did not seem strange to pretend that the Idol of Forbidden Knowledge—a tacky Chinatown souvenir—had real magical properties, no more than it seemed odd to play-act the sense of danger we felt as we entered the dungeon. I was beginning to get it. Though I never did find out if the Idol was "the most beautiful thing" or whether it would serve as the carrot on the stick for the next quest.

I did see battle. During a clash between we twenty defenders and an army of nasty, half-humanoid, half-plant creatures called mandrakes, I watched that pyromaniac goblin toss fireballs. I saw a fairy named Dusk Whisper use healing potions and spells to patch up the wounded fighters. And I wondered, What drew him to that character? Did he have to care for a sick family member? Perhaps all escapers suffered some kind of trauma. Did he have a mommy complex, too? As for me, pacifist, passive-aggressive monk—why had I chosen that role? (Never mind; don't answer that question.)

In the end, I proved my mettle. The FoD handbook describes combat this way:

Any attack that hits a legal location takes off points of Resilience equal to its damage. If a character is struck by an attack that does more damage than their remaining Resilience, they take a wound to the location that is hit. A wounded arm is unusable, a wounded leg means you can only move by crawling, and a wounded torso means you are Critical (dying).

I had no idea what my Resilience was. No matter. As the mandrakes attacked, I was caught up in the melee:

"Power Strike!"

Bam!

"Parry!"

"Get in there! Flank him!"

"Two more mandrakes!"

Fwaappppp!

"Power Strike 2!"

"Dodge!"

Ffff-bapppp-pah-pah-pah!

"Mortal Blow!"

Argggggghhhhhhh!

I was swinging my mace and monsters were dropping. The surging adrenaline was real. By the end of the weekend, even a man of peace could justify violence in the face of pure evil.

SIR, YOUR WORDS ARE FROM YOUR HEART

What had ultimately made the LARP alluring was not the play violence, but the conversations. On Sunday morning, folks gathered around the tavern, eating breakfast and discussing their ragtag utopia. Saphrin, from the Arabian-like Desert of Brass kingdom and dressed like a belly dancer, complained about infighting to the bull-headed Magnus Tigersblood, Chris Jones's other warrior (you could sometimes play multiple characters over the course of the weekend).

"What is needed is two councils," Saphrin insisted. "A council of war, and one for domestic matters."

"Your world extends no farther than the end of your sword," Magnus shot back. What ensued was an argument about how to best govern their frontier settlement.

Saphrin complained that there was no place allotted for women.

Magnus replied, "If you want to lead people—"

"I am not here to lead people," interrupted a character named Sol, dressed in white with a gold mask and eating a banana. "If they want to follow me, OK."

Things got heated. Players discussed the issue—without a script, or jumping out of character . . . or giggling. (Though any player who wanted to exit temporarily "out-of-game" made a special hand signal, holding a closed fist or a weapon to his or her head, or by wearing a white headband. The other players would then ignore the person as if he or she were invisible.)

Finally Magnus apologized. "I am not a wise man. I know how to fight and how to draw a few runes."

"Sir, your words are from your heart," said Sir Talon. Wow. This kid was still on.

Sol, Magnus, Talon, and Saphrin continued their debate. In the end, nothing was resolved. Their story would be continued at a future weekend.

Game master Christopher Tang was right: He couldn't control the party, nor the plot. The LARP had its monsters and its adventures, but the most compelling action revolved around how, or if, everyone could get along. Just like in the real world. The appeal of LARPing was not the battles, but the collective storytelling, the camaraderie. As Tang had put it: "The quiet moments, just talking, is the heart of what we do."

And in truth, I was going to miss those quiet moments. My first night, as Ethor, I spoke for a half-hour with a pointy-eared, green-veined goblin named Heinrich Irongear. Completely in character, we compared the political economies of our made-up worlds. Mine, the Realm of Castles, a rich forest dotted with alabaster fortresses, seemed like paradise. His subterranean Goblin City, with belching iron factories, sounded like Dickensian London. I took pity on him, or his character (it was hard to say which). Heinrich seemed happier in the Forest of Doors than back home—wherever that was.

As for Saphrin, earlier that weekend her character had explained to me (well, to Ethor, anyway) how she'd arrived in this place. She said she had found a door while exploring ruins in her desert world. She went through the door, and did not want to go back. "I enjoy it here. The seasons change, and I have many friends here. And I feel free to be who I want to be. Given the option, I'd rather stay here." I—Ethan, not Ethor—later learned that the woman's real-life husband was off in Iraq. "My husband was not a kind man," she said. As she spoke in-game, I couldn't help but wonder if she meant her LARP world or her real life, whether Saphrin's story overlapped with the woman who played her, and how much truth had leaked into this fantasy. Or if any of this mattered.

Perhaps it will matter someday . . . but not that day.

My mind traveled back to the car ride to Flovilla three days earlier. I had wondered if, surrounded by digital culture, humans had lost the ability to think magically, and suggested to Tang

Characters from the Forest of Doors LARP: Saphrin, second from left; at right, Sir Talon.

that perhaps LARPs might not be able to compete with MMOs. We were stuck in a traffic jam on I-75, on the way to what would become—once Tang declared "game on," and once we walked through the portals—the place where almost anything could happen, the Forest of Doors. His response offered the contrary position. "What we do is closest to virtual reality," he said. "We're actually doing what we're doing." A weekend in the Forest of Doors proved not only a LARP was not silly. It was also as immersive as D&D, as a video game, as life itself.

As for that fantasy–reality divide that I had been struggling with, Nick Perretta could have schooled me on how to cope. He told me that he didn't think much about Forest of Doors once he'd returned home from a weekend in the woods. "I leave the game mostly behind," he said. Sometimes he'd scribble down an idea for Wolf's next exploits. "Most of the time, though, I just let the game have its time and my wife and daughter get me the rest of the time." IRL: in his real life.

Geeks get personal with tech

A geek is more likely to figure out how to customize toys and to design arousing environments for your avatars to play in than a non-geek. And that experience translates into a greater sensitivity to atmosphere and mood during sex—beyond lighting a candle.

Don't be surprised if your geek lover puts more thought into arranging the boudoir than you do, or if common household items ("pervertibles") soon take on a new dimension. More than one geek has told me that Home Depot is their favorite adult store.

Geeks dig consensual role playing

Geek lovers combine a well-developed and oft-exercised erotic imagination with their physical technique. It isn't a big leap from "I'm a level-13 thief, evil-aligned" to "I'm the prison warden and you're the new detainee." Scientists and therapists alike claim that the brain is the most critical sexual organ; a geek's familiarity with fantasy arouses your mind even as the handcuffs—or the bag of loot—bring your body to attention.

Geeks interact

A technophobe mostly talks to you in person, but a geek is happy to be with you by texting your phone, flirting with you in a chat room, Skyping you, Twittering just in case you're on your vibrating couch . . . seducing you by instant message. . . .

—from "The 10 Real Reasons Why Geeks Make Better Lovers,"
an article by Regina Lynn on Wired.com (2007)

Geeks in Love

Before I go any further, I must 'fess up: A big something happened about mid-way through my quest. A tic in my personal life became a twitch, and then became a series of oscillations and tremors that shook my world. On love's Richter scale, the seismic event hit a 7.8.

My relationship with my girlfriend—the one who didn't quite understand my penchant for quoting Tolkien dialogue in parking lots—collided with reality. Or, at least, with a major roadblock in her mind. Her doubts about me being husband-worthy material, being a manly provider type and possibly fathering offspring, festered in unhealthy ways. The fact that early on in our dating phase I made her watch all three *Lord of the Rings* movies probably did not help my cause. Nor had my weekend in Flovilla, Georgia, fighting terrorbeaks. Or my other medieval moments.

Like in the movie *Diner*, where Steve Guttenberg's character Eddie makes his fiancée pass a football trivia quiz before agreeing to marry her, I had wanted to gauge my girlfriend's tolerance of me as a once and possibly future geek. I had no final exam for her, but she had one for me. As our first year together drew to an end, I had somehow failed *her* test.

Naturally, this raised old specters. I knew my D&D past was not entirely to blame, but a horde of doubts still plagued me. Was I mired in some perpetual adolescence, or was I charmingly/innocently in touch with my inner child? Did that inner child need an ass-whupping? The two of us haggled over a potential future. We parleyed and parried and cried way too often. We spent so much time broken up, I felt like I had an imaginary girlfriend who I could visit only in an imaginary kingdom. I did not want my intimate life to become a fantasy life. I had been in one major long-term relationship, but ever since, with other women, I had fallen for that "fake relationship" trap: false closeness, words not action, and assuming e-mail love meant real love. I feared my ineptitude to find or stay in a normal relationship was a further symptom of an unformed, perpetually fetal me, and that this failure was emblematic of my larger escapist tendencies. Ever since the Momster, perhaps I was afraid to let a woman get too close.

My girlfriend and I took some time apart. I had to begin all over again, yet felt no wiser. I checked in with old flames, some of whom had married and made babies. Most of my friends and family had by now found their nine-to-five, soccer practice, and poker-night paths to domestic bliss. Why did I have none of this, and why did I still refuse to follow that well-trodden, time-tested life trajectory? How did couples find and sustain love, trust, intimacy, and understanding? How did they negotiate and tolerate each other's oddball interests and obsessions? I wondered if the woman of my dreams would also have to share my passions. At least she would have to refrain from passing judgment on them (e.g., my *Lord of the Rings* figurines, once she found them in my underwear drawer). Was there room in relationships for both sides to express rich fantasy lives, whether the same or wildly different? Could a geek find love?

I found some answers in a surprising place: Milwaukee.

THAT FLEETING MAGIC MOMENT

I met Elyse Boucher and Mike Scott through an online hospitality network called couchsurfing.com. I was headed to Milwaukee on assignment and figured a good way to run deep with geekdom while visiting would be to infiltrate a lair or two. I saw Elyse's online profile: "Interests: Art, living history, sci-fi, reading, archery, historical costuming, books books books." She maintained five Web sites, including two "in-persona" blogs. Her main Web site declared, "I am a well-adjusted geek who likes imaginative, social play." She was not "a basement-dwelling, no-other-social-skills geek casting magic missile to attack the darkness."* Better still, she seemed well matched with her partner. I knew I had struck it rich.

They agreed to host me for a night. I drove to West Allis, Wisconsin, just west of downtown Milwaukee, on a muggy summer afternoon. I parked outside their house and knocked on their door.

"Hello . . . welcome. Come in," Elyse said.

I walked up the steps, passed through the porch, and entered the house. It was a shrine to geekdom.

A medieval helmet sat on their CD stand. A couple of hefty steel swords hung from the walls. On every shelf, in every nook, on every flat surface, a something: a plastic or ceramic pop culture knickknack, a model car or spaceship, an action figure. Amid all the clutter, I still found it hard to miss the oil painting of two intertwined dragons as I headed up the stairs to my bedroom, or the longbow and quiver balanced in the corner next to the TV.

"We're looked at as geeks and freaks, but in our culture we're pretty lucky," said Elyse. "We're trying to find out what makes us whole."

---

* "Magic missile" is the name of a first-level spell in D&D. According to the *Players Handbook*, the missiles "dart forth from the magic-user's fingertip and unerringly strike their target," causing 2 to 5 hit points of damage.

"It's fun being a geek," added Mike. "Why be normal?"

Regular folks make more money, Mike went on, but they lead lives of drudgery. Not Mike, a fantasy artist and craftsman of retro-design televisions. Not Elyse, a case manager for the Milwaukee council on aging and former nuclear, biological, and chemical weapons specialist in the army. No drudgery, no boredom—not in this house. And no ugly, cocktail-party sniping of each other (drunk wife or husband to assembled dinner guests: "I can't believe he/she spends all his/her time doing X.") Mike and Elyse seemed to get along brilliantly. From what I could tell, geek culture—and their tolerance of each other's quirks—helped the two discover their true selves, whereas in my recent experience, lack of tolerance was the hurdle.

Elyse had met "this skinny guy"—forty-seven, big-rimmed glasses, salt-and-pepper goatee, quasi–Middle Ages mullet—at a Renaissance fair in 1992. They started talking. He said he was an artist. She was not impressed. All the guys say they are artists, drummers, actors. "What piece of garbage am I going to have to say is beautiful?" she remembered thinking. But Elyse's then eight-year-old daughter was impressed. The lithographs Mike had in his car weren't half bad: actual *Dragon* magazine covers and Spelljammer game art. When Mike recognized Elyse's penchant for making *Holy Grail* references, 'twas love at first sight. "I was the girl who was wooed by Monty Python," she beamed. When I met them, Elyse was forty-five, her daughter Angelique was twenty-four, and her granddaughter, Angelique's own daughter, was six.

As a kid, Elyse's mom had bought her the D&D boxed set. She ate it up and read as much fantasy literature as she could. A six-year army stint in the 1980s got her out of her small northern Illinois town, and got her a first husband. She played D&D with her fellow soldiers on an army base in Germany, and wrote interactive fiction. During college, she discovered the Society for

Elyse Boucher as Dame Merouda Pendray, the persona she plays in the Society for Creative Anachronism.

Creative Anachronism.* Her husband didn't allow her to participate. That marriage didn't last long. Now in a healthy relationship, Elyse had delved deep into a few subcultures. But D&D, like the SCA, wasn't something that she liked to blab about out-of-game. "I'm not interested in talking about characters, my twelfth-level ranger elf, at lunchtime." For her, the appeal of the SCA was to be fully in the moment of role-play. "If I'm sitting in a sixteenth-century pavilion wearing a sixteenth-century dress, sweating in a sun-drenched field, I don't want to talk about computers," she said in her precise and matter-of-fact way of speaking. "I want to be talking about gardens, family, potted plants, sixteenth-century stuff. You have to be willing to make that jump."

Elyse stood in her very ordinary kitchen in Milwaukee. The air was damp, and the light dimmed as cloud cover arrived. She described the SCA's "Knowne World," which consists of nineteen kingdoms worldwide, a place where she was known as Dame Merouda Pendray. As Merouda, she lived for that fleeting "magic

---

* The Society for Creative Anachronism (SCA) is an organization of 30,000-plus members "dedicated to researching and re-creating the arts and skills of pre-17th-century Europe," according to the SCA's Web site.

moment"—when even if but for an instant "you feel like you are in history. You see yourself in the sixteenth century." Thunderstorms growled outside. "I don't actually want to go back to the sixteenth century, because that wasn't a pleasant place." Living without penicillin, for example, would be a drag. Still, she wanted to feel that sense of enchantment as the "twentieth century fades away."

No more parking lots or potholes, no more custody battles or alimony, no more economic downturn.

I HAVE NOT YET DONE ANYTHING SAGA-LIKE

The present day fading away, clouding over, becoming something else. I knew that what Elyse described was an experience sought by many. Fantasy escapism, in both mild and immersive forms, has roots that run deep in human history. I've already iterated my reasons for D&D hooking me. But I'm just me—most of the time, anyway. Just one recovering, occasionally insecure geek dipping into his past. Excellent rationales explain why all this fantasy entertainment might appeal to others. As literature and story, it has proven a time-tested genre, with a solid and rich foundation beneath all these whimsical elves and foam swords. I wasn't sure if I understood why fantasy, more so than other genres, could cast such an intoxicating spell of immersion, or exactly why we human beings need to pretend we're someone else. But as I gallivanted along on my quest, I figured it had to serve a function higher than pure check-out-of-reality escape. Or else the desire was hardwired into our brains and psyches, and we had been a shallow, addicted culture of escapists since the first story was told around the first campfire.

It can be argued that cave painting inspired the original escapist fantasies. Our ancestors probably stared at pictures of animals they drew, play-acting or fantasizing about killing their mastodon or whatever they liked to eat. They had no books, but their minds were stimulated to imagine a kind of "make-believe" action in an imaginary space. Various rituals—how to make rain, become fertile, get the girl, slay the demon—served a similar purpose, giving early humans purpose and belonging, a mastery over the elements, and the ability to escape the confines of their flesh. The dances and trances were a way to deny death and provide a vacation from everyday thought. These mental gymnastics were not quite the same as our modern sense of fantasy, but were the beginning of humankind's efforts to create a convincing simulation of a real sensory experience, and a distraction from day-to-day life, aka "reality." Your troubles.

As we advanced as a society, we've come to understand our heroic campfire stories as make-believe, as metaphors for real life. Whether Greek myth, *La Chanson de Roland,* Norse *Edda* and *Völsunga* sagas, the Finnish *Kalevala,* or the German *Nibelungenlied* (and, in the East, the *Mahabharata* and *Ramayana*), nowadays we don't believe these legends actually happened.* Seen as real or not, these stories did impart values, and often had another purpose than to simply entertain. They modeled idealized behavior and embodied desires of what we could never do or be. *The Iliad* and *The Odyssey,* two narrative poems told in elevated language, celebrate the feats of heroes who struggle with worthy foes against a backdrop of gods and monsters. For these protagonists, slaying beasts is their principal activity, and they discover fame and pride through brazen acts of courage on the battlefield. The ultimate is glory and honor. Unapologetic ambition, fighting brutally, mercilessly—even dying is no bad thing, as long as the heroes triumph or go down swinging.

Sounds good, doesn't it? We all want to live a life of valor, action, romance. In the best flights of fantasy, we dream of a better self. This was the function of twelfth-century Norse works such as *Njáls Saga* and *Egils Saga.* These tales of valor taught

---

* Don't get me started about the Bible's tall tales; Stephen King once said something to the effect of, "The Bible? Some of the best horror stories ever written."

both psychological and moral lessons, and pointed the way to bravery. In Icelandic sagas, the character would say, "I have not yet done anything saga-like." These heroic narratives featured imperfect characters who accomplished great things, despite their flaws. This type of story was designed to fantasize the listener into better behavior, and served as a "how to be a hero" instruction manual.

But as we've progressed as a culture, we've become more disconnected from nature and have relied less on "faerie" or magical explanations for scientific phenomena. Longing for the way we were has become a formidable force, opening an imaginative space for nostalgia. As early as the late Middle Ages, authors were already romanticizing a lost, fantasy past. Sir Thomas Malory's collection of King Arthur tales, *Le Morte d'Arthur* (1485) and the poem *The Faerie Queene* (1590) by Edmund Spenser revived the ideas of knightly romance and combat, just as that way of life was dying. Like the Brothers Grimm, Spenser and Malory populated their works with fantasy stock characters like giants, goblins, and sorcerers to help breathe life into that magical era. Interestingly, *The Faerie Queene* was the first major literary work featuring elves, not men, as main characters.

Much later, in the nineteenth century, William Morris wrote *The Wood Beyond the World* and other works, which broke ground as the first fantasy novels set in an imaginary fantasy world. The path that leads us to Tolkien takes us through authors like Jonathan Swift, Mary Shelley, Edgar Allan Poe, Jules Verne, George MacDonald (*Phantastes, The Princess and the Goblin*), J. M. Barrie (*Peter Pan*), L. Frank Baum (the *Oz* books), and Robert E. Howard (*Conan*). These writers' combined dabblings in various genres made fantasy, gothic, horror, speculative fiction, ghost and vampire stories, mystery, and the supernatural all fair game for their literary descendants, and familiarized the tropes of magic, haunted houses, castles, secret doors, madness, curses, and adventure for a new generation of readers.

At the same time, a parallel path was taken by speculative fiction like H. G. Wells's *The War of the Worlds* and *The Time Machine,* and movies like *Metropolis* and *Modern Times.* These works expressed public anxiety in the face of urbanization and dehumanization. (Tolkien's colleague Jack Lewis tried his hand at science fiction—his "space trilogy"—while J. R. R. stuck with fantasy.) It's safe to say that as a culture, as we headed deeper into the twentieth century, traveling further from our agrarian pasts and becoming more industrialized, we became more skeptical of progress. We may be emotionally and intellectually sophisticated as a species, but we've experienced growing pains. We're still in the awkward adolescent stage of our evolution on planet Earth, one foot tentatively testing the future, the other hankering for the past. Hence, the greater our yearning for a pretechnological time, and this restless nostalgia for days of yore. Or perhaps a yearning to be elsewhere is simply the human response to anxiety.

STUCK IN THE MIDDLE AGES VS. FUTURE BOY

I had gone out for part of the evening. When I came back, Elyse was asleep, but Mike, a night owl like me, was awake. We shared beers in his living room and watched *Futurama* on TV. I soon learned that Mike and Elyse's geeky hobbies and fandom activities were polar-opposite subcultures. Elyse was in the fantasy camp. Mike was into science fiction. We drank some more, and Mike told me about his past.

A Milwaukee native, Mike was an outcast in high school. He used to dress up as KISS band members and spit fake blood. At sixteen he moved out of his house and started working in restaurant management, then for a cable company. But he always built stuff and loved art. "I wanted to do everything," he remembered. He made custom cars, did airbrush artwork, and painted fantasy-themed scenes. A guy at the cable company who was into D&D took him to Lake Geneva, home of Gygax's company TSR, Inc.

You should be doing this, the guy told him. He introduced Mike to TSR's art director. By the early 1990s, Mike was freelancing for TSR, creating art for its family of role-playing products.

Mike sat on a beaten-down couch in their living room. He showed a video of his first day at work at TSR: a shaky camera roving around the studio, shots of other artists like famed fantasy painter Jeff Easley. He had felt like the luckiest guy in the world. "I got to go to work and paint and do what I liked," Mike recalled. "It was a hell of a lot better than soldering cables and fixing converter boxes." If the company hadn't been bought by Wizards of the Coast and moved to Seattle, he told me he still would have been working there.

Eight years ago, with a business partner, Mike began a career creating reproduction 1950s Philco "Predicta" televisions for the high-end, collectibles market. "We make everything, even the knobs," Mike said, with an excitable, almost childlike level of animation. His company has been featured in national magazines. One of his TVs was used in the Emmy Awards broadcast. Elton John, Brad Pitt, and Alex Ross (fellow geek and famed DC and Marvel comic-book artist) have all purchased his Predictas.

Mike was electrified about many things: historical and ahistorical costumes, Beatles memorabilia, toys, models, and collectibles. Intrigued by 1950s science fiction design, he began re-creating highly detailed reproductions of props from his favorite films and TV shows. "It's a small hobby side project," he said. He wasn't some "big-time re-caster making a fortune." His was a one-man operation, making items from scratch to outfit small groups of people for conventions and occasionally to sell to private collectors. His work included replica manta ray–like Martian war machines from the original 1953 *The War of the Worlds* film, jet packs identical to the ones used in the film *The Rocketeer,* and Viper pilot helmets based on the new *Battlestar Galactica* series. He built a Mike-sized, silver fiberglass costume of Bender, the foul-mouthed cartoon robot from *Futurama*. Tired of waiting for a toy company to put one out, he made a super-detailed scale model of a car from the Jack Lemmon, Natalie Wood, and Tony Curtis movie, *The Great Race*. He had friends who helped him make *Battlestar Galactica* flight suits. "Some say these are more realistic than the props used on the set," he said. Which begged the question: What makes one prop for an imaginary science fiction scenario more or less "realistic" than the other?

Earlier that evening, Mike and Elyse had given me a tour of their treasures. In a back room, behind lit-up glass cases, he had arranged his collections: years of science fiction memorabilia, including a blaster used in the SF spoof *Galaxy Quest* and rows of *Star Trek* action figures. He didn't collect *Star Wars*. "I had to draw the line somewhere," he quipped. But in its own giant case, dominating the room, I saw what Mike explained was the original "Dr. Frank-N-Furter" leather jacket, smothered with pins and chains—the Real McCoy worn by Tim Curry in *The Rocky Horror Picture Show*.

Elyse also used the room to work on her SCA projects, like calligraphy. Mike would participate in SCA events; he had his period costume, and his SCA name was Miguel De Montoya el Artista. (The name was inevitably followed by the "You killed my father—prepare to die!" reference from *The Princess Bride*.) He had fun at annual events like Pennsic War, but the medieval era didn't quite light up his imagination like the future did. To me, his participation seemed more out of kindness to Elyse, in fealty to their relationship, so they could both enjoy attending the same events.

Watching him talk, it became clear that Mike was happiest making stuff out of fiberglass, creating molds, sculpting, and painting. He'd love to be making movie props full-time, professionally. That was his dream. His Holy Grail: to build a full-scale, walking Robby the Robot suit, from his favorite film, *Forbidden Planet*. His current project: an intricately detailed reproduction of the spacesuits used in the film *2001: A Space Odyssey*.

Mike Scott with his collection of science fiction memorabilia and props, most of which he hand-crafted himself. Bender costume at right.

"It's never been done faithfully. I'm a stickler for detail." At a recent convention called Wonderfest, *2001*'s lead actor Keir Dullea donned the helmet, providing Mike with "another incredible geek moment."

"That 'stickler for details [trait]' is common to model-making, the SCA, D&D, gaming," Elyse added. For the SCA, she has created documents in painstaking calligraphy, as well as illuminated manuscripts. She is into heraldry, embroidery, and archery. She makes her own paints and bakes her own sourdough bread. In the SCA these sticklers tend to be members of the Order of Laurel. They craft stuff, they weave, they make armor, they cook. In D&D, she said, they call these types "rules lawyers." Really into the minutiae.

She also took her role-playing onto the Internet. Between SCA events, she blogged from the point of view of her persona, Merouda, (using modern day equivalents for period typography):

17 AUGUST 2008

Vpon ye day of Saint Joachim. my Lord Miguel et I waited upon ye Baron et Baroness at ye yr tourney, et spent pleasaunt hours in discourse with many whom I hath seen little iin these passing months. Et so also did I see my old gossips, Lady Gabrielle and Lady Genvieve. and most pleased was I, fot it hath been many years since I was with them and able to speak of things we all enjoy. 7 we have all promised to gather again, having made oaths to one another to work on such documents and illuminations as we may. 7 so also did I spend time in ye companie of ye Countess Julia, for whom I have great regard, et ye Baroness Alice, et others, but I did not shoot in ye archery tourney et so am sad for ys.

Ironic that the role-play for a woman who supposedly lived in the Middle Ages was recorded not, say, on vellum in a leatherbound book, but as a blog. But the SCA, as I would learn later, was capable of embracing all kinds of anachronistic contradictions.

Elyse and Mike led me down to their basement. More stuff. One half of the space was a chaotic workshop crammed with supplies; the other half a tiki bar next to more glass cases for their museum of toys.

"I got the pack-rat gene," Mike said.

"Some of these toys are Michael's, some of these are the six-year-old's," Elyse deadpanned. Some of the stuff was hers, too. But the house was only so big. Their country house that they planned to move to someday would have more display space. Possibly. They'd work it out.

Whether or not they had room for all their stuff, they certainly had made room for each other, as other couples have done. I had heard all kinds of stories. There were those who had gotten hitched at SCA events, or other LARP groups like Dagorhir's Ragnarok (picture the wedding party dressed in period costume and the cake in the shape of a castle). Other couples gamed together—D&D, Warhammer, or World of Warcraft—or connected online and eventually married IRL. Some built their families around gaming culture; a boyfriend would get his girlfriend hooked on an online game and they'd come from work, each log on to their separate laptops, and their avatars would interact all evening. Romantic bliss. During my Summer of Imploding Love, I spent some time with a woman who had met her husband at a gaming convention. They had a young son, and she organized "play dates" with other moms in her social circle. The kids played with each other while the moms played RPGs.

What was the love lesson here? Pairings of geek and non-geek, what Elyse called "mixed marriages," usually didn't work. "Michael's other girlfriends didn't get his interests," she said.

All in all, their complementary mind-sets rarely came into conflict.

"I say she's stuck in the Middle Ages," he said, "and I'm future boy." Their dream house? Half Dr. Morbius's futuristic lair from *Forbidden Planet,* half medieval castle. "She could go off into her tower and I could go off and make coffee with Robby the Robot."

Regular folks didn't get them, but they couldn't have cared less. "I've got a partner who I still love intensely," Mike said. He leaned across the couch to kiss Elyse.

That was it in a nutshell: Elyse and Mike *got* each other. They respected each other's weirdness. It sounded pretty blissful to me. I became just a tinge envious of this union they had found. Out of turbulent pasts, they had made a solid home. Supported each other's quirks. When would I find my Hot & Nerdy gal pal? Or perhaps there would be no geek love for me.

Recently, Elyse told me, she introduced Mike to sock monkeys. She wrote sock monkey stories. Together, they made sock monkey costumes. They took pictures of their sock monkeys. *Sock monkeys.*

"We are adults who understand the purpose of play," Elyse said. Then she got serious. She motioned toward her fifty-five-pound draw longbow in the corner. "But . . . if the zombies come, we'll know what to do."

Mike laughed.

Elyse corrected herself. "*When* they come, we'll know what to do."

General Specifications

Range
-Designed to throw 250–300 lbs.
-300–400 yards with counterweight partially loaded with 50–100 lb. pumpkin.
-The ultimate range with a fully loaded counterweight has yet to be determined.

Actual Throws
-2004: 1394' World Record throw with 8–10 lb. pumpkin.
-2005: 1702' World Record throw with 8–10 lb. pumpkin.
-2006: 1476' World Championship throw with 8–10 lb. pumpkin.
-2007: 1658' World Championship throw with 8–10 lb. pumpkin.

What can Yankee Siege Throw?
-Trebuchets were designed to throw large round rocks that weigh 250 lbs. Yankee Siege is designed to throw the same thing. We substitute pumpkins and other such objects for the sake of safety.

—from the Web site for Yankee Siege, a 56-foot-tall, 52,000-pound trebuchet built in Greenfield, New Hampshire; winners of Punkin Chunkin 2008 World Champions, Trebuchet Division, with a throw of 1,897 feet (www.yankeesiege.com)

To Work Here, You Have to Forget

For some, games are not enough. Miniatures, maps, and graph paper are mere props. Playthings. Foam swords are for poseurs. Even the imagination is insufficient. They want to dwell in a real place, create an annex of a fantasy world, but in *this* world. They travel a step further away from LARPers. A level deeper into dedication. I went to see this fantasy, made manifest.

On a Monday morning, a crew of workers, mostly French, arrived at a forest clearing in Burgundy, three hours southeast of Paris. They were doing their best to stop the clock. If they couldn't actually hold back its hands, they were content to break off huge chunks of the calendar, months at a time, and ignore the twenty-first-century world as we know it. Already dressed in tunics stained ochre from earlier days of labor, they climbed out of their battered Renaults. They hit the "backstage" cantina to down a few espressos from plastic cups. Then, in an extraordinary act of denial, a sort of shared anachronistic reverie (or a delusion the *Diagnostic and Statistical Manual of Mental Disorders* has yet to identify), they tramped off to the Middle Ages.

I visited the site at Guédelon to see their crusade. Laborers and craftspeople were re-creating a medieval castle without modern technology. They wore period clothes and, with their graying beards, mops of hair, and ample bellies, some looked the part. But they were working, not pretending. No play-acting here. They wanted to know how to build castles like their forebears, so these architecture geeks gave it a try, one hand-carved stone at a time. There was nothing make-believe about shattering a slab of rock with a sledgehammer. As I arrived, I thought, What better backdrop for this stage of my quest than a real castle?

Sadly, no dragon would be blasting fire at its towers, nor would any orcs be battering in the front gates. But I was intrigued to see firsthand how the workers balanced that modern-day/medieval-day, time-travel divide. The project evoked the bittersweet dreaming of Don Quixote and the infinite drudgery of Sisyphus. I was here to see how they reclaimed the past. I wondered if I'd visit mine, too.

The workers clearly weren't hobbyist reenactors. This was their job. But fealty to realism ruled. On a thirteenth-century construction site, you wouldn't have seen any of the following items: sneakers, T-shirts, watches, calculators, trucks, power tools, boom boxes, or engines of any kind (except siege engines like catapults). Nor would these tools be found at Guédelon. The requirements for this kind of work were as simple now as they were then: a pale peasant's smock and trousers (no loud colors, please), a willingness to work hard, and, oh, two or three decades of your life.

"To work here, you have to forget," said stonecutter Clément Guérard, who was a seven-year veteran of the project. With a flint and tinderbox, he lit a hand-rolled cigarette—one of the few modern amenities permitted on the job. Walkie-talkies, steel-toed boots, and protective eyewear were also allowed. Then he went back to whacking away at a purplish, breadbox-sized stone with a hammer and chisel. On average, he finished three blocks a day.

Guédelon is the brainchild of Michel Guyot, a former riding instructor from the province of Berry in France. Inspired by a scheme to construct an eighteenth-century

Workers check to make sure a stone is level on the Guédelon worksite.

frigate in Rochefort, Guyot began work on this dream in 1995. He found the ideal location for his fortress—a 6.9-hectare (about 17 acres) abandoned quarry just outside the village of Treigny—and hired castle experts to draw up the plans. After assembling administrative staff, a foreman, and laborers, and raising the necessary start-up funds, he broke ground in 1997.

"When you love old buildings, cathedrals, you ask yourself, how is this done?" said Guyot, fifty-eight years old when I met him, whose passion for castles (he already owned four that he had restored himself) developed in adolescence. He was not interested in merely reconstructing the castle, but in creating an experimental medieval work site to rediscover ancient building techniques, such as the best recipe for a durable mortar, or the best angle, shape, and size for arrow loops.

When I visited, the *chantier médiéval* (medieval construction site) was a little under halfway along its projected twenty-five-year timeline to completion—give or take a few years. There has never been a strict deadline, nor should there be. Modest goals for one year, for example, might be to add thirty steps to the spiral staircase, finish the vaulted ceiling in the main tower's cellar, and raise the wall of the *logis* (great hall) another three meters. By the end of 2008, the workers had erected beams for the great hall and covered about a third of its roof. They might finish by 2025. Or 2026. Or . . . Progress happens when it happens, guided by the precept that the medieval way is the best way (although computer models help to predict the project's path down the road).

The medieval way is something of a mystery. "At the beginning, we didn't know the best methods," Guyot told me. "But after a while, the workers have an eye to cut stone. They can just glance to see if it's wrong." Guédelon is not an exact reproduction of period fortifications because few historical records detail the method for, say, constructing features like merlons and machicolations. To figure it out, Guyot and site supervisor Florian Renucci made several fact-finding trips to nearby ruins, where they looked at design features, analyzed building materials, and mused about which techniques might suit their own castle. For Guédelon's stonecutters, masons, woodworkers, carpenters, blacksmiths, rope makers, and basket weavers, on-the-job training was de rigueur, and the ability to improvise, experiment, and fall headlong into faith was crucial.

Outsiders could also work on-site for a week or more to see for themselves. I met Julien Bultreys, a Belgian student, amateur sword maker, and, not surprisingly, a *Lord of the Rings* fan. His week's experience as a stone hewer, mason, and blacksmith's assistant was diametrically opposed to the super-precise machines he was accustomed to using as an electrical engineering student. (That he was a science geek came as no surprise.) "You're encouraged to work slowly to avoid accidents," said Bultreys. "There's no deadline, no accountability. It doesn't matter how fast we work. Just do a good job."

On first sight, you might think that Guédelon's half-built stone walls and towers, rising from a wide moat cluttered with rock, were long-forgotten ruins being unearthed by archaeologists. The ferruginous sandstone, covered in moss and mold, appeared to have been in place for centuries. Its original design was based on period Burgundian fortifications set forth by Philippe Auguste, king of France, in the twelfth and thirteenth centuries. The king emphasized function over form, eschewing decorative embellishments in favor of battle-friendly features. Guédelon was shaped as a quadrangle, protected by *courtines* (curtain walls), and surrounded by a moat. At the corners stood four main towers; these and the two gatehouses were topped with conical roofs.

One imagines a castle construction site in the Middle Ages swarming with serfs, but Guédelon employs only thirty to thirty-five laborers; workers are far outnumbered by visitors. In my imagination, I supplied the beggars, religious fanatics, and the scary dude whipping the lazy peasants back to work. A woman led a horse pulling a cart. (I suppressed the urge to supply the extras' Pythonesque dialogue: "Bring out your dead!" "I'm not dead yet!")

Contributing to the project's overall sense of authenticity was the natural site, which provided workers with almost every material they needed: water, rock, earth, and wood. Tools and nails were hammered out in the forge. There were no cranes. Stones were pushed on wooden rolling pins; if they needed to be hoisted to the top of the main tower (which will one day rise to 100 feet), a mighty mason named Philippe Delage trudged inside a huge wheel, or "squirrel cage," which turned and lifted the load. And when Renucci needed to explain an idea to his head mason, he got down on his haunches and scratched a diagram into the hard-packed Burgundian dirt.

OVERTHROWING A NEIGHBOR'S CASTLE

While Guédelon was the extreme real deal, it was by no means the only such project. Kids turning corrugated cardboard refrigerator boxes into clubhouses and scrap lumber into tree forts constitute the roots for real-life fantasy world-building. Hard-core adult

LARPers may construct tower and dungeon facades out of plywood and paint them to approximate the pattern of stone. I heard of a luxury condominium project in Madison, Wisconsin (again, the heart of D&D country), "just a 9-iron" away from a golf club, modeled on a European village, with streets named Paddington Parkway and its 164 units priced at $278,000 to $700,000 a pop. "Bentley Green is quaint English villages, royalty, and historic stone architecture all rolled into one," the PR materials crow. "This unique replication of traditional European neighborhood living has all the warmth and character you experience while traveling overseas." In photos, it looked pretty Epcot-fake to me.

Tolkienites eager to travel and immigrate to a "real" Middle-earth build hobbit holes of their own to inhabit. Designs are based on actual movie sets, or merely inspired by a desire to lead some hobbity lifestyle. Homes are rounded, earthy, covered in sod. In Chester County, near Philadelphia, architect Peter Archer was asked by a client to design a structure to house a client's collection of Tolkien manuscripts and artifacts. His company built a small-scale stone cottage with handmade clay roof tiles, a 54-inch-in-diameter round cedar door, and a wooden ribbed arched interior, all befitting of a Baggins.

In Wales, Simon and Jasmine Saville created an earth-sheltered home, both eco-conscious and cheap, made of toxic-free materials from on-site trees, straw bales, stone, and mud. "The house does seem to have some kind of innate appeal. I think it touches something common, a romantic idea of some fantasy past/alternative," Simon said in an interview on his Web site, simondale.net. It's not necessarily a faithful hobbit dwelling. But Tolkien's pro-environment message clearly appeals to neo-hippies. "Everyone says it is a hobbit house; they all love *Lord of the Rings* at the moment. I think Tolkien draws the hobbits as the naive or innocent representation of humans in a wholesome natural state. People instinctively relate to this, especially in the context of modernity."

The Yahoo! Group "BagEnd2" is devoted to a similar ethos: "news and the exchange of ideas concerning the architecture, planning and construction of Hobbit Holes." Some members have built storage sheds and playhouses for kids from round culverts and fitted them with round doors. One Web site, www .ourhobbithole.com, charts the progress of a Frodoesque fantasy. The man behind the project laments why we can't adopt the hobbit lifestyle of food, drink, and the occasional adventure. But, alas, Tolkien's worldview runs afoul of the American Way. Technology, work, and responsibility mean we can't "break with society" or live in the middle of nowhere to "find a simpler way of life." The site's author complains about his slow progress.

Some hobbit dreams are alive, but just barely; others were started but went belly up. At a hobbit-like development called The Shire in Bend, Oregon—complete with artificial thatched roofs, gardens, streams, and ponds, and a "Ring Bearer's Court"— only two homes were built in the thirty-one-lot development. One sold for $650,000 before the project went bankrupt. "It basically destroyed my life financially, but that's the price of a dream," said Ron Meyers, one of the developers, in an interview in the *Bend Bulletin*. Fantasy is not immune to a mortgage crisis.

More obsessive is the brick turreted castle (with moat) that a man in California, near Yosemite National Park, has been building on weekends for the past two decades. The design is based on faint memories of his medieval childhood hometown in the Netherlands. Another guy in Iowa has been making a giant model of Middle-earth city Minas Tirith out of, at last count, 420,000 matchsticks. Still others have constructed full-scale siege weapons. A group in the UK constructed a re-creation of a Roman war machine, a ballista, and later put the $180,000, 12-ton device up for sale on eBay, with one caveat: "If you have aspirations to overthrow a neighbour's castle, the ballista isn't ideal." Others, like the Yankee Siege Team, compete against other siege weapons to see which can launch a pumpkin the farthest at an annual event in Delaware called "Punkin Chunkin."

I think the timeless tangibility of these projects combats the commerciality of the modern world. The retreat to stone, iron, cloth, and wood helps lift the weight of modernity from weary shoulders. When we think "fantasy," we think "medieval." That linking of simplicity to Middle-earth and the Middle Ages is what fuels theme parks, too. But the tradition of building fantasy structures actually dates back to the sixteenth-century European tradition of the "folly." Nostalgic wealthy land owners wanted castles and towers on their estates. Desirous of old picturesque ruins they'd seen elsewhere, they constructed faux abbeys and castles, one of the most grand being Gwrych Castle in North Wales, a massive structure with 120 rooms and 18 turrets.*

Disney's Magic Kingdom is the most commercially driven example of mutant medieval architecture used to evoke that storybook feeling. Now, every major kiddie franchise must have its own theme park. Not to be outdone, in 2010, The Wizarding World of Harry Potter is slated to open in Universal's Islands of Adventure in Orlando. The 20-acre, $265-million park will have rides and attractions that "will draw from all the books and the movies," Universal Studios announced. Expect a Wild Quidditch Ride, a Hagrid Hamburger, and a Voldemort Milkshake.

UNLIKE THE REALM OF MICKEY, GOOFY, AND CINDERELLA

Back at the Guédelon site, at the woods' edge overlooking the castle moat, I found a medieval hamlet still under construction. I wandered among the cluster of wattle-and-daub huts. Pigs dozed behind stick fences, and geese strutted around piles of drying willow and the huts devoted to artisans.

---

* More bizarre, the grounds of Ireland's Belvedere House and Gardens include the 100-foot-long, 50-foot-high "Jealous Wall," built in 1760 to block the view of the property next door. He constructed the wall to appear half-crumbled. The owner believed the neighbor, his brother, was having an affair with his wife. Just to be sure, he locked up his wife for thirty years.

"I get to come here and make baskets all day," Bernard Farges told me. "This is paradise."

Here, Diana Hajdu, a former lawyer from Paris, was busy forming hundreds of decorative clay tiles in preparation for the day a decade from now when the castle's floors will be finished. The eight years she has put in thus far may one day come to naught, as the kiln she will use to perfect her firing technique has yet to be built. She had no idea if her tiles would be able to withstand thousands of footfalls, but she kept on pressing clay into her molds, undeterred. When she's finished with the floor, another 78,000 tiles will be required for the roof.

Many of the site's full-time workers have pledged decades to the project, but they haven't come on board simply because they were seduced by Guyot's vision: Guédelon is also their employer, and they receive salaries and benefits. Administrative director Maryline Martin told me that 90 percent of the workers are not skilled laborers, but "intellectuals." Some fled the cities and white-collar jobs to invite this fantasy into their lives. Guédelon lets them work on something larger than themselves. The place appeals to a primal desire to have one's world in front of you, to live simply, to work hard, to expose one's body to Mother Nature's best and worst, to measure one's progress in wood and stone and sweat. The results of daily work are palpable.

Whereas other "living history" attractions, reenactment encampments, and theme parks are closer to movie sets, albeit with convincing actors and props, at Guédelon, there is actual building going on. Visitors can observe Guyot's crew perfecting their approximation of the old techniques: harvesting oaks and shaping them into beams, splitting massive rock slabs into manageable chunks, custom-chiseling the larger rocks into blocks, and assembling them into ten-foot-high curtain walls like elaborate jigsaw puzzles. Tourists also hit the gift shop and a medieval-themed cafeteria. When I was there, Guédelon had become the second-most-popular attraction in Burgundy.

"It's not a museum," said supervisor Renucci. "You don't push buttons or see a film. Here it's direct interaction between the public and the workers." This has its downside, as far as castle production goes: A largely spellbound public, and hordes of French schoolkids, constantly interrupt workers with questions and gawking eyes. The attention has been a blessing in disguise: 245,000 annual visitors paying seven to nine euros a pop have kept the venture in the black. But it's also invited some grumbling from purists who have labeled Guédelon a theme park. "Some critics call it Disney—fake," Martin fretted, "because we make money and are open to the public."

But unlike the Realm of Mickey, Goofy, and Cinderella, Guédelon is no phony fantasyland with a stuccoed facade. Inhale the smoke, stir the mortar, absorb the utter silence save the sound of chisel blows ringing into stone; Guédelon convincingly evokes another era. Were it still the days of lordly turf battles, a defending garrison could use every corbel, lintel, arrow loop, and murder hole, all in working order. In the unlikely event of an attack, a defending soldier will be able to retreat up the spiral staircase (designed to thwart right-handed attackers), raise the wooden drawbridge, or sneak out the postern for a midnight sortie.

That said, utility isn't really the point. Nor is efficiency. A castle could be built more rapidly with backhoes and pneumatic tools, and more perfect stones could be cut, but that would only mirror the twenty-first century, not open a window to the thirteenth. What drives the dream is not the finished product, but the process. "It will be less interesting once it's done," Guyot lamented.

A man's home is his castle, so the saying goes. Guyot's castle won't be his home. He and other workers probably won't see the castle fully completed during their lifetimes. It's the continuation that matters, he told me—the fact that "the project goes on without me." I was fascinated with this concept, which recalled the cathedral-building projects of yore and that obsolete, decades-long view of work and time.

Wandering the worksite, and chatting with the workers in my broken French, I found the appeal of the atmosphere powerful. I yearned to live in a castle, or at least be here daily. This melancholy for another age—a misplaced nostalgia, to be sure, but palpable—rattled my medieval cage. To escape into physical work, and to find refuge from my constant mental-emotional gymnastics. What ex-D&Der wouldn't romanticize the place? Guédelon was no imaginary fortress sketched on graph paper.

The Guédelon castle in progress, at the end of the working season, 2008.

This was no nebulous video game. Guédelon was the ultimate home, a stronghold of safety against all evil forces.

In 2009, Guédelon was in the year 1240. The place is real, despite its authentic fakeness, its simulacrum of the past, and its wrenching of medievalism into the present. This erstwhile monk would retire there in a heartbeat. I wondered if any rooms might be for rent when the castle was done.

On the last day of my visit, when the sun dropped behind the trees, another day of chipping rock, hewing beams, and forming tiles had ended. At 6:00 P.M.—quitting time—a worker blew a horn. They would go home to their twenty-first-century lives. Tomorrow would be much the same as today, as would the same day a year and decade from now. But no one seemed discouraged. When I asked about the day's progress, one of the masons raised his hands, measured a space in the air about a foot high, and called out excitedly, "Tell the world we did this much today!"

I hit the L shift-O to the quote and then dollar.
If you know the dir of the nerdcore rhyme, you holla.

Nerd-ho! Warm the mic up. Yo,
we 'bout to strike up
this band of nebbishes
who cultivate nebulous fetishes:
the FPS, RPG or MMPOG,
any obsession to blather over by blog
or BBS. Step and possess. Hone thy geekishness.
Your frame rate and frags to date both impress.
And yes, your affinity for a certain site of some amusement
(a classically adorned parlor of fun where you let loose pent-
up cent pieces to partake of flicker-dramas)
gets you branded a sniper bitch or rocket mama-
humper. (Oh no!) They said you're cheating,
but with coins in hand you got more game than Wil Wheaton. . . .

—MC Frontalot's "Penny Arcade Theme"

The Weapon We Have Is Love

Quest to date:

If my trip to England and meeting Tolkienite Mark Egginton had made me feel 50 percent less guilty about escaping into my imagination again, the real brick-and-mortar work at Guédelon revealed a fantasy trip via the reality of hard manual labor. As for tabletop RPGers and LARPers, clearly games could be the glue that brought people together. While I seriously doubted my own return to regular Friday gaming nights, I did have a better grasp of why folks would devote hours to rolling dice, building props, and swinging foam swords.

But thus far on my odyssey, the medieval-fantasy subcultures I'd encountered seemed cloistered, if not closeted. The participants reveled in what they did, but their activities existed in pockets, on the fringes. What about true mass appeal, or fame and fortune—gambling your life on a fantasy? In Asia, online gaming was huge. Gamers became celebrities. In this country, a twenty-one-year-old had recently signed a three-year, $250,000 deal with Dr Pepper to play Halo 3. His image was plastered on soda bottles. Perhaps he had groupies and endless green M&Ms,

but his celebrity was largely felt only within the gaming community. I wondered if a geek subculture could make the jump to mainstream stardom.

When I learned about wizard rock, I had my answer.

I DON'T CARE ABOUT WHATEVER FATE THAT PROPHECY SAYS

BUM-BUM-SHHHK-BUM. BUM-BUM-SHHHK-BUM.

"Are you guys ready to rock a little bit? Are you ready to rock a *lot?*"

The crowd erupts.

"That's totally awesome, because I am Harry Potter," says Harry Potter Year Four into the microphone.

"And I am Harry Potter," says Harry Potter Year Seven.

"And we are Harry and the Potters," says Year Four, "and we came to this place to rock this party down!"

Their gray V-neck sweaters already discarded, the two Harry Potters are down to their jeans and white, short-sleeved dress shirts and striped English schoolboy ties. Harry Potter Year Four begins a hoarse-voiced rant, inciting the crowd to move and groove and destroy all evil, to do so with love in their hearts, with the power of love, a force no dark wizard can penetrate.

He leads the crowd in a call and response. "Can you say love?"

About 14,000 kids, teens, and adults packed into the quad shout back, "*Love!*"

"Rock!"

"*Rock!*"

"Love!"

"*Love!*"

"Those are the weapons that we have inside us," says Year Four. "That's what can take down Voldemort in the end . . ."

It was Friday, July 21, 2007. The Hungarian Horntails (two kids, ages six and nine, whose "dragon rock" band hailed from Pennsylvania) and Draco and the Malfoys (a duo from Rhode Island who sang anti-Harry lyrics like "My dad is rich and your dad is dead") had already taken the stage. The brothers Joe and Paul DeGeorge, who comprised two out of three members of the band Harry and the Potters, were the closing act of this outdoor show of Pottermania tribute bands, aka "wizard rock."

The concert completed Harvard Square's transformation into Hogwarts Square. Pedestrians clogged the streets. Hundreds of fans, many in wizard robes and pointy hats—I saw one dressed as a giant Golden Snitch Quidditch ball—wended from the doors of the Harvard Book Store and around the block, all waiting to get their copies of *Harry Potter and the Deathly Hallows*, the seventh and most likely final installment in the Harry Potter series written by J. K. Rowling. Once the bell tolled midnight and they got their hands on the books, fans immediately parked themselves on stoops and subway platforms and began reading the fate of Harry and his friends. I wandered though the hullabaloo, repeated throughout America—though nowhere else quite like this.

Still before midnight, back in Harvard Yard, behind the university's staid iron fences and eighteenth-century brick dormitories, Harry and the Potters kept rocking. The band played its final song, "The Weapon," which begins a cappella. The two Harry Potters sang alternating lines:

> *HP Year Seven:* We may have lost Sirius Black
> *HP Year Four:* But we're not turning back
> *Seven:* We will fight till we have won
> *Four:* And Voldemort is gone
> *Seven:* And I'm gonna do whatever it takes
> *Four:* I don't care about whatever fate that prophecy says
> *Seven:* No, I'm not afraid
> *Four:* No, I'm not afraid
> *Seven:* 'Cause there's one thing that I've got
> *Four*: One thing that you've got inside you too
> *Seven:* One thing that we've got
> *Four:* And the one thing we've got is enough to save us all

They punched the air wildly with their fists, singing together: *The weapon we have is love.*

They made Pete Townshend windmill guitar motions with their arms. *The weapon we have is love.*

They pogoed up and down. *The weapon we have is love!*

Harry Potter Year Four ran off the stage to slap the hands of fans in the front row. In what could have been a scene from a Beatles concert, teenage girls screeched. Adults rocked their heads up and down, too.

Back onstage, both Harrys continued hopping.

Love, love, love, love!

Love, love, love, love!

The drummer built his beat into a crescendo. Year Four jumped behind his keyboard and hammered away. Year Seven picked up his guitar. Electric riffs blazed from his fingers like lightning bolts. The crowd exploded in ecstatic waves of jumping.

The weapon we have is loooooooovvvve . . .

How does a singular bookish reading experience transform into stadium-worthy concert theatrics? How did these fantasy geeks become rock stars? Who taught them leap-off-their-amps scissor kicks? This never would have happened back in my youth.

THE LABYRINTH OF BEIN' A TEENAGE BOY

Some collect action figures—*Star Wars, Lord of the Rings, Star Trek, Hellboy, Hulk*—to demonstrate their fealty to the franchise of their desire. Other fans dress up as their favorite fictional characters at conventions: Stormtrooper, wizard, elf. There are the "furries"—folks who wear plush costumes closer to a fetish than an expression of fandom. It's all only by degrees more zealous than basketball or baseball fans wearing a sports jersey with SHAQ or SCHILLING emblazoned on their backs.

Still others in pop culture and fantasy fandom want to participate and extend the experience of what they find to be so engrossing. They want to design new settings, write new plots, and add new characters. So they sketch pictures, write short stories, perform songs, and shoot movies. These works are expressions of faith, or boredom with knowing their worlds too well. Fantasy realms often leave plenty of "what-ifs" unanswered. A writer like Tolkien only mentions an uncharted territory like Ilmarin or Evernight. The door awaits, half cracked open, and fans can't help but wonder what or who lies beyond—so they paint that corner of the world themselves. The impulse reminded me of my D&D years, when we'd begun making up our own answers to clarify some ambiguous rule. Not to mention my lame attempts at writing my own *Lord of the Rings*–like fiction.

Fantasy entertainment more so than other hobby areas (say, sports, cooking, or academia) attracts this kind of extreme participation. With no elaborate backstory or creation myth, baseball and football don't have the imaginative narrative possibilities that Harry Potter does. The simple rootedness of a baseball diamond to the real world makes it harder to picture a Yankees–Red Sox duel in outer space, or a torrid love affair between Derek Jeter and David Ortiz. But some universes, like Tolkien's and Rowling's, offer entry-level toolboxes with plenty of materials like races, places, and languages to build stuff with. Or to shoot a movie. YouTube hosts a plethora of fan films, from teens in pointy ears creating their own *Rings* quests to ambitious animated Lego reenactments of *Star Wars* scenes.

While spoofs and unauthorized sequels go back to *Don Quixote, King Arthur,* and *Alice in Wonderland,* it was *Star Trek* fanzines in the 1960s and the *Harvard Lampoon*'s *Bored of the Rings* published in 1969 that pioneered fan fiction. Since then, more risqué "slash fiction," a subgenre imagining romantic/sexual relationships between same-sex characters, has arisen. A Captain Kirk / Mr. Spock, or "K/S," combo is credited as the first slash "pairing." Naturally, made-up flings between Harry Potter and Ron Weasley, and others, have followed. The Internet has caused the genre to explode. "Frodo wants Sam to love him another way," is the summary of one slash fiction called "Not Like That" on the popular fanfiction.net, a Web site with archived "fanfic" based on *The Da Vinci Code, Are You There God? It's Me, Margaret,* and *Pirates of the Caribbean.* Not surprisingly, Harry Potter and *Lord of the Rings* tend to inspire the most takeoffs. Even Mark Egginton, karaoke dwarf from the Tolkien Society meeting, told me he's working on a *Rings* parody called "The Lord of the Grins," written by U. R. R. Jokin.

When Led Zeppelin wrote songs like "Over the Hills and Far Away" and "The Battle of Evermore," it didn't take fans long to figure out the band was referencing Tolkien. Their song "Ramble On" envisions an alternate *Rings* plot where the Gollum isn't after the ring, but some hippie chick. They didn't know it, but Led Zep was writing "filk," a musical genre that has come to encompass music about novels and characters, computers, technology, and the culture of fandom itself.*

Hanging out with the DeGeorge brothers one day, I met Uncle Monsterface, a band that frequently tours with Harry and the Potters. Fronted by Marty Allen, the band play songs about breakfast cereals ("Chocula"), superheroes ("We Wear Capes"), and old-school Nintendo games ("I'm Sorry [But Your Princess is in Another Castle]"). Naturally, I was very happy to hear their song lauding a certain deceased inventor of a groundbreaking fantasy role-playing game:

---

* "Filk" is a play on "folk." "To filk" is to play the music, and filking often happens at LARPs and conventions. Offshoots include "Nerdcore hip hop" and "geeksta rap"; artists like Commodore 64, MC Frontalot, and MC Hawking rap about robots, lasers, and entropy. Harry and the Potters represent the wizard rock subset of the filk subculture.

Deep in a basement
With Kool-Aid lips
and store-brand chips,
a brand new world was born.
Orcs, beholders, a dwarven axe,
Dude! Way cool. Hey look at her boobs!
Gygax, Gary Gygax.

Gary Gygax, you brought us geeks together.
Gary Gygax, you made the world better,
Gary Gygax, you brought us geeks together,
Gary Gygax, you made the world a better place for me.

I am an elf, I slayed the dragon,
Berserker DESTROY!
With maximum wisdom
I climb into the labyrinth,
of bein' a teenage boy
(oh boy, oh boy!).

There's no graph paper map
for where you've gone.

Gary Gygax, Gary Gygax.
G-g-g-gary, Gary Gygax,
G-g-g-gary, Gary Gygax.

"The Gary Gygax Song"

When I left this pop-cultural world, it was disdained by the mainstream. When I returned, D&D *was* the mainstream.

VOLDEMORT CAN'T STOP THE ROCK

Upon learning my town was the home of wizard rock, my heart swelled like Harry Potter's in the presence of Cho Chang. Technically, Paul and Joe DeGeorge lived in Norwood, about thirty minutes from where I live. But I say they hail from my own backyard—Boston.

Most folks credit the brother-brother duo as the first band to write and perform songs inspired by the ridiculously selling, seven-part Harry Potter book series. Before they formed Harry and the Potters, both had been in previous bands. In the summer of 2002, Joe (then a fifteen-year-old high schooler) and Paul (twenty-three and working as a chemical engineer developing vaccines for a biotech firm) were supposed to host a rock show in the backyard of their parents' suburban home. When the other bands bailed, the brothers DeGeorge scrambled to write a few songs based on the Rowling books they had been reading.

"We asked ourselves, 'Who would be Harry Potter?' " said Joe. "We both would be." Harry and the Potters was born, five years on the heels of the first volume, 1997's *Harry Potter and the Sorcerer's Stone.*

"Harry Potter is its own subculture, but we come from punk rock which is another subculture," said Paul. "We wanted to bring those two worlds together. A concept on top of a concept." Think "Harry in his rage stage." A pissed-off boy wizard who knows how to jam and get the crowd rowdy.

"We took some liberties with the canon," Joe added.

With songs like "In Which Draco Malfoy Cries Like a Baby," and "This Book Is So Awesome," they hit the book-buying zeitgeist just as Pottermania had gathered steam and was boiling over. By the time *Harry Potter and the Deathly Hallows* was released in 2007, the entire series had sold about 400 million copies in sixty-seven languages. Good timing for wizard rock.

When I caught up with Joe and Paul in June, 2008, about a year after their Harvard Yard show, they were in the midst of preparations for their fifth and most ambitious summer tour: "The Unlimited Enthusiasm Expo '08." With three full-length CDs and 450 shows in forty-eight states, Canada, and Europe under their belts (plus 20,000 e-mails lingering in their harry andthepotters@yahoo.com in-box), they weren't playing child-friendly venues like libraries, schools, and bookstores anymore.

"Some kids have grown up with us," Paul said. Inspired HP fans have also gone on to form their own bands, with some 500 groups having joined the wizard rock revolution. Wrockstock 2008 in Potosi, Missouri, featured fifteen bands with names like The Whomping Willows, Ginny and the Heartbreakers, and The Butterbeer Experience, playing over three days, and snagging fans from Scotland, Quebec, and South Africa.

The six-week Unlimited Enthusiasm tour with Uncle Monsterface and Math the Band would bring them to rock clubs in forty cities nationwide. Their press release described the tour as a "DIY traveling summer-camp circus and crazy rock tour . . . aka Camp Jump & Yell for Boys and Girls and Wizards."

Paul and Joe were now way beyond summer-camp age (twenty-nine and twenty-one), but they didn't seem far from childhood. With curly mops of hair, they had a boyish and innocent ease about them. They were having a great time on the HP bandwagon. Still headquartered out of their parents' house, Joe was a sophomore physics major at Clark University. Paul had been living back home again since leaving New York City. As their mom popped in and out of the kitchen, we drank coffee and talked about their musical influences: They Might Be Giants, Jonathan Richman, and Weird Al (yeah!).

Then, as if initiating me into their secret society, they brought me down to their basement. Like entering Harry's under-the-stairs bedroom, I had to duck my head while they showed me their lair. But the low-ceilinged basement was not crammed with Harry Potter memorabilia as I might have expected. This was their band's brain center. I saw the "recording studio" (random equipment scattered on an old billiard table) and the "order fulfillment center" (towers of boxes of CDs, T-shirts, and padded mailers). They estimated they had sold around 10,000 copies of their self-published CDs, most via their Web site or at concerts. "It's pretty good for a band with no label or way to promote ourselves," Paul said. He talked about the other "merch"—bacon mints, Harry Potter toothbrushes, pins—they'd be selling. They wanted their fans to fill out 15,000 "Hello, My Name is _____" nametags at their shows this summer. They wanted the tour to feel like one big happy family.

"This is the giant squid costume," Joe said, pointing to a floppy mass of foam. "Sometimes he plays drums with us."

The DeGeorges sing songs about the plight of being a young wizard. Their character is always POV Harry—nothing that he wouldn't see, experience, understand. To the archetypal wimpy teen persona, Paul and Joe have added the aura of rock-star divinity. But Paul and Joe didn't call it role-playing.

A week later, rehearsing in a Clark University student café for their three-band circus of a summer tour, Paul said he "didn't fully understand role-playing" (though he had just started playing D&D, roped into the game by his roommate Marty Allen of Uncle Monsterface). "We're a band who performs," he insisted. Nor did he consider their show a tribute act (they were not performing the oeuvre of another artist). It was closer to performance art. "What we do is a combination of acting and music. We do draw on Harry's personality. Anything goes onstage. It's where we break furthest from Harry."

Joe, the more introverted of the two brothers, said that when onstage, "I am Harry Potter." But he also leaves meek Harry behind "and becomes a rocker." The HP persona liberates Joe. Of

Joe DeGeorge, Harry Year Four, of Harry and the Potters, performing in concert. Paul plays guitar in the background.

course, audiences have to suspend their disbelief that two Harry Potters could exist, both wielding microphones and not magic wands, and that one can play the keyboards and the other the electric guitar. It's not a complex concept to grasp, Joe explained. Young kids get it. So do grown-ups. "We've had people who have never read the books who said it was one of the best shows they'd ever seen. Maybe they're even inspired to read the books."

I caught several of their shows. The brothers were making a small buck—not megabucks—off the Harry Potter craze. But it seemed to me that their performance was a new kind of role-playing that defied classification. The faux-but-real heavy metal band Spinal Tap was a tongue-in-cheek send-up of rock clichés. Their boy-wizard act was also a parody, and a conduit to minor stardom in the real world. But its sincerity transcended irony. Their shows persuaded audiences to role-play do-gooders. Rock clubs and libraries became surrogate Hogwarts for an hour. Watching them perform, I felt elated and fierce and ready to defeat evil.

MAGIC IS NOT MORALLY NEUTRAL

Three weeks before they hit the road, the band, the two members of Draco and the Malfoys (one of whom is an occasional Potters drummer), and assorted friends and girlfriends all sat in the audience in folding chairs. Like hundreds of others, they listened with rapt faces to J. K. Rowling, who spoke during Harvard's commencement weekend.

"She's hot," Paul said.

It was almost exactly one year after the Potters' "stadium" debut. Paul and Joe now occupied the same outdoor space, Harvard Yard, but instead of rocking on the stage, they faced it, and drank beer from plastic cups.

"Unlike any other creature on this planet," Rowling said, "humans can think themselves into other people's minds, imagine themselves into other people's places."

"She's totally hot," agreed Meredith, Paul's girlfriend. Paul met Meredith, a Rowling fan, when she helped book one of the Potters shows in Kansas four years ago. At the time, Meredith was into Harry Potter fanfic and Nocturne Alley, an online, text-based role-playing game featuring a slash relationship between Harry and Draco. Of her relationship with Paul, Meredith said, "It's a dorky love story."

Rowling's pitch was to get Harvard grads, alumni, and families off their Ivy League butts to do some good. "We do not need magic to change the world," her voice boomed. "We carry all the power we need inside ourselves already. We have the power to imagine better."

It was the first time Harry and the Potters had seen Rowling in the flesh. "I thought it was great," Paul told me later. "She put a lot of thought into a speech that would impact those kids. Her speech could have gone in another direction. It was a call to action." Still, he seemed disappointed. "I still don't feel all that close to her."

The same feeling of disenchantment affected a family from Lancaster, Pennsylvania. A mom and her two daughters, aged twelve and sixteen, had gotten up at 5:00 A.M. and driven six hours to be there. They were serious fans. The whole family had attended a Harry Potter camp the previous year.

"I want to know who killed Fred Weasley," said the younger daughter, dressed like an English schoolboy with a cape and standing on her tiptoes.

"She wants secrets," Mom whispered.

But they were held back behind an orange snow fence, about 200 feet from the podium. "We're bummed," Mom said. "We wanted to get closer."

As for me, watching Rowling speak, I realized thirty years had passed since my own mother had attended Harvard grad school. Had she finished her master's, she would have been part of a commencement weekend much like this. But by October of her first semester, in 1978, the brain aneurysm had sabotaged her academic program. The Harry and the Potters song, "Save Ginny Weasley," rattled in my head: "Are you scared to walk through the hallways? / Are you worried that the spiders run away? / Are you petrified of being petrified?" I wasn't. Imagining Mom graduating here—seeing her in her cap and gown—helped close that door.

Then I saw a kid, all by himself, probably ten years old. He told me he was from Hong Kong, and his brother had graduated from Harvard earlier that day. "I'm going to get her autograph," he said, gripping his dog-eared Harry Potter tome in his hands. He said that orange fence wasn't about to stop him. "I'm the fastest runner in my school."

BILBO BAGGINS, LUKE SKYWALKER, AND JESUS

At Boston's premier indie rock club, the Middle East in Cambridge, the Unlimited Enthusiasm U.S. tour kicked off with a camp theme song. Then came a couple of hip-hop numbers by Dumbledore: Picture the combined band members of Uncle Monsterface, Math the Band, and the Potters in red tracksuits, with two rappers in yellow tracksuits hiding behind beards and sunglasses and wearing wizard hats.

"This is how Dumbledore rolls," an unidentifiable wizard chanted. One song, "U Down w/OOTP?," went down like this:

Dumbledore: Order of the Phoenix, let me hear you say
Backup singers: What's that, Dumbledore? What's that, Dumbledore?
Dumbledore: Voldemort's posse is totally lame
Backup singers: Voldemort's posse is totally lame.

Those DeGeorge boys, they've pioneered another filk genre, "wizard hop."

Songs by Monsterface ("Gary Gygax," etc.) and Math the Band followed, backed by video projections and sock puppet shows.

Flags made from *Star Wars* bedsheets were waved. Inflatable animals bounced through the crowd. It felt like a geeky update of San Francisco's multimedia, acid rock band happenings of the late 1960s.

During a break between songs, on a makeshift screen, a montage of movie scenes played—*Pee Wee's Big Adventure, Ghostbusters, The Neverending Story, Harry Potter,* and *The Two Towers*—as a voiceover of the hobbit Samwise Gamgee intoned, "It's like in the great stories, Mr. Frodo . . . Folk in those stories had lots of chances of turning back, only they didn't . . . They kept going. Because they were holding on to something."

"What are we holding onto, Sam?" Frodo asked.

"That there's some good in this world, Mr. Frodo . . . and it's worth fighting for."

The crowd roared.

Harry and the Potters launched into their set. When they got to "Voldemort Can't Stop the Rock," the audience had warmed to their lesson. When they hit "The Weapon," the audience morphed into a jubilant, bopping, grinning mob. The DeGeorge brothers entered the crowd. They became you. *You could be Harry Potter. That could be you onstage, Year Four, soloing on a shiny red saxophone. That could be you, Year Seven, laying down licks on a witch's broomstick guitar.*

Harry and the Potters turned the concert into a crusade. *You're on a mission to redeem the world. You can defeat evil.*

As if to counterpoint accusations of frivolity and please Ms. Rowling herself, the tour inserted real-world relevance adjacent to the merchandise table. At the back of the hall, the Harry Potter Alliance aimed "to spread love and fight the Dark Arts in the real world": torture, AIDS, genocide in Darfur, Zimbabwe's election stolen by Mugabe. Harry Potter fans had united around issues on message boards. They took action. The Wizard Rock community had also organized a "Wizard Rock the Vote" voter drive.

Joe and Paul DeGeorge rode the wave of nerdcool. Like

in alchemy, the DeGeorges transformed their geekiness into musical, Zeppelin-like, hammer of the gods heroism. A gaggle of young things asked Joe for autographs after the show. As he signed his name with a Sharpie on their T-shirts, I said, "Joe, you're a rock star."

Joe smiled meekly, uncomfortable with all the attention. "Sort of."

They were still geeks. Sort of.

It was hard not to admire, even feel envious of that metamorphosis—the brains getting their revenge by turning the tables, defeating the jocks who (I picture now, in my mind's cruel eye) long ago peaked at age seventeen and now lived bloated and lazy lives on their recliners, watching the sports they used to play, miserable in their marriages foretold and arranged ever since prom night.

Despite the excitement for this tour—which took them from Cambridge to New York to Athens, Georgia, then to Austin, Seattle, and Ann Arbor—after five summers of shows, this would likely be their last hurrah. Joe had moved most of his stuff to an apartment in Worcester. Paul was about to relocate to Lawrence, Kansas, to live with his girlfriend. The run would be over.

"This summer will be our last big tour," Paul told me back in Norwood. Perhaps he and Joe had become bored with their Harry Potter personae: that oddball, postmodern, hypertextual-musical concept of one fictional character bridging the space-time continuum across two real bodies. I wondered if wizard rock had a way of keeping the DeGeorge brothers mired in a perpetual yet largely innocuous adolescence. Did they want to stop being adored by the mostly tween and teen girl fan base? Were they ready to move on? Was I?

Who can say if any of us have fully healed from our childhood years. Certainly not me. But the Potters had shown me how to begin to embrace my inner geek, how to recklessly proclaim your love for a fantasy book and fantasy world. They had shown how to transcend and transform one's awkward teenage years into minor rock-star success. How to switch from getting your fanboy on to getting your own audience.

Paul and Joe DeGeorge were riding a wave of HP fandom, and yes, that magic wave had begun to subside. But when the waters finally recede, Harry Potter will have landed safely in the canon. As of 2009, three more HP movies were yet to come (adaptations of book six, plus book seven slated to be divided into two movies). An HP multiplayer online game was rumored. Not to mention the Florida theme park on some developer's drawing board. HP fandom would continue, flourish, and become institutionalized. The books and movies were too big to be dismissed as flavor-of-the-month. They'd become as ubiquitous as Tolkien. Someday soon, the DeGeorges would probably shed their HP uniforms for good, but the wizard rock genre will leech off the franchise's immortality. The stories and characters and songs will be passed on to the next generation, and the subcultural references will shine in that pantheon of godlike mythologies. Harry Potter will take his place alongside heroes like Odysseus, Paul Bunyan, Bilbo Baggins, Luke Skywalker, and Jesus. We need our heroes.

Unlimited Enthusiasm had captured an innocent, marshmallows-and-campfire-song experience. But my next stop was a different sort of summer camp—for medieval reenactors. On a massive scale. With free-flowing mead, wars to be won, and plenty of damsels, quite possibly in distress.

Konrad's point was a good one. Two weeks before he had gotten up at Warcamp and apologized to the kingdom for not understanding the politics that goes into being Pennsic king. Konrad's complaint is that Pennsic should be fought and won on the battlefield, and it isn't. Pennsic is fought and won in the eight months beforehand, as crown tourneys are won and new kings are chosen and are courted as allies. The Midrealm has created a well-oiled machine for courting allies (I've seen the ambassadorships they send to the West, sometimes at March Crown so they can begin courting them the day they win and become heirs). Konrad's point is that the war should not be fought through politics and pandering. But Lutr was having none of it. I am told that Midrealm kings who lose Pennsic take it hard (I saw one Midrealm king cry back in his camp after the war was decided against him).

—from a posting "Back from Pennsic"
on valgards.livejournal.com, by "Valgards,"
aka Michael Cramer, of Brooklyn, New York
(August 9, 2008)

In the Beer Line with the King

In the weeks leading up to Pennsic War, I sewed a tunic. I made a matching sash and shoulder bag. I was off to battle and I needed to look the part. Unlike Forest of Doors, no cast-off, thrift-shop puffy pirate maternity shirt or purple hippie-chick blouse was going to cut it.

In the Society for Creative Anachronism, wearing period garb, historically accurate and grounded in reality, is required. The SCA is no game, nor is it a performance for the public or some flight of fantasy. It is a society, a social activity, and above all, a reenactment group. Its "play" is based in history. Members inhabit what they call "the current Middle Ages."

While local and regional events and tournaments are held year-round, the SCA's largest annual event, Pennsic War, is the flagship. Each August, at a campground about an hour from Pittsburgh, some 12,000 medieval reenactors pitch a sea of period tents and gather for seventeen days to fight each other, take classes, and party like it's 1399.

How could I resist?

I had flirted with the SCA before. My freshman year in college, after I'd decided D&D was kid's play and gave it up for good, some dudes in armor swinging long swords arrived on campus. I wondered, briefly, if it was for me. But I couldn't risk my new cool friends seeing me in a floppy hat and flowing cape. I never went back.

Two decades later, I was in a different place. And Mike Scott and Elyse Boucher, the geek couple from Milwaukee, told me they planned to attend Pennsic 37. I figured it would be fun to hang out with them in full costume, consume home-brew around a campfire, and shoot the medieval shit. They might help me locate what Elyse had called that fleeting "magic moment" when, at an SCA event, you felt like you had shaken off the weight of the present day to travel to another era in history.

Besides, the SCA's educational angle made it seem more legit than other stops on my fantasy tour. "SCAdians" (SCA members) were probably as ordinary as Revolutionary or Civil War reenactors who found a rifle-and-bayonet worldview comforting. As a kid, my friend Kevin got dragged off by his father to reenact Vermont's Revolutionary War battles like Fort Ticonderoga with a group called Herrick's Regiment. "It was an opportunity to drink a lot of beer and make out with high school girls," Kevin told me. As an adult, he still did the occasional event in costume, and brought his wife and kids. "My dad runs the unit now, so we're trying to stay in the will."

If I could understand the lure of that, why not "recreational medievalism"?

There was only one problem. For me, the equation "magic + Middle Ages = escape" was uncontestable. Like Guédelon, the SCA lacked sorcery, dragons, and quests. Elves and faerie princesses, these were not tolerated. It all seemed terribly humdrum. Who would want to go to medieval camp without that anything-is-possible fantasy? My goal was simple: to show up, and to last as long as possible.

LIKE MY GRANDMOTHER'S MUUMUU

I arranged to camp at the 37th annual Pennsic with an SCA group from Boston. They agreed to give me a square of land for my tiny tent on their "household" plot, in exchange for my help with chores and cooking. Fair enough.

About two weeks before Pennsic, I grew a beard. I'd even begun sleeping outdoors. Like a LARP, the SCA is part theater, but it's also a camping trip. On the porch of my apartment, under a dim sheet of urban stars, I acclimated myself to my thin camping mattress. I needed to temper my body, and pretended it was not car alarms that woke me in the middle of the night, but trumpets calling me to war.

By coincidence, just before I departed for Pennsic, my old childhood friend JP came to visit. We had been in touch often, and periodically engaged in various collaborative projects over e-mail (our most recent was a postapocalyptic novel about giant mutant rabbits with automatic weapons). I was happy to see him. Naturally, he was excited to hear about Pennsic.

"Remember when we wore winter coats and sparred with those broomsticks?" JP said. "With garbage-can lids for shields?" It seemed like a stupid hobby for a kid like JP, who, because of his congenital disease, would break a bone every time he wiped out on his bike. We did it anyway.

"Yeah, in summer. I remember using car mats for armor. Talk about hot," I said, becoming wistful for our days of yore. "That was fun."

"Fun, until one of us lost an eye."

One of us almost did. We didn't use face protection. JP's mom swiftly put the kibosh on our little medieval reenactment society.

I showed JP my tunic. A local SCAdian from my "household" had found a couple hours to coach me through sewing it. What we'd thrown together was more rough-draft than finished product, but I figured it would work. I pulled it over my head and modeled it for JP.

"What do you think?"

"I don't know . . ."

I looked at myself: too tight in the chest, too short in the sleeves, a ragged and crooked hem. I was no period tailor. The plain brown fabric itched my skin. Knowing how dressed to the nines the other 11,999 attendees would be, donning this tunic would be akin to wearing a burlap sack to the prom.

At the eleventh hour, I grabbed an old white bedsheet and sewed a second tunic. This one resembled my evil grandmother's muumuu: baggy with a plunging neckline. I tried to salvage the tunic by dyeing it—why, I don't know. The package said "taupe," but the color came out a weak beige. I added royal blue. The end result was a tie-dyed, mottled Technicolor dreamcoat. Yes, pale purple. I was going to look marvelous.

THE SCA DOESN'T HAVE ESCAPISM

"If you're at an event, you don't say 'Dude, I couldn't e-mail you because my computer broke,'" Anna Bradley told me. "You say, 'I couldn't communicate with you.'"

Before I hightailed it to medieval summer camp, I needed to know more about the world I was about to plunge myself into. Bradley, a SCAdian from my local "barony," Carolingia, was my source. Perhaps, with an SCA crash course, I could be saved from any avoidable embarrassment.

We met on a weeknight in the most medieval-feeling place I could think of—an Irish bar in the Boston suburbs. The thirty-year-old Russian immigrant from Connecticut had been involved with the SCA since 1996. She explained how the society worked. Every member chose a unique heraldry and name, from the simple, like Harold the Farrier, to more oddball ones like Oin Glock Dubh mac Duwangle. Then, they researched who that person might have been and when he or she might have lived. In the SCA, Bradley answered to a different name, Constance. "But it's me, Anna, who recognizes the name Constance. There's no role being taken up. It's me." The casualness of role-play didn't mean members weren't deadly serious. Some wouldn't eat anything "out of period" (OOP), foods like chocolate, tomatoes, and potatoes, which had not been available in Europe from AD 600 to AD 1600, the rough bookends of the SCA's historical construct.

Founded in 1966 in Berkeley, California (surprise, surprise), the SCA has some 30,000 paid members and about 60,000 participants from the U.S., Canada, Europe, Asia, South Africa, and Australia. They live in a through-the-looking-glass "Knowne World" of kingdoms, each ruled by a king and queen. The imaginary political boundaries have fanciful names with real-world "mundane" counterparts. For example, there's the Kingdom of Artemisia (Montana, southern Idaho, most of Utah, northwestern Colorado, and southwestern Wyoming) and the Kingdom of Drachenwald (a chunk of Europe). Like in feudal Europe, kingdoms are subdivided into principalities, baronies, shires, and cantons. The barony of Carolingia, serving Greater Boston, was my homeland, a subset of the Kingdom of the East, which stretches from eastern Pennsylvania across the Northeast and into Canada. The SCA map overlays the real globe, an imaginative reconstruction of real lands shrouded by a mist of the unreal.

Bradley explained that SCAdians are many things—archers, brewers, calligraphers, dancers, equestrians, fencers. She enjoys sewing, spinning, weaving, and dancing, as well as helping to run the society. "I do the modern things so the medieval things can happen." She mapped out a typical busy week of SCA business: "I attend a meeting, I make sewing kits, I work on an illuminated manuscript scroll, I sew a cloak for a local princess, I scout a site for a local event, I mentor a friend, I embroider 'queen's favors,' I write e-mails as Constance." All in all, SCA-related activity consumes twenty hours of her week. It's not an escape from day-to-day drudgery; the SCA is hard work. "Someone has to do this," she said. "SCA is like quicksand. It will take all of your time." But she loves it.

Unlike a LARP, no specific plot drives the action of an SCA event. Instead, at gatherings people discuss, learn a new skill, spar, or feast; they just happen to be dressed in period garb. In the LARPs Bradley participates in, her characters "are better than me." She gets to save the world. "It's standard escapism— I'm going to put my life on hold and play someone else." But the SCA "doesn't have escapism," she insisted. "It has self-betterment and self-actualization. LARPing is my way to deal with things without consequences in real life. In the SCA, you are doing things in your real life. . . . It's you with a funny name and funny clothes," enmeshed with who you are in the modern world, with all the service, education, and camaraderie of a fraternal organization. "It's as much a game as being a Mason. You go, you wear funny things, and do funny things. It's not a game; it's a part of life." For many, SCA is family. "Some people are into it to beat each other with sticks. Some people do it to make clothing or medieval cheese. I got involved for the arts and crafts, but I stayed because it's my community."

I told her I was planning on attending Pennsic, and she said she'd be there too. Before I left the pub, she gave me some final advice: "Don't expect high medievalism," she warned me, invoking drinking bouts, pagan rites, and rumors of orgies. "There's some of everything. Some drink Bud and wear long T-shirts and are there to pick up chicks."

Sounded like my kind of gig. If only I had better threads.

PRIVATE, MEDIEVAL-THEMED ISLANDS

First I noticed the smell of wood smoke. Then I saw it: the 500-acre field of Coopers Lake Campground in Slippery Rock, Pennsylvania. Within eyeshot of I-79 spread the peaks and valleys of thousands of tents. I had driven ten hours and ended up in the Middle Ages.

I exited the highway, registered at the "troll" check-in area, hung my Pennsic medallion around my neck ("Remember to wear your site medallion at all times"), and unloaded my gear at my household's camp. I slipped on the brownish tunic, parked out of sight, and with a *chirp chirp* of my door lock, I left the twenty-first century behind.

On the long walk back to camp, I gawked at the period tents of every shape and size tucked among the trees and clogging the open fields. Each was pitched cheek by jowl, demarcated from the next by multicolored, decorated cloth partitions that reminded me of Christo's *Running Fence*. Some households were bound by wooden stockade fences or faux stone walls. Signs labeled each encampment like a fiefdom—Norseland, Raven Spittle, Shadowfire, Rogue's Refuge, Bog End. An elaborate pirate ship might abut a Roman villa complete with archways and columns and a Gothic cathedral sculpted from foam. Like an amusement park, each nestled anachronistically beside the next. Each home to a fellowship of friends, a private, medieval-themed island.

"Hello the camp!" I called out. "It's Ethan . . . I mean, Ethorain." I was running out of "Eth-" variants for my alter egos.

My household, Camp Crook'd Cat, was comparatively mundane. A plain green army tent served as the common space, kitchen, and dining room. My fellow campers had arrived the previous week. I had come for War Week, when the field battles truly began. But my campmates weren't fighters. They focused on taking classes at "Pennsic University" and cooking period food. The wood-fired, brick-and-mud oven they constructed each year was renowned. My first meal was an impressive spread of chicken, gingered carrots, salad, mead, and fresh baked bread. We sat at tables with linen tablecloths, and ate from wooden bowls with knives and spoons (no forks, which were OOP). My friend Ted back in Boston, rustic bread baker extraordinaire, would have loved the brick oven. I wished I had brought along my own posse.

Conversation at the camp was sedate. These were no raucous brutes or lofty knights. Order was paramount. A strict spreadsheet and chore book dictated who did what, when. The night I assisted with the cooking, a flowchart determined how and when to allocate resources like fire and prep time. But that's what happens when engineers and programmers are in charge of the kitchen.

I FLY MY FREAK FLAG HERE

Once I'd unpacked and eaten, I set off to wander the Knowne World. On the surface, Pennsic looked medieval, but few here truly roughed it. Non-period amenities included running water, shops of every stripe, and a daily paper called *The Pennsic Independent.** Camps draped offending twenty-first-century luxuries like ice chests and camping chairs in medieval disguises. Hot showers were labeled LORDS and LADIES. The e-mail and battery-charging center was called Mystic Mail.

A blast of true time-travel hit me when I wandered up Battle Road and down Plunder Lane, the high-traffic merchant area and food court. Here, merchants in white tents sold armor, books, cloaks, fabric, flagons, jewelry, and weaponry. Fantasy or science fiction paraphernalia were deemed inappropriate, but humor was not: I saw a shop called Hobbitronics and another called The Bored Housewife. Some items looked suspiciously like S&M wear. As the sun went down, I sat to watch the "populace." After a hard day in the battlefield, returning soldiers, with shields slung over their weary shoulders, shuffled back to their camps. "Have a fun day at the office?" someone joked. Others strolled about, bedecked in velvet, silk, and linen finery of every color. The SCA attracted lots of families with kids. Also in attendance were SCAdians with physical disabilities (shades of my mom) who covered the grounds in motorized scooters.

---

* Sample headline: MAGICIAN CLEARED OF WITCHCRAFT CHARGES; sample ad: NEW SHIPMENT OF UNTRIMMED GOAT!

I scratched the skin under my tunic, especially itchy in the August heat, while women passed, wearing simple peasant dresses or kirtle gowns with tight bodices. Men in garish tunics dangled swords, leather pouches, and drinking mugs from their belts. Below the belt, tight-fitting hose left little to the imagination.

"I'm a delicate flower!" shouted a six-foot-six half-naked guy in leather pants.

"Excuse me—I decided to be vain," muttered a woman in a brocade houppelande (a long robe with full, trailing sleeves) as she ducked into the camp's one bathroom with a flush toilet and mirror.

Thousands of campers thus outlandishly attired seemed ludicrous to me at first, but I was surprised at how quickly I grew blasé about my surroundings once I'd entered the SCA's communal medieval consciousness. After a while, I approached Sir Gareth Nikodemos Somerset, a knight with a graying pony-tail and trim goatee. When he wasn't fighting, he told me, he volunteered at Anshelm Arms, a high-end armory housed in a real timber-frame structure in the center of the marketplace. In return for sales help, the shop displayed and sold the padded coats (called gambesons) that Sir Gareth made himself.

He sat outside the armory while folks browsed among the polished-steel helmets, breastplates, gauntlets (armored gloves), greaves (shin guards), cuisses (thigh armor), and knee cops. I was curious about how much this gear cost and asked him to price out a basic armor package. He went through the minimum options, from an aluminum "shield blank" ($75) to a rattan stick ($15, "makes three swords, and you'll break swords regularly") to a helmet ($150). Sir Gareth said, all total, a no-frills "harness," or complete suit of armor, can be had for as little as $500, even less for one that was used.

"But you're going to look like a Yugo," he advised. You can spend as much as you want to, just like buying a car. His new custom-fitted breastplate with matching backplate cost $2,000, and he owned a helmet worth even more. For museum-quality armor, "if you want to look like a Ferrari," you can spend up to $20,000.

My face dropped.

"People don't complain if you spend thousands on a Jet Ski or downhill skiing," he gently fired back. "You're buying a piece of artwork, not just athletic equipment." You need solid gear to fight. Whether nerds in real life or not, fighters were "stick jocks," and it looked as if the well-built Sir Gareth, who hadn't played football in high school because it seemed too dangerous, could whup me soundly with one hand tied behind his back—despite suffering a motorcycle accident when he was twenty-three that broke his back and nearly severed his leg at the ankle. Most of his foot was saved, but a third of his heel bone was missing. "I was told I'd never walk right again." He walks fine now—and triumphs on the battlefield.

Sir Gareth said that SCA fighting was "the skeleton" on which "the flesh of all our other activities" had grown. "It is odd that fighting means so much, yet there are lots of members who never fight and there is no stigma against them." Sir Gareth was patient, generous with his time, and unfailingly nice. The mundane man behind the helmet was David Randrup, forty-one, the same age as me. He had been involved with the SCA since middle school in the late 1970s, a time when he was also playing D&D. Now he was a seventh-grade history teacher from Torrance, California. After ten years of teaching, he still saw the parallels between middle school and SCA. "We're all twelve-year-olds," he joked. "Everyone is the lead role in their own movie."

But the SCA was not a Renaissance fair. A Ren fair had actors who performed for spectators. "They are about entertaining," he insisted. "We do it for ourselves." No special effects, no star-fandom divide, no passive entertainment. Best of all, no peasants, lepers, or persecuted Cathars—everyone was considered minor nobility. Everyone was also pristine. That scene from *Holy Grail* made perfect sense here:

Peasant A: "Who's that then?"

Peasant B: "I dunno, must be a king."

Peasant A: "Why?"

Peasant B: "He hasn't got shit all over him."

The SCA meant having the guts to walk the walk, don the frock. Being social was about strutting around in full garb, making a good impression, and looking macho or fabulous. "I fly my freak flag when I am here," Sir Gareth said, "and when I am home I dress in jeans and wear normal clothes." One didn't have to speak in a faux British accent, but when addressing a stranger, one was expected begin with a "M'lord" or "M'lady." You had to make an effort to fit into the fashion show. Even OOP pirate types and stomach-baring gypsy hippie chicks, or "belly bunnies," were tolerated, both in vogue thanks to the Johnny Depp swashbuckling franchise. No matter your attempt at costume, the SCA embraced your version of the Middle Ages. For me, the hodgepodge of eras and dress felt disharmoniously jarring. I wanted a more consistent fantasy world. But the mishmash didn't bother Sir Gareth. "For me, it's totally normal for a Viking, a samurai, and an Elizabethan lady to be walking down the street together. Technical reenactors hate that."

Sir Gareth, and others I'd spoken to—SCAdians who were real-life flight attendants, midwives, and IT professionals—spoke of the "instant camaraderie" felt here. Extreme hospitability and good humor are legendary. "Yearly enemies, eternal friends" was a phrase I heard several times. "There is nothing cooler than being part of 3,000 in a battle, then afterward reaching out and shaking hands and saying, 'Want to have a beer?'" said Sir Gareth. Once "killed by someone's grandmother," later he had a laugh with that grandmother around the campfire.

Sir Gareth also told me the SCA is a great way to meet women. He'd met his "lady," Madeline of Owl's Nest, at Pennsic 36 in 2007, her first event. She went back home to Georgia, found her local SCA group, and reconnected with Sir Gareth via an e-mail. "We quickly struck up a friendship that blossomed into a budding romance and have been sort of caught up in our own fairy tale," he wrote me later. (He signed his e-mails to me "David/ Gareth.") They still live on opposite sides of the country, but hope to be soon "residing in the same kingdom, and look forward to many years of happily ever after."

As dusk arrived, I went off on my own maiden-seeking quest. This would be fun. I explored every corner of my new world. Folks wandered the hundreds of camps, dropping in on parties, chatting, and enjoying the free food and drink. Fire-eaters and jugglers performed. Dandies and centurions lounged in a Turkish teahouse; in one corner, two harem women sat on a topless fighter dude, giving him a massage. When full darkness arrived, oil lamps and braziers were lit. Encampments beckoned through wrought-iron gates and archways in 100-foot-long fences. Bards told stories around crackling fire pits, casting archaic shadows on the faces of lords and ladies who drank and sniggered into the night.

Ethorain the newb felt it all wash over him. He blundered from camp to camp, visiting a masquerade ball, a bagpipe contest, a Viking dance party. Sir Gareth had rightly warned me: "The first year, you don't know what's going on. Second, third, fourth years are the best."

No TV, no radio. Just ale, mead, and meat. Fire, story, and laughter. Ethorain hesitated to use the word "magic"—so he used three words: *Verily, 'twas enchantment.* But I hardly spoke to anyone all night.

Back at my tent that night, alone, no maiden by my side, I listened to the thunder rolling through the camp. Then moonlight blasted from above, turning the tattered clouds to blue-gray cigarette smoke. Half-buzzed on mead and other homebrews, I made a list of all the women I'd ever slept with. Not exactly a litany. I began to fret. Me, at Pennsic, for a week? What would happen if I hated this? If I enjoyed this *too* much? I want to go there. I don't want to go there.

Does not compute. I texted my sister: GET ME OUTTA HERE. EVEN 2 GEEKY 4 ME.

I WANT THEM BOTH DEAD

Aside from one excursion with a campmate to the local super-market—still in costume, shopping for turnips and stew meat, our Pennsic medallions dangling from our necks, we looked like escaped patients from the local psychiatric facility, but the cashiers hardly batted an eye—I stayed safely on-site. After a couple days, I settled into a routine: rise from my tent, slip on the scratchy tunic, forage for breakfast, check the chore grid and do my duty, slather on sunscreen, then head into the expanse of tents and costumes.

I found myself attracted to the fighting. Like workers trudging to the subway, at about 10:00 a.m. the populace began marching. They had a job, and that job was warfare. That particular Wednesday morning, a procession carrying banners and playing drums and horns stomped past a Dumpster and toward the battlefield whose edges were marked by hay bales. More armored legions arrived, each bearing a different coat of arms. They carried shields and pole arms. Flunkeys pulled carts stacked with piles of arrows and crossbow bolts. Others pushed small ballistas and catapults. Water bearers filled plastic jugs.

"Where's my brain bucket?" a burly guy asked.

Hand weapons made of rattan and pole weapons made of fiberglass lay on the grass. Pieces of armor piled up like car parts. Fighters, some with shoulder-length hair and beards, stretched in the sun. Others made last-minute repairs to weapons with duct tape. An experienced swordsman explained his technique to a youngster: "You know the baseball player, Paul Molitor? All the power's in swinging the hips."

Strategy was discussed, like before the big game. And this *was* a big game. Pennsic field battles could involve 7,000 participants, the largest mock medieval conflicts in the world.*

"It's all about killin' people," said another guy from inside his rusty helmet. He wore a blue tunic with a yellow lion on the back. "There's a king of the Middle and the king of the East out there, and I want them both dead. Whichever I can get to first."

Despite my broomstick-and-trash-can-lid apprenticeship as a kid, and my stint as a passive-aggressive mace-wielding monk who went down to Georgia, I was not allowed to fight. Combatants had to pass rigorous SCA training; it typically took six months of practice and safety instruction before being authorized to fight. But I did talk with other warriors. At this point, I was escorted by Joyce Oswald, the SCA's deputy media liaison, aka Aoibheil of Dunholen. She toured me around the site in a golf cart. We drove up a hill that provided a panoramic view of the entire camp as she recalled her glory years as a fighter, before she took her current job. She said in the old days of the SCA, the introduction of the fairer sex on the battlefield was confusing. "How can you be chivalrous and hit women?" she asked. Now women combatants were far more common. Weapons and armor were "the great equalizer."

We drove back to the battlefield, which bustled with royal activity. Current and past royalty got to wear "pointy hats"— crowns and coronets. In lieu of actual bloodlines, royalty ascend

---

* The first Pennsic War, in 1972, was a turf battle between the Kingdom of the East and Kingdom of the Middle (Ohio, Indiana, Illinois, and parts of Kentucky, Michigan, Iowa, and Ontario). The loser got the territory around Pittsburgh, which neither the East nor Middle wanted to claim. (The name Pennsic = Pennsylvania + Punic.) Each year, a grudge match between the East and Midrealm was restaged for the amusement of fellow SCAdians. Other kingdoms and armies chose one side or the other in an ever-shifting tide of allegiances.

A water bearer refreshes a "stick jock" during a break during a battle at Pennsic.

to the throne by winning semiannual Crown Tournaments.* We met a man named Paul Acks who wore glasses, a graying beard, and a straw hat. For thirty years, he has been known to most here as Viscount Syr Bear the Wallsbane. Like an afterthought, a crown sat on his hat, a sign that the real-world draftsman from Erie, Pennsylvania, had once been king. Now, the fifty-six-year-old Acks is a "simple country viscount."

Acks alluded to "sacrifices" he'd made—career and relationship choices—to devote time to the SCA. He said he'd give away money to his SCA comrades—a thousand dollars, no questions asked—even if he didn't know their real names. Many SCAdians had returned to Pennsic year after year. They were friends with

---

* Anna Bradley, my local SCAdian in Boston, had deadpanned that any royalty "is just a guy who is good at hitting things"—joined by his girlfriend. But sometimes women ascended the throne by fighting in tournaments themselves, and winning.

personae who essentially did not exist in the mundane world. Acks lit a cigarette. "I build my life around the SCA." As he fastened his gauntlets, he told me of stick jocks who kept fighting well into their sixties, even seventies.

He lowered the grille on his helmet. "Now, excuse me," he said, grabbing his spear. "I have to fight." Acks walked over to join his comrades, who were gathering at a structure about 100 yards away: a 2-D wooden facade, perhaps, but a castle to him and everyone else.

THE THUNDER OF SHIELD AGAINST SHIELD

Unlike in a LARP, SCA combat flew at full force, like in football. Weapons were wooden, but not padded. Players got knocked over, banged, and bruised; they even broke ribs and jaws. So, armor that protects the neck, solar plexus, kidneys, elbows, lower arms, head, and hands is kinda important. No weapon tip was narrower than the widest gap in a helmet grill. Marshals watched for safety and crowd control. Struck on the arm and you can't use that arm; hit in the leg and you fell to your knees. A solid blow to the head or body spelled death. The combatants themselves judged the force of the blow to be sufficient to wound or kill.

"Someone who gets hit but refuses to acknowledge is usually talked to by the knights and some understanding is hopefully reached," Sir Gareth told me.

Battles were staged in any number of scenarios: on bridges, in the woods, around castles. Open field battles were all-out melees, the win being called when one side was wiped out. In one Town Battle scenario I observed, lines of hay bales marked imaginary walls and streets. The battle was won by protecting five banners. Banner possessions, noted at fifteen-minute intervals during the skirmish, earned a War Point. War Points from this battle and others were added up over the week to determine if the East Tygers or Midrealm Dragons won the overall war.

Armies with names like Ironlance, Northshield, Atlantia, and Clovenshield fought for the East Kingdom. They mustered from the field's south. The Midrealm armies—Ealdormere, Calontir, Trimaris, Tuchux, and others—attacked from the east. Stick jocks kissed maidens before mustering. "Give me a shot of Gatorade," barked the I-want-them-both-dead guy at a water bearer, before marching away.

The signal sounded, and the soldiers stormed toward each other. A cheer rose from the field as the forces collided like crashing waves. The thunder of shield against shield, the *thwack* of weapons hitting metal breastplates and helmets sounded like gunshots, making me jump.

"Advance! Advance!" "Spears to the front!" "Shields! I need shields here!"

Attackers used pole arms to pull down a line of shield-bearing soldiers. Defenders held their ground. The locus of battle shifted from one spot on the field to another. I moved to one corner, where the fighting was more free-flowing. "Get the banner!" a unit commander yelled. I was quite close to the action. A falling knight tripped over a hay bale and nearly knocked me down.

From logjams of bodies, dead soldiers walked off the field. "I *know* it's a two-hour battle!" one fighter wheezed to his friend. "I wanted to last longer than ten minutes."

It had seemed that the East was ahead, but counterattacks by Midrealm forces turned the tide. In the end, they entrenched themselves around more banners. After an hour and a half, a four-to-one win was scored for the Midrealm.

But which side had won the battle didn't matter. In a move that stunned the camp, King of the East, His Royal Majesty Konrad, upon seeing that most armies had sided with the Midrealm, declared, "I do not wish to shed the blood of people I hold in such high esteem." He had conceded all War Points to the Midrealm before War Week had even begun." In protest, makeshift signs proclaiming MAKE WAR, NOT LOVE had sprung up all over Pennsic.

The warfare impressed me. But was the bravery real?

As if to counter my skepticism, I saw a woman in full armor wielding a sword. As she charged into battle, her comrade-in-arms pushed her in a wheelchair. To me, she looked like a knight on horseback.

IN THE BEER LINE WITH THE KING

"What will it be, Your Majesty—beer or the happy juice?"

"The happy juice," King Lutr replied.

At the Midrealm's royal encampment, huge tents housed the king and queen and the various members of the court. The grass was thick. The place was posh. I had crashed the Midrealm feast, had mooched some chicken wings and M&Ms, and snaked my way to the bar. Woo-hoo. I was in the beer line with the king.

"Hi . . ." I stammered. I looked down at my ragged brown tunic and quickly added, "M'Lord."

"Hello. How are you?"

"Good . . . uh, thanks." And then His Royal Majesty Lutr, king of the victorious Midrealm, went back to discussing a pressing matter with a sharply dressed knight.

I faced the fire pit with my beer and candy and began to brood. Clearly, heroism could be had in Pennsic's mock battles. The SCA built character and provided camaraderie. But also I suspected SCAdians found solace in this hierarchy. Though not nearly as grim, the organization was as highly stratified as the real Middle Ages. Having a pecking order at work, with a weaselly boss-over-lord at the top, was one thing. But on some level, wouldn't we all prefer being ruled by a goodly king? Face it—on some level, we fear choice, we fear freedom, and we fear democracy. We recoil from dystopian science fiction and the chaos of an uncertain future. Comfort could be had in everyone knowing their place, kings and queens and countesses on down to the wretched of the earth, each fixed to his or her place in society. Of course, the SCA had upward mobility: squires could become knights. But O! were chivalry and the pursuit of pure love to command our every action! If we focused on what my mother called the "Higher Questions": knightly principles like Courage, Justice, Mercy, Generosity, Faith, Nobility, Hope, and Strength. A medieval mind could put us closer to a time when such concerns consumed people's lives. When encounters with alchemy, angels and demons, and primal things were possible.

Fighters prepare to charge into field battle at a Pennsic War.

I thought of the knighting ceremony I had stumbled upon that morning.

"Their majesties call forth those companions of the Order of Chivalry here present!" a woman had cried to some hundred members of the populace assembled on the battlefield an hour before the day's fights had begun.

"Do you find this lord worthy?" the king asked.

An ample-figured woman stepped forward. "I have had the occasion to observe this man at many events and many tournaments," she boomed in a commanding voice. "And I have seen him, even when weary from battle, carry out with grace, with courtesy, with humility, any task asked of him." Other lords and ladies spoke to the would-be knight's good character. A white belt was affixed around his waist, and a fellow knight handed him gold spurs. A gold chain was hung about his neck. And like a scene out of a Sir Walter Scott novel, the king touched a sword to the knight's shoulders. From that point onward, this knight would be addressed as "Sir."

I sipped my beer. I looked around at the crowds in costume. The SCA's structure was as socially tidy as high school. Of course, SCAdians could gain renown not only through prowess on the battlefield, but also as artisans and volunteers. The SCA has three orders of Peers. There were those who fight—Knights; those who do arts—Laurels; and those who serve—Pelicans. (Sir Gareth was rare in that he was a peer in all three areas.) Supposedly, cooks and calligraphers were as celebrated as stick jocks. But come on: What lady wouldn't swoon for a knight in armor? It was like comparing an A/V club president with the captain of the football team. Barbarians, not monkish scribes, would be getting some between the sheepskin blankets that night.

DISAPPEARING INTO THE MISTS

In the end, I never connected with Anna Bradley. I'd forgotten to ask where in the maze of tents, paths, and kiosks to find her. Although I tried to locate Mike and Elyse from Milwaukee, I kept missing them. But I did have an encounter with Dame Merouda Pendray.

Merouda was Elyse's SCA persona. She was attempting to stay in character for the entire Pennsic War. I found myself spooked to be conversing with her in period language. I had associated Elyse with twenty-first-century suburban Wisconsin, not sixteenth-century Tudor England. But I understood Elyse was trying to conjure that magic moment. Back home in Middle America, Elyse captured our encounter in her blog:

> I sought ye goodman Ethan of Gilsdorf, who had spent some time at Marihaus several fortnights past, and whose conuersation gave me grete pleasure. Et he was in attendance within hys encampment and we spoke several moments, but owing to ye lateness of ye hour, I staid not, but noted the pleasauntness of ye camp et thought to learn more of ye company with which he staid.

Reading her chronicle made me feel I had visited the Middle Ages after all.

As many told me during my week at medieval summer camp, the SCA preserves the Middle Ages the way it should have been, not the way it was. The ideal, not the real. Forget the beheadings, the unjust taxation, the Black Plague. Women had equal standing. Just keep the good parts, and add the Internet, portable toilets, and duct tape. "We'd be nowhere without duct tape," Sir Gareth said.

The day before he had to pack it all away for another year, Sir Gareth / David Randrup paused to reflect on his annual, two-week Pennsic sojourn. "Is this an escape? Maybe it's an escape from the mundane or real world, the outside modern world, but it's also a world of its own with its own politics, its own concerns, its own trials and tribulations. And it is as much a break to go back to the modern world as it is to be in this world." To return to the twenty-first century made him sad. As we talked, the populace began dismantling tents and loading up trailers. The modern overlay of SUVs and jobs back home encroached on the Knowne World again. Randrup likened Pennsic to Brigadoon, disappearing each year into the mists. Pennsic was a temporary utopia. I think there was a reason why it only lasted two weeks; any longer and the fabric would begin to dissolve. Real-life problems would intrude and ruin this shared dream that 12,000 held aloft each year.

Randrup was raised as an atheist. Visiting churches as an adult left him disappointed. No chanting, no being "overawed with magisterial edifices," he said. "I didn't get any sense of wonderment." No sense of higher purpose—until he found the SCA. "This is my moral compass. Chivalric ideas. Here it is an attainable goal."

I asked Randrup about his knighting ceremony years ago. "We like to say that we don't 'make' a knight—we just recognize them. They were already that way even if they didn't know it." Being knighted made him proud. But with the title came a price.

Sir Gareth in armor leaves the battlefield at Pennsic.

"Once you're knighted, it's for life," he added. "I also felt a heavy burden of having to live up to what others thought a knight ought to be."

When faced with a thorny problem, like a conflict at his school, Randrup asked himself, How would a medieval noble face this situation? "While it may be tempting to wreak havoc with a broadsword (OK, the mental image never gets old)," he later wrote me in an e-mail, "the ideal is to face a situation with courage, mete out justice while expecting it from others, show mercy as you'd expect others to, be generous without regret, have faith in humanity, show nobility in adversity, have hope for the future, and have the strength to do it all over again the next time."

If the SCA began in the 1960s as a protest against the modern world, today it *was* the world for many of its participants. For those who stick with it, like Sir Gareth or Syr Bear, the SCA becomes part of the warp and weft of their lives. The SCA celebrates a code of conduct, a mentality and way of being that modernity has lost. Anna Bradley said the SCA was "a way to maintain a part of the world so it's there in the future." What had begun as educational—to learn to handle a sword, or sew a dress—ended up educating SCAdians on how to be better people. Nothing pointless about that, I concluded.

I could not figure out what it was about Randrup that was so compelling, until it finally hit me: It was his confidence. Randrup did not make excuses for his love of the SCA. He had a sense of humor, but did not ridicule his passion. The SCA occupied an important place in his life and he wasn't afraid to admit it. His demeanor made me feel confident to embrace parts of myself and my offbeat interests—even if they weren't 100 percent acceptable to others (i.e., a certain erstwhile girlfriend). He was a geek in jock's clothing. Randrup only wished he had a greater cause to fight for. "I'm sorry it's nothing heroic nor spectacular," Randrup said. "The day-to-day life of your modern medieval reenactment knight has few dragons to slay, nor damsels in distress."

No matter. The value in the group was in the doing: the being, the fighting, the drinking. "This is what I do," he said. Whether Sir Gareth Nikodemos Somerset was the alter ego of David Randrup, or the other way around, he—or they—couldn't quit anyway. "I have too much armor," Sir Gareth/David said. And he planned on being buried in it.

My last night, I walked by the lake. I wandered among the hundreds of camps that ringed the water, trying once again to find Elyse and Mike's household. But they had already left for Milwaukee, along with their SCA selves Dame Merouda Pendray and Miguel De Montoya el Artista. Dusk arrived. I watched a crowd of about a hundred gather at the shore. Each year, a man named Baron Garwig of the Kingdom of Ealdormere built a six-foot replica of a Viking boat. He brought it to Pennsic, where people added small shields painted with the coat of arms of a loved one who had passed away. The boat was launched into the lake. I watched as it was set aflame, and slowly burned away like memory, perhaps, or a glimmer of pain. One woman quietly sobbed. Fireflies bobbed like will-o-the-wisps in the reeds.

Another fleeting "magic moment." Were it not for the car whine of I-79, and the glowing Golden Arches hovering over a distant hilltop (which SCAdians had unsuccessfully petitioned McDonald's to switch off for two weeks each year), I nearly believed.

Be polite when you make item trades. Thank the person for their purchase or for selling the item to you. You can also wave and bow. Whatever happens, keep your cool and be polite. Take the high road in any item disputes . . .

Cast Buffs on other players you meet along the way. They won't be expecting it and it could help them in battle. Often other players will return the favor by casting whatever buffs they have on you also!

If someone is about to die fighting a monster, save them! You can heal them or help finish the monster off. Of course, don't let the other player take advantage of you by continually fighting things they cannot defeat on their own . . .

Give away items. You don't always have to sell items you do not want. You can help another player instead.

If you notice a person is about to attack a monster, let them have it. Find another monster elsewhere to attack.

—from "How to Be Nice," the World of Warcraft Game Guide
(www.worldofwarcraft.com)

I'll Only Go to Level 10

This is the story of a mother, a daughter, and a game.

The daughter plays a game. The mother watches over her shoulder. She watches, she watches, she watches. The daughter and the husband leave for a ski weekend. The mother doesn't like skiing. Like a child finding a liquor cabinet unlocked, the mother discovers the daughter's computer, her account, the password. The world. She starts to play.

I'll only go to level ten. OK, twenty. Then I'll stop. Just until 30, no more . . .

Days pass. Weeks pass.

The daughter no longer gives the mother advice, like "Ma, you're supposed to get a chest plate before you get a belt." The daughter gets pissed when the mother levels her. Now the daughter hardly plays. She's a teenager. She's moved on to other things.

You're in this world where it's life and death. Adrenaline rush. You kill. I'm really happy.

The mother keeps playing. The mother is an expert. The husband does not like to play. He thinks it's a waste of time.

It's changed the way I interact with people in the real world.
The mother, the wife, plays during the day. She stays up after her husband has gone to sleep. Sometimes she sees the sun come up, mouse in hand. Her family doesn't know how much she plays.

I am less patient. I am more forthright. I blurt out what I think. It's about fucking time. It's like breathing for the first time.

WE'RE ALREADY ROLE-PLAYING

In late 2008, in a mock news video circulating on YouTube, World of Warcraft (WoW) avatars were asked which presidential candidate, Obama or McCain, they'd support, and the newscaster predicted which lands in Azeroth, WoW's digital world, would go red or blue. William Shatner, Ozzy Osbourne, Jean-Claude Van Damme, Verne "Mini Me" Troyer, and Mr. T hawked the game in TV commercials; a *South Park* episode, "Make Love, Not Warcraft," lampooned it. Video games like Halo were being adapted for the big screen. Obama's campaign was even running ads *inside* the Xbox 360 version of the racing game, Burnout Paradise.*

To say that video games, particularly massively multiplayer online games, are popular is like saying *Oprah* has decent Nielsen ratings. According to Strategy Analytics, in 2008 they generated $1.5 billion in worldwide subscription revenues, a figure that's expected to balloon to at least $2.5 billion by 2012. Variously abbreviated as MMOs, MMOGs, and MMPOGs (or, if of the role-playing kind, MMORPGs), these games have become an integral

---

* D&D also popped up in the presidential race: Official McCain campaign blogger Michael Goldfarb equated *New York Times* and *Daily Kos* editors and writers with parents'-basement dwellers, "ranting into the ether between games of dungeons and dragons." After incurring the wrath of the gaming community, he later issued an apology: "If my comments caused any harm or hurt to the hardworking Americans who play Dungeons & Dragons, I apologize. This campaign is committed to increasing the strength, constitution, dexterity, intelligence, wisdom, and charisma scores of every American."

part of our social revolution and evolution, altering how we act and interact. But for good or evil? That's what I wanted to know. And how to square my idea of fantasy play—D&D-style "real world" interaction—with all this ether?

Society still considers gamers to be as introverted, inarticulate, and emotionless as their armored avatars. Sure, some serious gamers who play for dozens of hours per week seek shelter in other worlds. But I suspected otherwise. Some of these new games had a kick-ass macho culture—not a passive, wussy geek air about them. I wanted to test-drive WoW because it was the least-familiar fantasy for me, and perhaps the least fanciful. Heck, even soldiers played it.

I noticed gamers playing everywhere, even in my corner cafe. Being online with WoW and other MMOs has become an acceptable use of public space. However, penetrating the MMO subculture proved more difficult than showing up for a weekend event in a purple shirt. Online gaming runs silent. Online gaming runs deep. And it takes place both everywhere and nowhere, and the spaces in between. As I learned more about online gaming, and spoke to players and game developers, nothing seemed black and white. I kept reading stories that linked gaming to either escapism or heroism, antisocial behavior or community. Both warm fuzzies and red flags kept popping up.

I knew that alternative electronic identities were a part of life. I'd already participated in online dating, MySpace, Facebook, and e-mail: In my profiles and flirtatious texts, I'd put forth my best, most seductive versions of myself. Safe behind the barrier of a computer screen, I was tempted to rewrite my personal history, or claim to be passionate about something—say, ending world hunger—just to snare a date. Wasn't I already role-playing, even if not in a heroic fantasy realm? But at what expense to me, not to mention the millions of MMO players whose interest in gaming seems to fill a psychic hole in our culture?

News stories told of how virtual relationships had wrecked real-life ones. Spouses were ignored or cheated on. Or even more heinous behavior occurred: virtual muggings, harassment, racial incidents. In a recent case in Belgium, authorities were trying to decide if real-world laws applied to a case of avatar-on-avatar rape in Second Life. At first, it was easy for me to cast aspersions (and fireballs) at finger twitch–based games like Halo or Grand Theft Auto. As I'd wanted to believe back at the Chainmail table in Lake Geneva, "healthy" fantasy like reading Harry Potter books or sketching dungeons with pencils had to be better than "bad" fantasy like WoW. Not that I blamed the computer gamers. Poor suckers, it wasn't their fault. The gaming industry churned out irresistible if pointless escapist digital experiences. They killed time. They numbed minds. And they clearly couldn't have any redeeming value.

But I soon discovered I was missing the point. MMOs and other computer games offer something powerful. Perhaps it was enough to tempt me to return to that other world that I had loved during my D&D days: the video arcade. In the spare hours after school, when I wasn't shopping for graph paper or dice, primitive games like Galaga, Defender, and my personal fave, Robotron, ruled my pocketful of change. Online games might not be all bad. Look at how I turned out.

WHO WOULDN'T WANT TO HAVE PERFECT BOOBS AND KILL SHIT AND BE BORN AGAIN?

Phyllis Priestly was the one who compared playing World of Warcraft to breathing for the first time. An elfin woman, slight and bookish and perky, she wore glasses with zebra-striped frames. Her reddish-brown hair was streaked with blue. Huddled over a café table in New Haven, Connecticut, she flashed her fingers across her white MacBook, directing her avatar Euphey, a level-70 night elf hunter, through the realm of Aggramar. While college profs and students ate pastries, slowly sipped lattes, and leisurely thumbed through the Sunday paper, Euphey ran like a gazelle through fields and across frozen landscapes, leaping over bridges, and firing her bow at foul creatures. Arrow after arrow hit their mark in a display of grace and perfection.

"Where would you like to go?" she asked me. Priestly had been playing WoW for several hours a day over the past two years. At the time, the game world had fifty-one regions on three continents.

"Wherever you think would be fun," I said.

With Euphey (short for "Euphonious") as my guide, my eyes, and my emissary, I strolled the streets of Darnassus. I explored the Temple Gardens. I gazed from The Warrior's Terrace. I entered the city of Stormwind. I crossed paths with hundreds of other avatars: Death Knights, Druids, Hunters, Mages, Paladins, Priests, Rogues, Shamans, Warlocks, and Warriors. Euphey hardly said (or typed) a word.

"I've spent a lot of time here," she said. "Stormwind reminds me of Avignon."

Hours or eons later, we walked across Tanaris and left footprints in the Abyssal Sands. "I want to take you to what I think is the prettiest spot in the game," said this fifty-one-year-old mother and wife. She held a comparative literature PhD in Greek mythology and had founded a primary school, but at the moment, WoW was her world. She took me deep into the vast Caverns of Time. The tunnel spiraled down to a network of caves, some filled with sand, some lush with vegetation. "I want to live there," she gushed. "I want an apartment there." We gazed at the huge looming statues. Meteors streamed by, and a purplish cosmic mist shrouded the scene. It looked like a location for a cheap B-movie set in the distant past, or far future.

Priestly recalled how hyperconscious she had been on a raid—a joint battle vs. a common foe—during her first weeks of playing WoW. "My first raid, I fired the opening shot. I was nervous. I could feel my heart pounding." She wanted to appear cool in Azeroth. With Priestly at first clumsy at the controls, Euphey stumbled around, fell in some water, and couldn't attack fast enough. Priestly worried that other players had noticed. Now she was confident, and after countless hours of playing, Priestly felt the game had made her a better person. WoW also leaked into her real world. All that rapid-fire picking off of wolves, quilboars, and troggs had sharpened her reflexes, quickened her reaction time, and heightened her senses. She claimed gaming had made her a better driver: The windshield became a rectangular viewfinder into a world of obstacles and foes. "I keep expecting something to jump out and kill me," she told me. WoW, she also said, had turned her into a more skilled writer. WoW was a literary and textual experience for Priestly, and she was beginning to write fiction affected by her experiences. Dealing with "self-proclaimed pricks" in the game, "it makes my text crisp." Assertiveness training through MMOs. "It's freed me up to say what I want to say." In her mind, she had become more confident, more daring, more connected.

The orc in the ointment was that playing an avatar had caused Priestly to question her marriage. "You can be anonymous but you can be anyone you want to be," she said. "This mind-body stuff goes back to Plato." She called it "multiplicitude," having multiple avatars, and it made her fantasize about sex, relationships, and designing her own partner. She flirted online. She talked about a recent five minute "Lancelot and Guinevere moment" between her and another avatar, one of pure "emoting"—a spontaneous pantomime of laughing, sobbing, touching, "boiled-down desire, unrequited need." I sensed her marriage was in a rut, or inexorably doomed. She seemed to be starved for adventure and romance, or she simply craved the focused affection of someone new.

"The game rewards you for your time and attention," she admitted. In hindsight, she realized she was "ripe for this addiction."

Priestly liked the way Euphey looked. She admired the way

she moved. "Who wouldn't want to have perfect boobs and kill shit and be born again?"

I agreed. Watching Euphey was transfixing. Priestly also had a level-55 druid (who could shape-shift) and a level-38 priest (good for healing during battle). A character named Bluthia "does all the shopping" for her other 'toons (short for cartoons, or avatars).

While Priestly played alone, she chatted or texted with in-game friends. Conversations became linked to in-game places. "I can't quite differentiate in my head between being in that ballroom in Karazhan and doing a raid, and being at a beach"—a real beach—"two years ago." A WoW memory lingered whereas a real-life memory faded. Once the experience had passed into memory, its origin was irrelevant. But Priestly was careful not to cross that fantasy-reality divide; she never gave out her e-mail address to fellow players. "I need the boundaries to not disintegrate entirely," she told me.

That difference between "in-game" and "out-of-game" activity reminded me of how a LARP handles the same issue, or how the SCA distinguishes between "in-period" versus "out-of-period." Still, reality leaked through in disturbing ways. Some of the real people behind the avatars were scary. Priestly had heard some disturbing confessions. "I need a friend," one gamer she had known for six months wrote in-game. "I just beat up my girlfriend." He had knocked her teeth out. "He was looking for confession," Priestly said. Then he disappeared.

"You can get very lost in here," she said of yet another land, city, port, or island we sailed through. On a purely visual level, Warcraft had endless nooks and crannies to explore. She described how Warcraft sometimes distracted her from basic duties like brushing her teeth, going to the bathroom, and taking a shower. When she'd finally look into the mirror after a long gaming session, she'd half-expect to see Euphey, not herself. "Where are my elf ears?" she'd wonder. Then she'd realize what happened. "They fell off."

"Wait till it affects your dreams." She looked up and smiled at me. "There you have it—my other life."

And here I was, entering the dungeon once more.

FROM ARCADE TO MASS ENTERTAINMENT

Clearly, the dungeons of modern fantasy-themed MMOs owed their fealty to Dungeons & Dragons. But the technology of video games had leapfrogged a zillion times since my glory days as an arcade wizard. The new visual tricks of the graphics and the complexity of the game-play scared this forty-one-year-old grumpy old man.

As the fan base of D&D expanded into the 1970s, the first computer games were, not surprisingly, fantasy-based "text adventure" MUDs (Multi-User Dungeons) like Adventure and Zork, originally run only on mainframes. We wanted stories that involved us, battles that felt real, and dragons that scared us. The technology was beginning to make these dreams more believable. The 1980s brought the first wave of 2-D games made for arcades, home computers, and console game systems. By the 1990s, video games appeared with even more graphically satisfying environments. Wolfenstein 3D, Doom, and Quake debuted on home computers just as video arcades began to go out of business. Many included Tolkien-type medieval fantasy or first-person shooter (FPS) scenarios. Players could spend not just 50 cents for a ten-minute thrill, but hours in complex virtual places that could be explored and conquered. "Graphical MUDs" allowed characters to communicate with each other; an early online role-playing game called Meridian 59 pioneered the 3-D, first-person point of view (and introduced players to the monthly fee scheme). But it was Ultima Online in 1997 that blazed the trail for other MMOs; this game was among the first to be played simultaneously by thousands of players on multiple servers, with graphics which, at the time, were considered state-of-the-art. EverQuest and Final Fantasy laid the groundwork for

Warcraft, the current sales and subscriptions champ. Since then, dozens of MMOs have debuted, the most popular typically with science fiction, superhero, and fantasy settings. It was only a matter of time before the worlds of Gygax and Tolkien spawned their own online counterparts: D&D Online, launched in 2006, and *Lord of the Rings* Online, in 2007, both born and bred by Turbine, Inc., a gaming company in the suburbs of Boston.

As U.S. computer and video-game sales have grown—tripling since 1996 to $9.5 billion in 2007, according to the Entertainment Software Association—the user base has exploded. A whopping 65 percent of American households, and 97 percent of children ages twelve to seventeen, now play some kind of video game. As technology has increased processor speed, realistic look and feel, and the size and complexity of game worlds, two gaming tracks have emerged: console gaming and online gaming. Console gaming (Xbox, Nintendo, PlayStation) generally focuses on shorter game sessions that mimic real activities such as car racing, snowboarding, and basketball, or FPS games set in wartime or postapocalyptic scenarios. In the mega-selling Halo, for example, there's no real "role-playing." Still, Halo spins an elaborate backstory about hybrid cyborg-human soldiers battling an alliance of alien races, and its game mechanics allow players to fight collaboratively, and text or speak to each other in real time.

Online games, especially MMORPGs, tend to focus on longer narratives, quests, and relationships that can last months or years. Thousands of players inhabit a "persistent" game world; for example, even if Euphey (or Priestly) is snoozing, game plot and events go on for other players. A persistent world also means a player's avatar can affect the outcome of game play experienced by other players. That innovation makes a game like WoW more "lifelike." It also induces anxiety when a gamer is offline: For every moment wasted in IRL (in real life), in-game stuff is happening without you, and that world is leaving you behind.

The games can go on forever. The worlds haven't quite figured out what to do when real players die, and their avatars keep on living.

SUCH A BEAUTIFUL WORLD

I jog softly across the silver-blue snow, my white beard and braided hair bouncing as I go. I am Ethorian, level-1 dwarf warrior. All is quiet, except WoW's incessant electro-classical theme music that functions like that *Lord of the Rings* soundtrack of trumpets and kettle drums. I leave my homeland to find adventure, hunt beasts, and collect booty to complete quests. I run. I leap. I do heroic stuff.

A gangly ogre-like creature, a trogg, stumbles past me. No need to fight it unless I want to. Plus, I don't know the keystrokes. The interface is about ten times more complex than a D&D character sheet. Not intuitive. I grow tired of the soundtrack and turn it off. Other avatars run through me. I'm a clumsy ghost.

I chat with Euphey in a little text box in the lower-left corner of the screen.

Ethorian: so how do I kill stuff?

Euphey: see the bar at the bottom? click on the little icon of the sword . . .

She shows me how to draw my ax, target a foe, and rack up the corpses. Her priest character, Laknar, has made me a mage-weave bag, which I stuff with booty. We play for an hour, Priestly puts her IRL daughter to bed, then she joins me again for more killing.

Euphey: fun!

Ethorian: yesssss . . . so, what's this icon that looks like a goblet?

She rockets off. I hear Euphey off-screen—*shhhooofkkff!*— her arrows hitting targets, shrieking, grunts, weapons slashing flesh. My dwarf trudges after her across the snow. I feel like an explorer. I find running across WoW's (almost) infinite landscape mesmerizing.

This was around the time I started sleeping outside to prepare for Pennsic War. I was playing WoW a couple hours a day, to level up Ethorian (who also slept outside, in Coldridge Valley, a mountainous area in the dwarfish homeland of Dun Morogh). I was also having MMO anxiety dreams—the equivalent of showing up for the SATs, naked, without my number-two battle-ax. I ran and fought in this dimly lit shadow world of pixels, reaching for a control panel in the sky that I could never touch.

Some days later, bored of being stumpy and inelegant, I retired Ethorian, and rebooted as Edenwyn, a female night elf hunter like Euphey. (Why not a little digital cross-dressing?) Priestly exited the game and reentered as Nusala, a third-level character, closer to my level. We bounded off like BFFs through the fairy-like forestland of Teldrassil.

Edenwyn: such a beautiful world . . .

Nusala: also ugly. you should see the assholes out there

Edenwyn: nice boobs

Nusala: you've got nice boobs too. better to have a drop dead gorgeous toon since you gotta spend a lot of time with him or her

On the way to "the wondrous city of Darnassus, the new refuge of the reclusive Night Elves," we paused to kill stuff. Nusala danced, laughed, bowed. She was gorgeous. I forgot that it was Priestly behind the keyboard, miles or light-years away. Nusala was not quite a person, but she was an essence, a life form. The hours passed. The whole world became a thirteen-inch screen. Ethan disappeared, as did his girl troubles. A new me emerged. I was one with Edenwyn, alive, and real. Real enough.

IN-GAME HE IS MY BEST FRIEND

Most fantasy MMOs like World of Warcraft are still based on D&D's basic mechanics and scenarios: make a character, go on adventures, kill the monsters, get treasure. As in Gygax's D&D, the higher the level, the more prowess your character has. But unlike D&D, WoW offers instant visual gratification. No dice rolling, no paperwork, no lame pencil sketches of your avatar. Like online shopping, you click through on-screen options for race (human, dwarf, night elf, etc.), class (mage, rogue, warrior, etc.), skin color, body type, hairstyle. You create your own unique name. You choose a side to fight for—Alliance (good guys) or Horde (bad guys). And you select a server so you can play with your friends. With so many millions playing, the WoW universe needs to be divided into concurrent worlds, or "realms," each on a separate server, or else the taverns and marketplaces would become mobbed with avatars. For further crowd control, most MMOs use "instancing," or multiple copies of certain content. Imagine multiple Frodos trying to destroy multiple rings, a multidimensional/multitemporal premise to ensure there's enough monsters and treasure to go around for everyone.

In D&D, the game is collaborative. You and your fellow players work together against whatever the Dungeon Master has dreamt up. You never backstab the other characters in your party unless you don't want to get invited to play the next time. In some MMORPGs, player vs. player, or "PvP," combat is acceptable. But not everyone likes to kill their fellow players. In player vs. environment (or "PvE") games or realms, you take on computer-generated foes. Like at an SCA event, WoW also has alternative fun for pacifists. There are skills to learn, professions to pursue, and avatars to chat up in the tavern. WoW also has its fan-fiction subculture, those who make YouTube tribute videos, and costumers who dress up as avatars at conventions.

I spoke with players who eschew raids and group play. They travel deeper and deeper into virtual worlds, exploring and fighting solo, while other players fly past, each on their separate quests. To me, this seemed a lonesome way to game, even more so when a non-gaming spouse (often a woman) tries to lure her loved one out for a night on the town. The phrase "World of Warcraft widow" exists for a reason. Typically, it's the wife who can't understand why her husband would spend so much time in a world *that doesn't exist.* "Does [your husband] describe Republicans and Democrats as The Horde and The Alliance?" lamented one woman in an article on ehow.com. "Have you overheard him 'buying gold,' and mistakenly thought he was preparing for your retirement? If so, then welcome to WoWoW—Widows of World of Warcraft!" A game can be a place to escape a boring home life or a relationship drained of intimacy and spark. Like Phyllis Priestly's.

On my quest through the rat race of Warcraft and other MMOs, I encountered the nice and not-so-nice. Nice players did nice things, casting buffs, which are spells and effects that enhance other players. Not-so-nice players—the worst offenders are called "trolls"—disrupt play and trick newbies. Diligent players spend hours grinding through low levels and monotonous quests to achieve power. Cheaters in rich countries pay "gold farmers," often Asian gamers, to level up characters or acquire powerful items for them. Just like in real life, I realized you can either play by the rules or find an easy way out.

Most of the unpleasant behavior falls under the category of "griefing," the general term for nasty behavior like stealing online booty and account passwords, and wantonly attacking other players (exploiting mismatches for fun is known as "ganking lowbies"). In 2006, one well-known incident brought widespread attention to griefing. In WoW, a guild of players held an in-game funeral honoring the real-life death of one of its members. The location was in territory hotly contested by a rival guild called Serenity Now. In the middle of the memorial service, Serenity Now attacked the funeral party. Commentary flooded the blogosphere, ranging from outrage ("Yes, it's real easy to be an asshole behind a keyboard and get away with it") to amusement ("This is the best thing I have ever seen").

But for every ruined marriage or sociopath I read about, I heard happy stories about players who had integrated gaming into already-full lives. Take Jerry Lustig, a former metallurgical engineer and currently a car dealership owner from Parsippany, New Jersey. He read science fiction as a kid, played Pong in the 1970s, and even used to DM D&D sessions for his son's friends. He told me he had always had a "predilection for fantasy and daydreaming." As an older adult, Lustig dabbled a bit in Xbox, but he mostly played WoW and Ultima Online. He was not a hard-core gamer—he played about ten hours per week, more in the winter and less in the summer. That's because in the warmer months, he raced cars (he owned three race cars and was part of a semipro racing team). Despite his limited game time, reduced further after he developed lymphoma and lost a whole year of playing, Lustig had done pretty well for himself. He played two characters, a level-69 shaman named Dran, and a level-70 rogue named Rismo, named for the Gran Turismo race car. Not bad for a seventy-year-old.

Lustig found PvP "sort of interesting." He considered himself a very competitive person (he played football and threw the javelin during his school days). But he mainly played WoW for relaxation. "If I need anxiety and frustration, I can just go to work." If he wanted real-life, hand-to-hand PvP activity, he'd spar in his martial arts studio. To experience extreme competition, he had his racing, a world of noise, fumes, and heat. "The consequences of errors in the race car are much greater, and the intensity level is very high." He took it seriously. A bad race, he said, "leaves me as someone you don't want to talk to for a day or two." He didn't rely on gaming for thrills. "I enjoy the fantasy and problem-solving. Engineers tend to like problem-solving, and I want my gaming experience to provide diversion and relaxation."

There weren't a lot of seventy-year-olds playing computer games in his town, so for gaming camaraderie, Lustig joined The Syndicate, an international guild for WoW and Ultima Online players, one of hundreds of player guilds worldwide that support socializing in and outside the game. Guilds can be based around common games, game goals, or, surprisingly, around a religious belief. (For example, Tribe of Judah is one of many Christian guilds; others have silly names like "Defenseless Old Ladies" and "When Fat Kids Attack.") At 620 members, The Syndicate, founded in 1996, is the largest in online gaming. Members of The Syndicate might gather "in some basement somewhere, playing games and drinking beer and eating pizza for a day or three," said Sean "Dragons" Stalzer, the father and a husband who runs the guild and plays a Guildmaster character, a level-80 Tauren shaman. Members consult on game design, produce strategy guides and books, and support programs to keep youth in school. "The Syndicate was once a guild but has evolved into a virtual community," Dragons said. "Gaming these days is not really about the game itself. The game is just a tool used by a large group of friends to have a good time together." Warcraft could be a team sport. Like on a basketball court, gamers knew each other's body language, moves, and nonverbal cues. "Over here!" "You got him!" "Kill 'em!" The Syndicate's motto was "In Friendship We Conquer."*

MMOs let you hide your body; no one was picked last for the raid team based on superficials like appearance. Playing online was the ultimate equalizer. You could find heroism, grace, agility, and victory. In the Asian Pacific, home to about three-quarters of the world's estimated 30 million MMORPG players, competitive gaming was a hugely popular sport, and players of strategy games like StarCraft and WarCraft III were as recognizable as pro-

---

* Actress and gamer Felicia Day, of *Buffy* fame, has produced a hit web sitcom called *The Guild*. While not explicitly about WoW, the show is obviously inspired by the game and its players.

fessional athletes. Gamer sports stardom had made some inroads here in the States. Annual "arena tournaments" pitted trios of players against each other. Games were announced like sporting matches, with play-by-play and post-match interviews with players. (To get into the game, even Boston Red Sox star pitcher Curt Schilling has launched a company, 38 Studios, as has Vin Diesel with Tigon Studios.) I had seen the North American World of Warcraft Arena championships, held in Boston and won by a team that included a 17-year-old young woman named Rumay Wang, from suburban Boston, the only female in the whole competition. When her team "Fnatic" won, shy young men flocked to her and congratulated her; she more then held her own in WoW's mostly man-centered universe, not quite a hero, perhaps, but a minor celebrity, and very much desired by the boys. (A recent study suggested that while male gamers outnumber females 60/40, the most dedicated and hard-core players of MMOs are women.) At the world championships, Fnatic finished second.

Guilds like The Syndicate, I learned, even brought families together. "We have members who play," "Dragons" said, "and then got their spouses to play and they are now hooked." Mom, Dad, Sis, and Bro log on to their separate computers from the four corners of the world. Social gaming had come a long way since Monopoly or Parcheesi. "Dragons" was kind enough to connect me with Syndicate members Darkfeather and Trainwreck, the mother-son duo of Lisa Champion, forty-four, and her son William, twenty-eight, both from Okeechobee, Florida. They played Ultima Online together and were Squad Leaders in The Syndicate. Trainwreck was in the Marine Corps Infantry Division. When I heard from him and his mom, he was about to be shipped off to Iraq, for the third time.

"For me, crafting drives me nuts whereas it's fun to her," Trainwreck wrote to me. "I like the fighting and exploring, so [it's] always cool when she asks where something is in a dungeon, etc., and I can help her out." Their online socializing and Syndicate duties helped them stay in touch. "It really boils down to us being able to hang out and play together [and] help each other out."

"I miss him and worry so much," Darkfeather wrote. "It's like a huge part of your heart gets ripped from you. You cry and pray a lot. While he's gone I continue to play UO (it keeps you busy along with real life)." To keep her son updated, she sent a weekly newsletter about Ultima Online, which he and the other Marines enjoyed. "It's mainly about what's going on in-game, stories, and jokes, never about real life. Due to me wanting only to bring a smile, it's the safest way I could come up with to make him feel like he's at home (in the States) without actually making him homesick, if that makes sense." The newsletter kept him from thinking he'd been forgotten. Trainwreck and Darkfeather couldn't play much when he was on tour in Iraq; she'd sometimes level up his character in his absence. Before Trainwreck left for one tour of duty, she said, "it was my job to have all the skills up to grandmaster prior to his return."

Darkfeather felt that gaming has brought them closer together. And it had also changed their mother-son relationship. Darkfeather is still the mother, she insisted, but "in-game he is my best friend." When I last spoke with Darkfeather, in the weeks before Trainwreck's next deployment, she told me he had just gotten married. Plus, this news: "I will have a new grandson around late June."

WE BATTLE AND LOSE—AND LOSE—AND LOSE SOME MORE

I knew a guy who'd had a promising basketball career. He was headed to college on a scholarship but blew out his knee and dropped out of school. End of sports career—beginning of interest in console games based on *Lord of the Rings*. Had he substituted swordplay in Middle-earth for hoops heroism? Was that a self-soothing move, or an outlet for frustration? I hadn't met many gamers who claimed WoW made them better people—but I did wonder if MMOs made players feel more heroic. Might raiding a dungeon, destroying a city, and killing a troll give us that taste of danger which our psyches have craved ever since society insulated us from death by sword?

Sean "Dragons" Stalzer felt strongly that most Syndicate members didn't play the games out of some misplaced desire for vicarious risk-taking or play-acted heroism. He did agree that some younger players might get swept up into power trips. "You get to be an extremely powerful entity that can do things far beyond your human abilities," he said, "and can conquer what would normally be impossible objectives." But older players didn't seem to be "'fooled' by the false sense of heroism." For them, gaming was social, more about fun and "an escape from their normal lives."

"We're not trying to be heroes," said Jim Sanborn, thirty-nine, another Syndicate member from outside the Twin Cities in Minnesota. He worked as a data-integration consultant, served on his school board, and played a shaman character named Chamois in Warcraft. In a particularly long e-mail to me, signed "Chamois the verbose," he pointed out how people used to write letters, which took weeks to get to their recipient. Culture had changed exponentially since the telegraph and the telephone, followed by cell phones, e-mail, texting, and YouTube. So too with video-game culture: We've simply adapted our playing habits. People have always had both "competition and recreation" in their free time, and have always enjoyed playing in groups, be it golf or bowling or poker. "Now instead of having to get twenty-two people together to play football, you can sit down alone with your TV and Xbox and play Madden '09, and you never get picked last, never pull a hammy, and you get the ball as often as you want it," Sanborn said. He can play games with hundreds of friends and family spread across the globe, in real time. And while he can't beat his boss at golf, he can "kick his ass at Half-Life." Take that, manager scum. "Just because our golf course has dragons or spaceships on it, doesn't make it any less competitive, valid, social, [or] real."

From my D&D days, I understood this need to band together in guilds, to create a brother- and sisterhood, much like in the

Fighting a troll: a screenshot from Lord of the Rings *Online.*

military, bound by common cause and necessary killing, even if the killing *was* virtual. The desire to cheer with each other after a hard battle, to share the victory and the spoils, was probably genetic, even if today, those battle cries and cheers were transmitted over headsets—"Yeehaaawww!!!!"—to disembodied players separated by thousands of miles.

"We don't need video games to simulate battles or be heroic; in fact, we need just the opposite," said Sanborn. "So many times in our jobs and family lives, we battle and lose. And lose. And lose some more. Video games are something we can play and win."

THE GAME MADE ME MORE "ME"

I had first met Phyllis Priestly in May. By November, she was forced to close the school that she had founded six years before, after it had been declining for months. Her family had moved to a new house, and she was up to her windpipe in renovations. Her thirteen-year-old daughter, who had taught her to play, had planned to let her Warcraft account expire. The blue streak in her hair was gone (but she was contemplating going purple). With all the changes, I wondered if WoW was still a fixture in Priestly's life.

A mage uses a frostbolt spell in battle in this screenshot from World of Warcraft.

I caught her in a reflective mood. She told me she was deflated after the failure of her school. "Warcraft gave me solace," she said, sipping a mocha latte in the same café where we'd met before. "I needed to go off and lick my wounds." She now had mixed feelings about playing. But after almost two years, Priestly was also feeling more bold and confident about changing her world. If she could complete a quest, perhaps she could talk to her husband. She continued to play WoW, but not as much as before. Still, Priestly knew her husband would prefer if she didn't play at all. Now that the crises had passed, she hoped her interest in the game would fade. She said she was waiting for that moment when she would disconnect from it. When, like I'd experienced with D&D, she wouldn't need WoW anymore. "When I will want to go outside again."

I was glad I wasn't the only one who, having reached midlife, had experienced that dazed-deer-in-the-headlights freak-out, wondering where to run next.

For the moment, WoW continued to hold sway in her life. Warcraft was a kind of family for her. Over two years, she had come to really "know" players: where they lived, what they ate for dinner, when they put their children to bed. "There is a basic need to be loved, to be listened to, and to be heard. That's what these games provide." She congratulated game-makers Blizzard Entertainment for doing a great job. "It's powerful." It's not called World of WarCrack for nothing.

The week after I visited Priestly, Blizzard released the game's next expansion pack, a long-expected infusion of new content called Wrath of the Lich King. Millions of fans lined up at midnight on November 12, 2008, to buy, load, and enter. In its first twenty-four hours, it broke all records, selling 2.8 million copies. EverQuest II (aka "Never-rest" and "Ever-crack") released its update, and *Lord of the Rings* Online launched their Mines of Moria expansion the following week: "an immense network of tunnels, chambers, mines and huge halls beneath the Misty Mountains . . . one of the largest and most dangerous online underground environments ever created." Each game a labyrinth, a mirror reflecting a mirror, encased in or behind or within a computer screen.

"It's far more compelling than my real world," Priestly said, smiling. "That can't be good, can it?" She felt that the draw of World of Warcraft and other games was almost primal. "We're hardwired for battle. That reptile part of the brain. The saber-toothed tiger on the savannah jumping out." Priestly paused, and looked sad. She did not want to go back to the person she'd been before she played. "I'll always treasure it. It's done so much for me." The game, she said, "has made me more 'me.'"

We provide 12 power leveling service for mmorpgs including World of Warcraft,
Final Fantasy XI, Guild Wars, Maple Story, Ever Quest, Ever Quest 2, Dungeons &
Dragons Online etc. to our loyal customers. You will get the first class service as
a cheap price for power leveling. We provide many special cheap packages on hot
sale at the moment. WOW Power Leveling 1 - 60 only cost $159.99. Take a look our
special cheap packages and get the cheapest and securest power leveling service
from us. There are 13 special packages for you. Choose one and save more. We can
provide the cheap power leveling service at the first time when it came out. Such
as the Burning Crusade comes, we provide the power leveling service for any level
to level 70 at the lowest price. The price of power leveling for the two new races
(Blood Elf and Draenei) is as the same as the original races. It is much cheaper
the any other website. Hoping to serve you and nice to help you to have a wonderful
mmorpg life.

—from an advertisement for a power-leveling service Web site
(www.wowpls.com)

An Outlet for Souls Who Could Not Rest

"I believe that online games can destroy people," Rajeev said.

Rajeev was a brainy, clean-cut, thirty-one-year-old business student who had ambitions to become a writer. Within a few minutes of our meeting, he began to spill forth his story. As an Indian-American, he had felt family pressure to attend medical school. He applied and got into a prestigious program, only to realize later that a medical career was not for him. He stayed in med school, but just barely. Rather than confront his parents, he became obsessed with computer games: Baldur's Gate (set in a high fantasy milieu), Icewind Dale (D&D-based), Civilization (empire building), and Birth of the Federation (*Star Trek*). "They became a distraction," he said. "I would call it an addiction."

Addiction? As I talked to more and more gamers, it became clear that these fantasy worlds are not harmless. Nor are the people whose hands eagerly click away at keyboards unaffected or blameless. As Phyllis Priestly demonstrated, players can develop almost psychic connections to their avatars and what their avatars do. Stories are legion about gamers descending into deep depressions when their avatars are killed. I heard tell of Chinese men who died from exhaustion at their computers after two- or three-day gaming marathons, and Korean kids spirited away to outdoorsy reeducation camps to wean them off their Internet dependency. A Japanese woman was so distraught by her real-life divorce that she sought revenge by killing her online husband's digital persona in a game called Maple Story, and was arrested, IRL, for hacking.

It struck me that humans haven't quite caught up—emotionally, psychologically, or behaviorally—with their avatars. The puppets can do stuff, some of it misanthropic, that the puppeteers could not or would not do. Who controls the mouse—the user, or their "'toon?" Priestly admitted WoW was powerful. I believed her. I wanted to hear more radical stories like Rajeev's, about how falling into online fantasy has the potential to both improve and implode lives.

At the height of his descent, Rajeev would wake up in the morning, head to his computer, and play all day, twelve hours at a time, drinking nutritional shakes. He lost a lot of weight. He also frequented strip clubs. He'd do the minimum schoolwork to stay afloat in his classes. His girlfriend at the time told him he had no close friends. "All you do is play video games," she said.

"For the first two years I could manage it, but not the third year," Rajeev said. He seemed relieved, almost eager to confess this to me. "I did not realize it at the time, but I was really unhappy to be in med school." He was sabotaging his career. At one point, he tried to kick the habit. "I remember, I would mail games to my sister and say 'Please don't ever give this back to me.'" Eventually, he quit his four-year addiction. In order to quit, he had to hit rock bottom. He failed out of med school, and moved in with his parents. They eventually forgave him. He slowly rebuilt his life and applied to business school. As the self-help parlance goes, Rajeev considered himself a recovered addict.

Perhaps Rajeev was already predisposed to fantasy. He played D&D in middle school and remembered constructing elaborate characters and civilizations that were "perfect in every way." As an adult, computer games were a logical, and allowable, medium for escape. "I come from a family where I could never become addicted to drugs, never to alcohol. [Gaming] was a socially acceptable addiction. My family could say, 'This was bad.' But they could never disown Rajeev."

Exactly how anyone decides when their gaming activity has morphed from "passion" to "problem" is unclear. The twelve-step group On-Line Gamers Anonymous has existed since 2002, to "help each other recover and heal from the problems caused by excessive game playing." OLGA claims all video games can be addictive, but singles out MMORPGs as potentially the most dangerous, because among other reasons, "Success in these games is highly dependent on the amount of time you put into them," "People may become attached to their new online friends," and "They never end." In an interview in the *Boston Globe*, psychiatrist Dr. Jerald Block discussed treating people for gaming addictions. He has found that gamers harbor considerable shame about their habits, even more than pornography addicts. That's because people understand a porn obsession; gaming addicts have a harder time explaining their obsession to family, friends, or their therapists. He believed that "Internet Addiction" (although he prefers the term "pathological computer use") should become a new diagnostic term.

Now and again, Rajeev will play a few games. Was there any danger of backsliding? He didn't think so. "I find them very boring. I cannot believe that I played them. The reason is I'm happy where I am. When your real world is good you won't be drawn to these worlds." He realized, in retrospect, that a computer game was just an imaginary world. It did not exist. "Playing a computer game, I'm not helping to build myself into a useful person," he said. "Now I try to make my apartment as nice as possible."

But here's the catch: Rajeev had graduated to self-help tapes. Anthony Robbins–type motivational programs, David DeAngelo dating guru "how to meet women" talks. "I just listen to these things all the time. When I'm in my car, instead of listening to the radio, I'll listen to self-help tapes. You get a lot of insight into yourself. You can have a life and listen to an audiobook." He paused. "Maybe I'm obsessed with that now."

A SYMBOL OF ALL THAT IS GOOD IN THE WORLD

Because WoW is not D&D or a LARP, where the play is face-to-face, avatars make it easy for the socially awkward to be bold. The anonymity of the game gives players the courage to overcome fears and act out. Many online gamers would never fly their freak flags, as Sir Gareth would put it, in person. "I know very few people that would take off their clothes and dance in front of the post office," said Jim "Chamois" Sanborn, "but you see it all the time in Azeroth." Sanborn believed that this shift in behavior was a two-way street. "People who would help old ladies across the street in Pittsburgh will gleefully stand by and do nothing while you are eaten by a giant dinosaur in the game." With an MMO's focus on battle, I expected schoolyard bully tactics and social Darwinism on steroids to be the norm.

That was before I heard from Levi Hunt, a member of the North Carolina National Guard's Infantry Medical Platoon—aka, Geistprophet, a voice for the victims of abuse, an outlet for souls who could not rest, and a symbol of all that is good in the world.

When I caught up with Hunt, age twenty-six, he was living in Wilmington and feeling quite anxious. He was a few months away from his first overseas deployment, where he would serve as the medical supply noncommissioned officer for his unit. "Needless to say, I'm a bit freaked out," Hunt said, "but I'm excited." It would hurt to leave his wife, Courtney, and his child behind for so long. But he was confident the family bond was strong. He and Courtney endured a lot together. Besides, it was Courtney who got Hunt into The Syndicate in the first place.

It was striking to me how many people in the military play RPGs—both D&D and online. I wondered if these folks were drawn to games like WoW specifically because they offer a black-and-white, good vs. evil, Horde vs. Alliance scenario. Iraq War soldiers surely performed heroic acts. But perhaps they fought without the same irrefutable sense of righteousness as World War II vets, who were confident their mission (and necessary killing) was for a just cause. Iraq is murkier. Perhaps that explained why Hunt was a serious gamer.

Or perhaps gaming was in his blood. Hunt's brothers were raised on D&D and Tolkien. "I was surrounded by 'geekdom' from the day I was born," he told me, taking a break from packaging his gear and personal items for shipment to Iraq. He played early *Lord of the Rings* games, Nintendo/Super Nintendo, Sega Genesis, Ultima Online (UO), and now WoW. When he first got into MMOs, he'd hole himself up in his room, log on to his local network with his buddies, and play UO for hours. He called that period in his life one of "Drinking, partying, and just goofing off with people the world over. It was good times and probably kept us from doing a lot of dumb stuff." When he met Courtney, he showed her the ropes and she became an avid UO player. She saw an ad for The Syndicate, applied, and, "because she is the amazing lady she is," got in. Her avatar was named Geistmaiden. Hunt joined next. The guild was founded on ideals that both he and his wife shared: "An online community of people who want to fight the good fight, and to have a hell of a lot of fun while we're at it." The typical lament of male gamers to their non-gaming womenfolk—"Honey, I can't go to the mall with you, I'm busy saving the world, OK?"—would never apply to the Hunt household.

Hunt's reasons for playing video games with role-playing components, like WoW or UO, went far beyond the usual beer, pizza, fun, and escapism. He and many others fell for that familiar high-fantasy narrative that many MMOs spin. To give a taste, here's a snippet of backstory taken from Warhammer Online: Age of Reckoning:

> In the lands of the far north, where tribes of savage barbarians worship the abhorrent gods of Chaos, a new champion has risen. His name is heard on the howling of the icy winds and the shrill cries of ravens. It is proclaimed in peals of thunder and whispered in the nightmares of men. He is Tchar'zanek, Chosen of Tzeentch, and he will shake the very foundations of the Old World . . .

Legends like these cycling in your mind, the horns of battle echoing across the virtual realms, and a rousing movie-like "game trailer" playing before you enter the game—how could you *not* answer the call to duty? Dedicated gamers like Hunt tapped into the soldier-samurai-knight bloodstream. The guild was like a tribe that embodied the best qualities of nerd (a mind for stats and strategy) plus jock (the brutish body and guts to stomach death). To play was to enter the timeless warrior myth, updated for our modern, quest-starved psyches.

"I've met several people in other guilds who love to fight because of the sense of community that's built on honor and valor," he said. "No, we don't get those chances in real life, without the drawbacks that real life carries, i.e., death, pain. In gaming, people feel more free to get in touch with an older side of our history that dates back to the first days of man." Online combat, like real combat, was a way of coming to understand one's self, through victory and defeat. "I will gladly salute a fallen enemy or one who has been better than me. That is just plain respect, which is so hard to find nowadays that sometimes we have to fight to find it. If I defeat someone, I will always honor them before [celebrating] my victory." In-game behavior provided a window into the soul of the characters he encountered. Hunt felt that players who bowed humbly or helped pull each other back to their feet, those people, deep down, had good and genuine motives IRL. Poor sports who cried and complained—well, that said "a world of things about that person in a short time." From those in-game experiences, he knew who was worth associating with, and who was not.

In real life, he did not get that pleasure. In Iraq, if he had to bear arms against someone, his foe remained nameless. "Chances are I will never see them eye to eye and it will be over only fast enough for me to think about when I ask for forgiveness from whatever powers may be later." In real life, justice was rarely served. Murderers walked from insanity pleas. Children died during warfare. Terrorists disappeared into the crowd. "It's depressing," he said.

Playing MMOs let Hunt restore balance to the cosmos. In the virtual community, Hunt became Geistprophet, who could avenge a loss, punish a criminal, and deliver retribution. His avatar stood for these values. "If someone wants to hurt my friends, strangers, or myself, I have all the powers in that world at my disposal to stop that from happening." The word *avatar*, before it came to mean a movable icon to represent a virtual being in cyberspace, used to refer to the manifestation of a deity or released soul in bodily form on earth. An avatar was a divine teacher made incarnate on earth, or the physical manifestation of an idea.

In the Ultima game series, Hunt explained, you were placed into the role of "The Avatar, the very essence of the virtues that make a good soul: Humility, Honor, Compassion, Valor, Justice, Spirituality, Sacrifice, and Honesty." It reminded me of Sir Gareth's code of knighthood. Even as a kid, Hunt craved that power to right the world's wrongs. "For me it made me feel good to come home from a hectic time in a broken school system, where I was the underdog that most kids used as a scapegoat, and become a symbol of all that is good in the world and fight back the evil that plagues humanity. I had no worries of death. I could resurrect if needed." Over the years he carried that persona, Geistprophet, from one game to the next, most recently to WoW, where he now resided "with my family in The Syndicate."

Trained as a medic, Hunt had served with ambulance units and treated soldiers and refugees, but he understood that 99 percent of the time, people didn't get credit for being good Samaritans. He helped others for the way it made him feel—what he called the "rush of sacrifice." "When you can don your own angel's wings, surround your patient with them, and work a sort of real-life magic into them and improve their quality of life, there's no feeling like that." He believed soldiers were some of our last true heroes. Had Hunt lived a thousand years ago, he might have been a knight. Or a saint. When he was unable to do good in real life, he carried that sentiment into WoW or UO, aiding players with a raid, or, seeing a stranger in trouble on a quest, offering a helping hand or sword. "If I see John Doe getting run over by a monster, I can step in. I don't need a 'thank-you' even. I've been there and others have done it for me, and I know the feeling of gratitude I had toward them is now directed back at me. Hopefully John Doe will do the same later."

Hunt took his games seriously, but none of his sober game playing muddled his understanding of real life. "In the gaming world, if I screw up, 99 percent of the time we can pick ourselves up, figure out what we messed up, and move on with little to hold us back." How he performed as a medic could affect the rest of a soldier's life. Screwing up, he said, would be unforgivable. He could not accept anything less than doing his best; it was no game. "The stakes are real in the world we are in."

Hunt had not become a football star or a dashing Hollywood lead, but in gaming, he found himself on equal footing with

Art commissioned for the World of Warcraft and Ultima Online guild The Syndicate. Their slogan, "In Friendship We Conquer," celebrates hard-core gaming.

others, in a milieu where the only real advantages were personalities and brains. Anyone could achieve greatness, claimed SPC
Levi Hunt. You didn't even have to be a soldier. Plus, if gaming
helped people get their minds off the world and the grim outlook
that is constantly shoved in their faces, even better.

I BEND DOWN AND PICK STUFF UP IN-GAME JUST AS WELL AS YOU

When I spoke with Nissa Ludwig, she was bent on fighting the
ignorance of the non-gaming world.

"I think society is predetermined to think gaming is a bad
thing," she said. "That is the societal view—that we're all crazy
and going to kill each other and ourselves. I'm certainly not. I'm
the music director of my church." Any opportunity to change
the perception that gamers were not all "devil-worshipping murderers" was welcome. Then she deadpanned, "I met my husband
at a devil worship club. Just ask him."

In fact, Ludwig met her husband, a computer game developer, at a LARP. Her father was a game developer too. She
couldn't remember when there wasn't a computer in the house.
"I was going into IBM with my dad and playing Zork on the
mainframe at age four." Ludwig played MUD-type games like
Dungeon, Zork, and D&D in junior high. In the interim, she had
played all the major MMORPGs: the superhero/supervillain City
of Heroes and City of Villains; Ultima Online; Lord of the Rings
Online, EverQuest and EverQuest II; WoW; and Star Wars Galaxies. Her main character, Kaylasara, traveled from game to game.
Her friends traveled with her from game to game, too. Many
hailed from Dragon Realms, a text-based game she began playing in the 1990s. "My character in that game is married and has a
family. My husband and I, we considered that my first marriage.
We invited my in-game husband to our wedding," she said. "My
[real] husband calls me Kayla as much as he calls me Nissa."

Ludwig, age thirty-nine, lived in Seattle and was unemployed.
Behind glasses and a mane of long reddish hair, she recounted

her lifelong relationship with gaming. She wasn't cocky, but she spoke confidently of her mastery over some games, and her impatience with others. In-game killing didn't appeal to her; rather, she was a maker, a doer, and a trader. "My interest is not going out there and beating the crap out of things. In my mind, it's very contradictory, the killing of another player. I'm not a PvP person; I'm a crafter, I'm a merchant. I'm a much more cooperative person."

That said, in wartime, armies need materiel, and Ludwig was more than happy to provide. "If there's war, they want my weapons," she said. In *Star Wars* Galaxies, the MMORPG that lets players become jedis, bounty hunters, and traders, she said, "I was *the* weapon smith on my server."

Surprisingly, Ludwig's more peaceable side was enjoying her latest game, Warhammer Online: Age of Reckoning, a fairly battle-heavy MMO that pits factions against each other. "I used to play the Warhammer tabletop game a little. I was not overly impressed with the world, the mythology of the game. But I'm loving the online game." She found the group-vs.-group play focus empowering. "They included one thing no one has done to this point: war with siege weapons. I can fire a big nasty cannon and take out a bunch of players. I can sit behind a bolt thrower and inflict 900 points of damage."*

For Ludwig the pacifist, running a trebuchet had thrilled her. I wondered if the shift was connected to her deteriorating health. An undiagnosed muscular disorder keeps Ludwig at home most of the day, in a wheelchair or using crutches. "The muscles in my body are slowly rotting," she said, rather matter-of-factly. She and her husband lived in a tiny brick bungalow ("like the one you picture in kids' books about where you'd grow up"). There was a computer in almost every room, and her husband had an

---

* To discourage ganking, Warhammer has an amusing punishment for any high-ranked player who attacks a lowbie: The game turns the offending player's avatar, temporarily, into a chicken.

office, his "cave," in the basement. Ludwig also got around on a battery-powered scooter with all-terrain wheels, which helped her participate in games like LARPs. She tended to fare poorly in any combat-heavy computer game that demanded her brain and muscles to work in concert, in a rapid-fire way. "But I type really well, and I'm a musician." She regularly played bass online in Rock Band; her band, PyroTechniqueMusic, included a singer from Peoria, a drummer from Cincinnati, and a guitarist from Fort Worth. They covered the likes of Avenged Sevenfold, Bon Jovi, and Deep Purple. "They are my three best friends other than my husband. There isn't a day that goes by I don't play, or get a text from all three of them. Granted, it's not a fantasy setting. There are no dragons involved. It's not the Dungeons & Dragons format, but it's not any less real." To be a rock 'n' roll hero was another kind of battlefield stardom.

Ludwig said plenty of disabled people play computer games. "I'll be playing and not do well in a battle and I'll say, 'Sorry, my hands don't work that way.' It's amazing how many other people say, 'Me too.'"

An organization called Able Gamers advocates for universal access to games. Their Web site announces that war vets and others with missing limbs can play Guitar Hero one-handed via a customized foot pedal, or that researchers are developing a "tongue-driven" game system for paraplegics. The International Game Developers Association's Game Accessibility Special Interest Group estimates that as many as 9 percent of all gamers claim some disability, whether visual or auditory, or a motor-coordination issue. The disabled community wields, or could wield, significant influence on game design. ("Two heads are better than one," one gamer posted on a message board, "but one arm is more than enough to kick someone's ass.")

While online anonymity may sometimes cause antisocial behavior, in Ludwig's case, it became a liberating cipher. In the same way that, in WoW, you could role-play a hoofed and horned,

Concept art for Lord of the Rings Online: a Moria orc in armor.

eight-foot-tall, 600-pound tauren and no one would guess that you were a twelve-year-old boy behind the keyboard, no one knew Ludwig was disabled unless she told them. No one passed judgment. No one immediately pigeonholed her as different, or dumb. "My brain works just fine, thank you," she said with some frustration. "Just because my body doesn't work doesn't mean my brain doesn't." Online gaming created an alternate world where no one saw her crutches or wheelchair. And that was, in her words, "a beautiful thing."

As I spoke with Ludwig, as she explained her bond with gaming, an odd paradox struck me. Only in a game such as Warhammer Online, where Ludwig could portray a character from any of six races—Dwarves, Humans, High Elves, Greenskins, Dark Elves, and Corrupted Humans—did she feel "just as normal as everyone else." The somewhat freakish, cartoony body types of the warrior elite—pointy-eared, yellow-tusked, demonically possessed, or otherwise mutated—made her an average, indistinguishable, part of the rabble.

Gaming also helped her escape the ravages of her body. "I'm a narcotics-laden pain [magnet]. I'm in pain all the time. There are times you can get out of the body. In gaming, there's a Zen part to it. In the heat of a massive combat, I'm not in pain. I'm thinking, 'Holy crap! He's firing at me! He's got a big sword—bad!' So there's an escape from that, too. It's unbelievably powerful." Ludwig-as-Kaylasara, moving from universe to universe, transcended the limits of her failing body. Not only did the gaming distract her from the pain, but it also allowed her—via her avatar—to do things that she could not do in real life. And she didn't mean ultra-heroic exploits. "I can't run through the grass barefoot anymore. It's something I cannot do. But my avatar can."

I have a sharp memory of teaching my mom a video game, circa 1984, on our Intellivision console. She didn't perform well. The pre-aneurysm "Old Sara" was dexterous, athletic, and quick-witted. She would have jumped in without fear. "Sure kid, I'll play. Bring it on." Probably would have beat all the kids in the neighborhood. But the game was too confusing for the post-injury Mom, saddled as she was with a paralyzed hand, a broken body, and scrambled brain and vision. The graphics flew by in a kaleidoscopic blur. Any of these modern MMOs would have been lost on her, too. Unfortunate—because Ludwig helped me see how my mother would have taken to MMORPGs, had she been less diminished. The prospect of Mom playing again was an intriguing fantasy. Mom remaking herself. Choosing a new body. Becoming whole. Mom running again . . . Wow.

As we spoke, it was hard not to be shaken by Nissa Ludwig's story. "Sometimes just bending down and picking up stuff . . ."

she began, and paused. "I bend down and pick stuff up in-game just as well as you." Games give disabled people a new social life, new social skills, a new home, and a new way to interact. "I don't even think game designers know what they are doing. You're not staring at the wall, watching TV, eating food and getting fat until you're dead." Sitting at home all day, she said, you wish you had a project; if you can't get out, "it starts feeling like a cage." When she told me, "I'm sitting here almost in tears because they gave that back to me. To have that taken away and have it back," she wasn't the only one about to cry.*

Then, to end our conversation, Ludwig threw in this zinger. "Getting sick is one of the best things that happened to me. When the sun comes up, it's a celebration. My legs don't work, but my arms do. Right on. I don't need a machine to breathe. You learn to be grateful for things you don't even see."

Earlier in my quest, I had held online gamers to a different standard than RPG geeks. Initially, encountering D&Ders and LARPers, I worried about how nerdy they were, and asked if I could still be a part of that tribe. With WoW players, I wondered if they were addicted crazies, and I struggled to understand their game's appeal. But both standards were incomplete. And there were hidden aspects of MMOs—benefits that went beyond mere entertainment—that I was beginning to see.

While my descent into MMOs was edifying, I was wearying of video screens and worlds I could only see. I wanted touch. Real 3-D. I was eager to visit the real world of fantasy again. And I was ready to see a few more freak flags flapping at an event called Dragon*Con.

---

* When I spoke with Ludwig a few months later, her health had deteriorated further. "I'm having a hard time getting a keyboard to work," she said. "The disease is progressive and degenerative. It's getting worse, that is part of it. . . .I have good days and bad days." Lately, she'd had "about 60 of those [bad days] back to back."

Rules and Policies

We reserve the right to ask you to leave the convention and refuse to refund your membership money if you are behaving—in technical terms—like a jerk.

NO CAMPING IN THE HALLS OR LOBBY! If you are found sleeping in the public areas, you will be asked to go to your hotel room. If you do not have a room, hotel or venue security will be forced to ask you to leave. Check the message board for people looking for people to share rooms and costs.

Please do not abuse our hotels or convention facilities. This includes putting signs on walls. Public locations for notices are provided. Room Parties and other announcements may also be dropped off at our Information Desk for inclusion in the Daily Dragon. Please don't eat the facilities; we'd kinda like to do this again, and under a roof . . .

Costumers, remember that no costume is NO costume, and there are public nudity laws in Georgia. Please wear appropriate (or at least enough) clothing in the common areas.

—from the Dragon*Con program schedule (2008)

You Have to Become the Con

My Journey to Atlantis: A Description of Native Races, Comprising Remarks on their Peculiarities, and Other Personal Observations, by Ethor-An3

DAY 1, 4:00 P.M.: I had heard tell of these creatures—some humanoid, others not—who assembled at every summer's end to overrun a certain lost city, Atlantis. Such was their custom for the past twenty-two years, this gathering at Dragon*Con. They mix freely with the permanent inhabitants and proceed to over-run four camps (Hyatt, Hilton, Marriott, Sheraton). They unload their battle gear: dragon wings, wigs, and fuzzy tails; contraptions called coolers and laptops; mammoth rifles and suits of gleaming armor. Some wear helmets or combat boots, or ordinary shirts emblazoned with slogans from their homelands: HAVE YOU HUGGED A HOBBIT TODAY? and KILT INSPECTION TEAM. The thousands in atten-dance appear to be linked by social, religious, or blood ties, each tribe with its own common culture, dialect, and way of dress.

With help from a friendly Amazon named Wonder Woman, I record the names of clans: Darth Vaders, Gandalfs, Superwomen, Klingons, Hellboys, Indiana Joneses, Wookies, Spidermen,

Pirates, Ghostbusters, Cylons, Ewoks, Transformers, Board Gamers, Geishas, Skeptics, Captain Kirks, X-Men, Harry Potters, and Has-Been-Stars. I find a thick pamphlet entitled DRAGON*CON 2008 POCKET PROGRAM, which contains much useful advice and administrative dicta. I am comforted to read the following regulation:

> Please abide by our weapons policy: All weapons must be non-working and peace bonded. No functioning projectile weapons includes water pistols, silly-string guns, and ping-pong pistols. Bladed weapons must be cased or sheathed at all times. No clowning around or showing off in the common areas. Any weapon used in an offensive manner will be confiscated. . . . We do not post bail.

I'm not certain what "peace bonded" is. I avoid tribespeople carrying the heaviest weapons and largest fanny packs.

DAY 2, 11:00 A.M.: I do not think these forces are here to conquer Atlantis. I think they came to absorb some higher teachings from the elder and wiser of their respective clans. I, too, I spend many an hour soaking up what knowledge I can. In "panels" and "seminars," humanoids dressed in plain garb sit at a dais or other place of honor. Followers, often dressed alike as "gamers," "marines," or "elves," listen attentively to a lively discourse on a variety of topics: "How to Survive a Zombie Apocalypse"; "An Hour with Lex Luthor"; "What Makes a Hero?"; "Freedom of Speech and Privacy Issues for Sex-Positive Bloggers and Podcasters"; "MMO Etiquette School"; "Japanese Sword Smithing"; "Reflections on a Decade of Paranormal Investigation"; "Aiya E'rendil Elenion Ancalima!: Learn to Speak and Read Elvish." Dragon*Conians flock to concerts, parties, workshops, sing-alongs, Q&As, quizzes, screenings, robot battles, and parades. One contest looks amusing: The 2008 Miss Klingon Empire

Beauty Pageant. Afterward, the clans disperse back into the general chaos. Some congregate and purchase beverages. Others return to their domiciles to rest. Or to become ill.

DAY 3, 7:00 P.M.: At night, the most outlandish and brazenly adorned tribespeople—shirtless men, women in tight-fitting bodices—leave the safety of their domiciles to mingle with the general populace. They examine each other, and record their images with devices called "digital cameras." This may be a mating ritual, or an outlet for exhibitionist tendencies. I overhear one creature, dressed quite minimally herself, say, "Some people just want to walk around in their underwear."

DAY 3, 2:30 A.M.: Though I am an unknown here, having consumed a few intoxicating brews, the tribes now accept me. It does not matter how one is dressed, or whose religion or philosophy—*Starship Enterprise,* Yoda, Speed Racer—one espouses. Yes, yes, yes . . . All belief systems are welcome. All is equal! I now think Dragon*Conians inhabit the essences of their tribal leaders. Like some cultures in other lands that I've observed— the ones who wear masks and animal skins—they mimick their spiritual gurus, and in doing so, they gain power and respect. They become gods and monsters themselves. Or, here, what they call "superheroes" and "stars."

I sip an elixir called "Jack and Coke" and muse. Would a Goth vixen, an Amazon, or an undead nurse accept me? Be lured by my masculine charms? Alas, my camp is not "centrally located." And it is filled with invaders of another kind, other tribes, so-called "businesspeople," "trophy wives," and "football fans."

WE'RE INTERSPECIES

It was fun to pretend I was not myself visiting Dragon*Con, but that I was Ethor-An3, a visitor from another time or another world. To be at Dragon*Con was to be from a different universe, and that four-day Halloween party embraced every known subculture. The event resembled a gaming convention plus a LARP plus a camping event plus a fashion show. Dragon*Con also felt like an academic conference: go to panels in the day, party at night. Except no one here was dressed as T. S. Eliot or Virginia Woolf (that I saw, anyway). But virtually every stripe of fantasy and science fiction fandom was represented. Probably half of the 30,000 attendees came in costume. Ethor-An3, Ethor, and Ethorian would have all been welcome here. You could game for four days or party for four days or play dress-up for four days. This was a place to find your kin. My idea of geekdom was again turned on its pointy ear.

At Dragon*Con, the people-watching alone justified the price of the $90 pass. The mobs warped the space-time-fandom continuum. Oppositional forces coexisted. Batman, Robin, and Catwoman talked to Medusa, Obi-Wan Kenobi, and Raggedy Ann. Alien palled around with Predator. Those in *Star Wars* costumes tolerated their *Star Trek* rivals. Even DC comic superheroes would speak with their Marvel counterparts. I saw a familiar furry blue bipedal creature carrying an AK-47. "Cookie Monster gone bad," someone muttered. "That's just not right," said a mother, shielding her toddler from the beast.

Over at the Marriott Marquis, the area where taxis pull in served as the perfect backdrop for anyone wishing to make a dramatic splash. A clan of vampire slayers, a brace of Jokers, a stray Shrek, and various unaffiliated undead paused and posed. Inside, the display continued. The hotel interior was a vast, white 470-foot-high hollow cut by bridges and mezzanines, like the fifty-story rib cage of a spacecraft designed by H. R. Giger. Two, twin six-foot-six women, Amazons in fact, tromped by in heels that made mere mortals tremble. In succession, they posed with a Klingon, a zombie, and a Superman. I saw a Tusken Raider mugging for the camera with two hot *mamacitas* wearing fire-engine red latex shorts and licking giant lollipops. They had come to flaunt their bodies, and many had buff and slim ones. Others displayed tattoos, piercings, and leather garb. I imagined the nonconventional relationships and sexual experiences. These geeks were not to be messed with. The only thing missing were onomatopoeic comic book noises—WHAAAA? KA-POW! OWWCH!—floating midair. Actually, I saw a few of those, too, that characters hoisted on signposts.

At the Walk of Fame, a large ballroom where rabble could meet their favorite stars, I talked with a couple from Texas. She was dressed as Aayla Secura, a blue-skinned female Rutian Twi'lek Jedi from the *Star Wars* universe. Floppy blue tentacles dangled from her head. Her mate was a *"Battlestar Galactica* marine, tactical."* I asked them if it was the custom for inhabitants from different realms to be so friendly. They said they experienced no cognitive, emotional, physical, or reproductive disharmonies by combining "different fictional universes."

"There is no chaos, only harmony," Aayla said. "It's the Jedi code."

"We're interspecies!" the marine told me.

I was interested in some interspecies action. With an action figure of my own. Dragon*Con had quickly answered one of my quest's burning questions: Can geeks be hot? You bet your light saber. This wasn't feeling like the same journey anymore. As a teenager, I was terrified of girls. Redemption time. In truth, I had come here to bed my Lady Geek.

Too bad I had no costume. Immediately, I regretted being in street clothes. I would have even settled for stepping into a phone booth and emerging as Purple Shirt Man: Woman-Slayer. Roll for damage.

YOU EVENTUALLY FIND YOUR PEOPLE

My first night at Dragon*Con, getting oriented in the paparazzi zone of the Hyatt, I was accosted by a robot. It looked like a studded gold cone with a gun turret.

"It's a Dalek," a woman next to me said, as it whirled toward us, then at some guys in futuristic military outfits. "It's a *Stargate:*

A contestant from Dragon*Con's Eleventh Annual Dawn Look-a-Like Contest.

Atlantis–Dr. Who crossover." The woman's comment saved me from the embarrassment of not being able to ID the respective fandoms. Her name was Loretta Painter, from Philadelphia, and she brought me up to speed on the whole fan-star scene. "I've been doing this for a long time," she said. "I do the Walk of Fame." Painter dressed plainly: She wore glasses, jeans, and a T-shirt. She was not into costuming. She was here for shows like *Stargate.* "I hang out with the stars. I am a fan of actors. I will spend my hard-earned money on autographs."

Painter brought her *Stargate* action figures with her, too, and was photographing them in various locations around Dragon*Con. "This is the way we express our fandom," she said. The con is a public way of showing one's affection for certain shows. And it helps people connect. Costuming is an easy way to identify like-minded subcultures. "Some people come here dressed as Indiana Jones and they meet someone carrying the ark." (That is, the Ark of the Covenant, from the first *Raiders* movie.) Thus pegged as members of the same fandom tribe, they'll spend the rest of the weekend together. "You eventually find your people. You're not alone."

Painter explained that unlike many cons, Dragon*Con is a fan-run convention. There are enough fans to support each "track." A "track" refers to the interest-specific way Dragon*Con was organized. Tracks mean, for example, that Tolkien, World of Warcraft, or *X-Files* fans are steered to events that interest them. "We're all here for something. We respect each other's fandom. I'm passionate about my fandom and someone else is passionate about theirs." She went on to talk about how Dragon*Con made her and others feel close to the stars. She had once met George "Sulu" Takei, from *Star Trek*; later, Takei recognized her at a different event. Fans want to feel they have a special relationship with the actors who have embodied their heroes (or antiheroes). At actor panels and Q&As, I heard more than one fan approach the microphone to ask a question and begin by saying, "It's a pleasure to meet you." In fact, the fan had not "met" the star at all. They were 100 feet apart in a ballroom. But it didn't matter.

Fans also want inside information—to feel they know something about a favorite show that no one else would know. Nerd culture thrives on specialized knowledge, and Dragon*Con was overflowing with it: news on when such-and-such game/movie/episode/artwork would be released. On my way into a panel about the upcoming movie *The Hobbit,* presented by the *Lord of the Rings* fan site TheOneRing.net, I overhead a woman gloating to her friend, "I can't wait. I'm going to know stuff that Steve doesn't know." There was also stuff to purchase. The merchant area was a Geek Mall: *Star Wars* replica costumes, colored contact lenses, custom vampire fangs, dice, latex ears (ogre, high elf, or orc), and LARP swords, all for sale. You could have your custom zombie portrait drawn. If a fandom made it, you could buy it.

But Painter wasn't entirely happy in her SF paradise. *Stargate: Atlantis* had just been canceled. "I was upset. I am upset," she said. "Like any fandom—football fandom, baseball fandom—you want to have that weekly fix. You have a cast of characters in your home for twenty weeks." The light of real life dimmed when a favorite show passed on into immortality, and reruns.

Painter was nice, but we didn't exactly hit it off. Strike one on Sub-Quest for Lady Geek.

THERE ARE WORSE THINGS KIDS COULD DO

"You can't observe the con," one woman I'll call Jill told me. "You have to *become* the con."

Jill and I had met at some point over the weekend. We spent some time talking about these gatherings and why people would travel from faraway places—Boston, California, England—to be here. Jill was young, about college-age, wild and outspoken, and seemed to have a checkered past. She was about twenty years my junior, but liked to call me "Darlin'." She was into LARPing and other games, and was interning at a small prosthetic makeup special effects company. Jill didn't seem to have a home, and when I asked where she was spending the night, I got the impression that when she wasn't crashing on friends' couches, she slept in her car. She said she had a boyfriend, but he wouldn't come to Dragon*Con. She told me her mother had been (or still was) a drug addict. And she didn't elaborate.

In a comic strip called *Monty,* the title character, a nerdy inventor, is dressed as a superhero. He faces questions from the media, who ask if he suffered any childhood trauma that led him to become a crime fighter. This is the backstory of countless superheroes like Batman, Spiderman, and Superman. They overcome a harrowing past and channel that bitterness or despair into a saintly mission. They gain superhuman prowess, but pay for that by living a double life. They get cool gadgets and amusing sidekicks, but suffer from crushing isolation. They can't tell most people around them of their true identities. No wonder superheroes tend to hang out with other superheroes. They can understand each other's pain.

In the comic, Monty says, "I had a perfectly normal, happy childhood. Totally normal. Very, very normal." Pause, blank frame. "OK," Monty continues, his lips quavering, "well, maybe my mom was just a tad intense when it came to p-p-potty training."

A joke, but that comic was on to something. A desire to be heroic could stem from some unresolved childhood crisis. Playing with alter egos allows superheroes to escape themselves, to do good. Jill, like me, had leaned on fantasy and role-playing when times had gotten emotionally tough. Not every role player had a troubled past, but enough of them did, and the fact that both Jill and I shared this made me wonder who else among the Dragon*Con swarm had escaped trauma, or was still trying to.

When Jill and I next connected several hours later, I told her about a conservatively dressed couple I'd seen sipping cocktails in the lobby of the Hilton. They had come to Atlanta from a rural town in Georgia to see a screening of a Christian film and decided to make a quiet weekend of it. They had booked a room at the hotel, unaware that Dragon*Con had invaded. They didn't realize "this kind of thing" existed "at this kind of scale."

Recovering from their shock, they sat in armchairs outside a karaoke lounge where a woman in a chain-mail bra sang "Carry On Wayward Son." I asked them what they thought of Dragon*Con. I could tell they were trying to look on the bright side.

He: Some are here just to express exhibitionism. It's been interesting. It's so diverse.

She: Everyone's been so nice.

He: Most people have noticed we have not been part of the crowd.

She: It's a little freaky.

He: I watched some *Star Trek* reruns, but never became a diehard fan. We grew up with *Star Wars* but never got into it. I read comic books but never injected myself into it.

She: And they're in their forties and still dressing up. There're some real neat costumes. You can tell some of them spent some serious money.

He: To me it's a little scary. What draws you to create this other life? It breaks my heart to hear these kids' stories, what they went through. If you can do it and not lose your sense of self, it could be fun. There are worse things kids could do. . . . I once dressed as a creepy Alabama fan for Halloween.

Did I want to "become the con"? What crime did Jill and I want to fight? Perhaps an outlandish costume would have helped me focus on the injustice I wanted to avenge. Jill had offered to help me throw together an outfit. She wanted to come to my hotel room to put on her makeup. Later in the weekend, we lost track of each other; she didn't return my texts. But she wasn't single anyway.

I never heard from her again. Strike two. And no hero getup for me.

THE STORIES LEAVE THE *STURM UND DRANG* OF LIFE BEHIND

If I couldn't find my Superhero Hottie, I'd set my sights on something almost as elusive. I was determined to get some one-on-one time with a star. A major star.

I was surprised by how much I enjoyed the Walk of Fame, where I loitered at least half a dozen times. I liked trawling the vast ballroom. TV and film stars of cult science fiction, fantasy, and horror sat patiently behind tables while fanboys and fangirls lined up to pay their respects—and paid $30 for an autographed photo with the likes of Linda (*The Exorcist*) Blair or George (Peter (Chewbacca of *Star Wars*) Mayhew. That year, the largest lines were for Avery (*Star Trek: Deep Space Nine*) Brooks, Nathan (*Firefly*) Fillion, and Robert (*A Nightmare on Elm Street*) Englund. Like a gelatinous cube patrolling a dungeon, I sucked up the stardust.

I watched the expressions on the faces of the besotted as they finally got to meet the objects of their affection. I looked for moments of humanity in the stars. When did they let their guard down, or seem sad, or unfriendly? Would I see Walter "Chekhov" Koenig get uppity with an annoying Trekkie? Not so many were lining up for Mickey "The Monkees" Dolenz, and I wondered if he was pissed. (Why was Dolenz even at a fantasy sci-fi con?) Lou (*The Incredible Hulk*) Ferrigno's table was a ghost town. He bailed by Sunday, tearing down his booth, I pictured, in a fit of rage.

But the real reason I kept hanging out was to interview Sean Astin, best known (and likely to be eternally best known) for his role as Samwise Gamgee, aka "Sam," Frodo's trusty sidekick in *The Lord of the Rings.*

Compared to, say, Jake Lloyd, the Anakin Skywalker of the lame *Phantom Menace,* Astin was A-list. Three Q&As with Samwise had been scheduled for Dragon*Con, with several hundred fans in attendance each time. A line spilled from his table whenever he held court in the Walk of Fame. But all weekend, his handlers had rebuked me. The more I tried to arrange an interview, the more I felt myself succumbing to latent fanboy impulses. I was tempted to jump the line and march up to Astin's table to speak to him directly, but decided against it. I tried Astin's handler again on my cell phone and left a message.

While Sam was a no-go, meeting Beau Bridges was a snap. He sat in front of stacks of headshots from his best-known movie roles, like *The Fabulous Baker Boys* and *Norma Rae.* Bridges' stature in the geek community had been cemented ever since playing General Hank Landry in various permutations of *Stargate.* I got to chat with Bridges, in between him shaking hands with fans and signing autographs. I watched as a fan dressed as a blood-stained chef wandered over. "Are you looking for a hospital?" Bridges said, straight-faced.

Bridges told me he had been to other conventions, like ComicCon, but this was his first Dragon*Con. "This is a totally new phenomenon for me, these conventions," he continued.

"Science fiction fans are so devoted and passionate. Performers are nothing without their audience." I asked him about the appeal of *Stargate*. "The stories leave the *Sturm und Drang* of life behind. There's a sense of fun about it." Were there any particularly memorable fan encounters? "Once a guy asked me to sign the architectural renderings of his house. He had his house built like Stargate Command." Nevertheless, Bridges seemed blasé. Either he had seen it all, or he was bored. Or he was jealous of the huge lines over at the *Star Trek* universe table.

I tried Astin's handler on my cell phone again. No answer.

To kill time, I talked with a real cop on security detail. Weren't all the weapons that space marines and superheroes carried a concern? What if some Stormtrooper had a real gun (or laser blaster) and opened fire? The cop was not distressed. This was his first Dragon*Con, he said, but the display of fake firepower didn't faze him. I guess he figured geeks were pretty harmless.

I wandered back toward Astin's table. I chatted with folks who came with binders of plastic sleeves to hold freshly signed photos. A father and son passed carrying *Star Wars* lunchboxes. I wondered how much actors made over a long weekend con like this. The equation seemed lucrative: $30 per signed headshot times hundreds of fans over four days. One woman said, "I'm just here stalking." She wouldn't pay the $30, but had come to soak up the aura. A young guy in a Darth Vader costume was on a quest to get all four actors who'd played Vader to sign the inside of his black reproduction helmet.

"You happy now?" a woman muttered to a man who'd just gotten an autograph from Lance (*Alien*) Henriksen. She looked unhappy.

"I'm happy," he said, not at all sheepishly.

Back at Astin's table, time was running out. I had stopped by so often, I felt like I was stalking him. Inexplicably, embarrassingly, I felt compelled to speak to him.

Mr. Astin . . . I mean . . . Can I call you Sean? I rehearsed. *I was just wondering if . . .*

I attended every one of Astin's talks and panel discussions. I listened to his stories of being on Peter Jackson's set. I heard about his weight loss and weight gains to bulk up and down for various roles. I chuckled with the hundreds of other fans as he described water fights between Dom (Dominic "Merry" Mon-aghan) and Vig (Viggo "Aragorn" Mortensen), or the crusty per-sonality of John "Gimli" Rhys-Davies, or his awe for Ian "Gandalf" McKellen. How he had cried when he was offered the role of Samwise. The stories may have been five years old, but I lapped them up like a starving fanboy. Surely Astin was sick of this? Then I imagined Takei and Koenig having to rehash *Star Trek* anecdotes from forty years ago.

I was mainly curious to learn how Astin felt about playing such a beloved character as Sam. Because of the movies, Astin *is* Sam for many, many millions. What a burden that must be, being the flesh-and-blood embodiment of a beloved Tolkien character. Or an honor. I wanted to know.

I checked my cell phone. No messages.

In the end, I didn't get my Sean Astin tête-à-tête. Instead, I succumbed to the crass, superficial siren call of fandom. If I couldn't get an interview with Astin, I thought, I'll stand in line with the rest of the would-be hobbits, elves, and civilians. I'll pay my thirty bucks, snag a few words with him, and get an auto-graphed photo. Not for me, of course. No, no, no. For my sister, who I had converted to *Rings* fandom. The freak.

So what if I was a sucker? I just wanted to take home some-thing that proved I'd had my moment with Sam. I did know one thing: My fandom was mild next to others'.

I had met Kyle Presley waiting in the Sean Astin line. He had driven from a small Georgia town about two hours from Atlanta, just to meet Astin, and he bore an impressive gift. "The reason I came here was to get this signed," Presley said, showing me a photo of a drawing depicting Sam holding Frodo in his arms at the climactic moment of their journey to Mount Doom. He had drawn it himself, and it must have taken him hours. It was quite accomplished. "I'm going to give him the original and have him sign the copy."

"You're going to give him the original?" I said. "Are you sure you don't want to keep it, and give him the copy?" Why would he do such a thing?

"He's given me a lot of years of entertainment. The movies. The DVDs. And I want to give him something back." Sweat gathered on Presley's brow as he waited next to me. I watched him walk up to Astin, but what he said escaped me. Astin seemed pleased by the picture. Then Presley slipped into the crowd and was gone.

I inched to the front of the line. I suddenly wished *I'd* brought a gift. A macramé *lembas* pouch or something. My turn arrived, I forked over my cash, got my photo, and approached Astin.

"Hey . . . Sam—I mean, Sean."

"Great to meet you," Astin said. Right. I was probably his 700th fan that day.

I decided to tell him about my quest. I blurted something about D&D, and Tolkien, and Peter Jackson, and me being a reformed geek, and my mother, and Elvish *lembas.*

He just smiled and said, "Hey, great." And it was over. When I shook his hand, I couldn't help sensing that spine tingle as his star power coursed through my body.

"Thanks." And yes, I even said, "I'm such a big fan."

NORMALLY, I HAVE NO INTEREST IN FANTASY

After a couple days dawdling at Dragon*Con, you can't help but notice familiar faces in the crowd. There was Silver Body Paint Guy, Knight-Riding-Dragon Man, and Big Boob Wonder Woman (OK, a few of them). And, of course, Frodo.

As it turned out, I had seen Daniel Gauthier before. In a previous year's photo of Dragon*Con's infamous Saturday-morning parade, Gauthier as Frodo was shown marching in costume at the head of the Middle-earth contingent. This year, I watched in person as hundreds of devotees hailing from every known universe marched through central Atlanta. Fandom after fandom passed by: a legion of about 100 Stormtroopers, Pez Vader carrying a sign that read VOTE VADER THE DARK FORCE PEZIDENTIAL CANDIDATE. X-Men, chanting for mutant rights. Behind a "Young Adult Literature" banner, librarians wagging their fingers and hissing, "Return your library books!" Klingons on motorcycles. Mad scientists carrying MWAHHHAAA! signs. The Wonder Twins, a group dressed as Green Lantern, Bat Girl, Ace Ventura, video-game characters from Halo, Warcraft, and Super Mario, the Spanish Inquisition, Spartans, the Muffin Man (from *Shrek*), The Beatles (Sergeant Pepper's version), and parade grand master Adam West, from the '60s *Batman* TV show, riding in a Batmobile. You get the idea. Gauthier had marched in four previous parades and this year was no exception. I saw him again as Frodo, walking beside various-sized elves and hobbits (not to scale). I had also seen Gauthier the night before at the Village of Bree party, an annual gathering of Middle-earthlings and other Tolkien faithful.*

It wasn't until after I'd seen Gauthier at a Sean Astin session the next day that I finally approached him. His costume was impeccable. He had sewed his own vest. With help from an effects shop where he lived in Montreal, he had made his own hairy hobbit prosthetics from a cast of his real feet. He'd purchased other items, like a cloak made from the same cloth used for Elvish cloaks in the movies, and the gold ring on a chain around his neck. He'd sunk good money into his costume, but it

---

* At the party, I briefly spoke with Gandalf, who called himself "the Abraham Lincoln of the fantasy world," and other characters, including a guy named Chuck, a tractor trailer mechanic, who wore a four-foot, hand-made reproduction of the tower of Barad-Dûr, Sauron's HQ, on his shoulders.

also helped that he physically resembled a hobbit: Gauthier was on the short side, a bit portly, with a hobbity mop of hair.

I asked a forty-seven-year-old French Canadian how he'd gotten into the *Lord of the Rings,* and he surprised me by saying that up until a few years ago, he hadn't even liked Tolkien. "I was dragged kicking and screaming into the theater," he said, recalling seeing the first movie. "Normally, I have no interest in fantasy." That all changed in one evening. "I fell in love with Frodo and everything he represents," he said in his soft voice.

The more I talked with Gauthier, the more he opened up. He was excited to tell his story. Once upon a time, he had identified more with science fiction and technology, which gave him the pessimistic outlook that humans could not live together, that we're destroying the planet. Disillusioned about politics, progress, and civilization for much of his adulthood, Gauthier felt lonely, introverted, and detached. "My outlook on life was that only 20 percent of the human race was worth redeeming." I gathered that Gauthier had been through a dark time.

Then, he saw the *Rings* movies (fourteen times since 2003), and he read the books. He was transformed. "It changed my life," said the former computer programmer. "My main interest has shifted away from technology to people." Not only that, but his take on the human race flipped 180 degrees. "Because of the fandom. It has turned my outlook around." Through Dragon*Con, Gauthier found fellowship. "Someone who comes from an environment with no friends, to come here . . ." His voice trailed off. "Now I have friends." To Gauthier, those bonds were as strong as Sam and Frodo's. After his first con, he found it very hard to return to real life. "I cried for two hours driving north, going back to Montreal. It was the parting. I had no idea I might be back. I thought, 'This is the high point of my life. It's all downhill from here.' It's like leaving your family." But he did return, and now he shuts down his Montreal home for a couple of months each year and drives south to be with those friends and attend cons.

Daniel·Gauthier as Frodo, walking with the Middle-earth contingent in the Dragon*Con parade.

At Dragon*Con, Gauthier also found a cause to believe in. A woman involved in the Tolkien community had been diagnosed with amyotrophic lateral sclerosis (ALS), or Lou Gehrig's disease. She was dying—"slowly losing her mobility and having more difficulty talking"—but the Tolkien community was going to help. "She's holding on till the end. She's stronger than before," Gauthier said, his eyes filling with tears. I had seen her at Dragon*Con, in a wheelchair, also dressed as Frodo Baggins. The November after I met Gauthier, fans dressed in their Tolkien and Harry Potter garb once more to march in a different sort of event—the ALS Association of Georgia's Walk to Defeat ALS.

Gauthier said that his experience of finding a new community through Tolkien fandom, and the plight of his friend, gave him the self-confidence to be a leader. He volunteered with the Red Cross. He also helped organize "A Long Expected Party," a re-creation of the birthday celebration that begins *The Fellowship of the Ring,* at a Shaker village in Kentucky that September. "Our target is 144 people. That was the number of hobbits at Bilbo's party."

Over four days, the festival would include food, drink, storytelling, guest speakers, musical performances, bonfires, and hikes. "We're trying to remove as many modern trappings as possible." The party was, he later wrote, "A great time, and for a few it was even a life-changing experience." A spiritual retreat for hobbits—simple beings who represented "what we were meant to be."

I had to admit that this was one of the reasons I'd been drawn to what many called a silly, pointless fantasy story: because of the hobbits. They stood in for us, representing what we might be able to do in an idyllic world—live in harmony with nature and each other, drink ale, share food, laugh, dance, and make music.

What exactly had Gauthier found in Tolkien? I believe it was a kindred mind. Gauthier shared Tolkien's idea that industrial and technological society was the coming Mordor. Like Mark Egginton, he believed that the politicians and the media spoke in the voice of Saruman. The ring that Gauthier carried around his neck became "a symbol of everything I despise in the world." I sensed that he wanted to cast it into the fires of Mount Doom. But through studying the themes in the book—fellowship, sacrifice, perseverance—Gauthier didn't despair anymore. In his escapism, he was inspired not to escape, but to turn full circle, to be courageous, to emerge. "One of the responsibilities of being human is making your own decisions. It took me forty years to learn that lesson. It's hard to do the right thing; it always has been. You have to develop the strength. Not physical strength." By which I think he meant, the strength to turn the course of your life around, to engage with the world, and find hope again.

As the elf queen Galadriel says to Frodo, "Even the smallest person can change the course of the future."

THROUGH THOSE DOORS AGAIN

Cons weren't just places to pursue hookups; they were also places to connect with old colleagues and friends. Knowing that

Dragon*Con was held in Atlanta, I was looking forward to seeing some of the players from the Forest of Doors. More than a year had passed out-of-game, and they had all returned to their lives, just as I had returned to my life in Boston. I was curious to hear what had happened in the interim.

I went to the live-action role-playing zone, where a Forest of Doors banner hung above a table. I recognized Sir Talon immediately. Charles Kelley was there, and another FoD game master. They were entertaining themselves with a tic-tac-toe game, searching the crowd for individuals who fulfilled certain criteria written in each square: "Inorganic character eating" (such as a robot); "Any ape creature"; "Group of four guys with goatees"; "Darth Vader on cell phone"; "+3 bodice avalanche." They had a long day ahead of them.

"I'm so glad you came to Dragon*Con," Kelley said. He wore an EVIL GENIUS T-shirt. "It's the epicenter of nerd culture. You can be the Michelin Man if you want."

Other than his shaved head and face, things were more or less status quo with him. He still wrote for game companies, and because he had "dual citizenship in nerd culture and hipster culture," he also hung out with his punk rock friends. "I lead a double life," he said. "Thoughts of Apsara and refugees from the Dark Mountains don't really weigh on my mind when I am seeing a Mogwai show or drinking PBR with guys who wear Nintendo-controller belt buckles. Two differing fantasies, I suppose." Acerbic as always.

But plenty had changed for other Forest of Doors dwellers. Christopher Tang couldn't make it to Dragon*Con; his wife was due to have their first child, a boy, that same weekend. I wondered how his gaming life would change. As the pressures of family and fatherhood mounted, would more or less fantasy be the answer? The gaming geeks were growing up, but they weren't letting go. "Being a father has taken me away from gaming more than I expected," Tang later told me. "I have hung onto the Forest of Doors, though. It is something I helped create and it is my one space where I am not an employee or a family man."

As for Chris Jones, who had played Leif Thorsson and Magnus Tigersblood, he and his wife Rachel now had a daughter. They named her Katriel Arwen (fans, check your Tolkien encyclopedias). The baby had been cramping their gaming style a little, and they'd taken a couple months off from LARPing. "I love my daughter, but I'm not going to condemn her to a life of nerdy geekiness," he told me, changing a diaper. "We're going to do things. We're going to travel, camp, hunt, teach her to fence, do gymnastics. Not sit around and play tabletop games." Still, Chris and Rachel had brought Katriel Arwen along to the con.

Since I'd last seen Jones, he'd begun playing a third character at Forest of Doors: Jack of the Spear, a less violent, fairy troubadour-hunter who wrote songs about other characters. He and other players had regular music rehearsals. "My goal is to have, like, twenty songs written per realm and at least twenty songs that are unique to the Forest and performed on a regular basis." The songs spanned several genres: folk, blues, bluegrass, country and western, and rock. He was researching Indian, Eastern, and Far Eastern. He wanted to write two operas, one "a goblin opera—imagine Queen's 'Bohemian Rhapsody,' that kind of rock-style opera." The man had dreams.

At one point, Rachel left, and Jones and I had time to talk more about his fascination with fantasy. As we pushed Katriel in the stroller, Jones reminisced about his days playing World of Warcraft and Diablo, another MMO, with his father and brother. "It was a bonding thing."* Jones said he didn't play Warcraft anymore, but another MMO had hooked him—the evil counterpart to City of Heroes, a game called City of Villains. "With diabolical craft and guile, players forge new super-powered villain char-

---

* At one point, Jones' dad had gotten deep into WoW. He had met a woman online and eventually became romantically involved with her. She asked him to lend her money. Jones had to stop his father from running off to Texas with her.

acters," the official game Web site proclaims, "in an attempt to dominate the world." Wicked.

We took in the passing costume drama. His take on Dragon*Con? It let people "show an idealized self, or what one will never be." I was reminded that Jones was a war veteran, and thought of that old U.S. Army slogan, "Be all you can be." Given how many at the con were dressed in pseudo-military garb, I wondered how many saw the armed services as some hugely funded role-play.

I had been burning to know about Jones's experiences in Iraq and Afghanistan. Had he seen action, and had his gamer background affected his take on the war? "You mean bullets flying, people dying, stuff like that? Yeah, a couple of times," he said. Jones served as a crew chief on a C-17, responsible for loading the aircraft and seeing them launched. "In a hot zone," he said, combat "was normally due to a mobile hospital coming under fire." The tents came under fire, personnel inside were wounded, but his C-17 didn't get off the ground until it was full. He said the violence around him "mostly became 'noise,' if that makes any sense. I could hear it and was aware of it, but I pushed it to the back." Several of his friends had died. "Still are [dying], actually."

His war experience made it hard to take seriously play combat and violence in an RPG or LARP. "I know when people make 'heroic' sacrifices or suicide or anything like that in-game, they have very little concept of what they are doing." Games have the luxury of calling "hold"—everyone freezes—nothing like the real thing. "If you're asking if real combat made me a better fighter in-game, not at all. The two are totally different. I may have a better concept of logistics, or even a better idea of other people's tactics, but I keep the two separate in my head." Jones didn't like to talk about the war and he became emotional when he reflected on his losses. But here he was a regular guy, dad, husband. No perfectly coiffed action star. A real fighter, and a war hero. And a survivor. Like me, my siblings, and my mother.

I wondered if his choice to play Jack, instead of Magnus, wasn't related to being a father, or having achieved some inner peace about his military service. "It was more of the character's attitude and goals," he replied. Magnus was a bullheaded brute. Jack was more playful and positive. But he insisted Jack was no pacifist. "He is a hunter."

Rachel rejoined us. They pushed Katriel Arwen in the stroller through the throngs of Dragon*Conians. We waited in line for an event and one guy gestured at Katriel and said, "Way to start them young!"

Jones loved his baby. But he had not expected babies would be much fun, or so real. "She's a fantasy made manifest. She is magic that I can actually hold." He paused. He seemed spellbound. Then he added, "We are not letting her play games till she is at least sixteen years old."

THE ENDLESS STREAM OF CHARACTERS

Geeks having babies. Was someone trying to send me a sign? The real world began to leak in. Later, at the posh bar at the Marriott Marquis, alongside *Battlestar Galactica* soldiers, yet another Wonder Woman, and a real security guard, I watched Barack Obama give his acceptance speech at the Democratic National Convention. So this could be the new America.

Then I saw an older man by himself, sipping a drink, looking down from the mezzanine. Tall, and wearing a dress shirt, he must have been in his early seventies. He didn't have a Dragon*Con badge. I wondered what he was doing here, and what he thought of the endless stream of characters below. After my weekend's pursuit of illusion, here was a regular guy. Street clothes. The anti-freak.

"That's an impressive one," he said in a British accent, pointing out one costume of a Warcraft avatar.

I realized I knew who he was, but I didn't want to put him on the spot. So I wished him good night and blended into the hubbub. A few minutes later, I had regrets. I screwed up the courage to ask him some questions and wended my way back through the crowds. But when I returned, he was gone. I had been speaking to David Prowse, the man who'd played the *real* Darth Vader (not to be confused with Vader's voice, James Earl Jones). In Prowse's wake, only faux Dark Lords remained, and Jedis and Stormtroopers, all mingling with drinks in their hands. Players. Not the real thing.

I didn't find my Lady Geek. My *Rings* fanboy was only partly sated. To end with the Dark Lord of the Sith felt like poetic justice. But, as Ethor-An3 might say, observing the scene in a partial state of inebriation, I was as welcome here as anyone. The great bat wings of Dragon*Con embraced all types. This was the lesson of the con. Even if I personally did not end up embracing anyone.

I trudged back to my hotel, passing through the real Planet Earth, that brash zone of Hooters and Hard Rock Cafés and warring football fans who had descended on Atlanta, or Atlantis, or wherever I was. Folks lingered at tailgater parties in parking lots, each side dressed in matching uniforms—one fandom (Clemson) in orange T-shirts, polos, and baseball caps, the other (Alabama fans) in scarlet. They stumbled about, smashing bottles, trying to find their hotels, clinging to their gods and heroes, no more or no less freakish than the rest of us.

My quest through fantasy realms was nearing its end. After my expedition here, and to Pennsic, Lake Geneva, Guédelon, Oxford, Forest of Doors, Azeroth, and the basement of my local game shop, my gamer-geek identity had been tweaked, tested, and terrified. One final place on my list remained: Middle-earth. Or, the closest thing to Middle-earth on earth that I could find.

Charlie Rose: *Your fascination with the notion of escapism is what?*

Peter Jackson: *Well, I believe—strongly—in breaking the barrier when you go see the movies. And what I mean by that is that, obviously, the movie-going process is one in which you walk into a darkened theater, you sit in a chair, and twenty feet away is a screen. And you watch the screen. When I was a kid, as we all were—I'm sure the same to you—every time I used to go to the movies when I was twelve, I'd leave my chair. I wouldn't be in my chair anymore. I'd just go into the screen. And I'd be there. And I would be just lost in the film. And as an adult, that doesn't happen very often to me anymore. Now, I don't know whether it's because I'm getting older, or because the films aren't doing that anymore. But I tried as much as I possibly could with* The Lord of the Rings *to re-create that type of movie where the audience can just get lost, and just go into the movie, and become part of the film.*

—from *The Charlie Rose Show* (February 22, 2002)

There, or Nowhere, and Back Again

At thirty-something thousand feet, somewhere over the Pacific, some of my fellow passengers on flight NZ7 were headed to New Zealand. I was headed to Middle-earth.

Before departing, I bought *The Lord the Rings Location Guidebook,* which painstakingly matched movie scenes to the places they were filmed. I mapped out a plan to land in Wellington, at the southern tip of the North Island; rent a car, and drive northwardly to Auckland; fly to Queenstown in the South Island; then jet back to Wellington. I fired off e-mails to movie tourism companies that organized sightseeing tours of *Rings* locations. I planned to see as many of the hundred filming sites as I could in two weeks. I wanted to talk with the similarly obsessed, those who had made the voyage to sate their secret quests, and see what made them tick (or what caused their nervous tics). And long shot of long shots, I tried to arrange an interview with Peter Jackson, the director of my beloved trilogy. *That* was my fantasy.

What would it feel like—thrilling? silly? mortifying?—to be traipsing across a country to witness mere shadows of scenery from a film (and book) whose influence on me I was still processing? The only way to face this question was to embark on my own pilgrimage. I wanted a high-fantasy geek-out, but could I walk in the footsteps of hobbits and elves with a straight face? I hoped New Zealand-as-Middle-earth would be what I had imagined in the books and the movies—but mostly in my mind. More than I wanted to see this place, I *needed* to see this place.

I was reminded of Bilbo Baggins's words just before leaving the Shire to stay with the elves. (I always suspected Bilbo—traveler, dreamer, and writer—was the character closest to J. R. R. Tolkien himself, the one he would have wanted to role-play.) Bilbo didn't know exactly what he'd encounter on his journey, but he'd hoped for closure. "I might find somewhere where I can finish my book," Bilbo said to Gandalf. "I have thought of a nice ending for it: *and he lived happily ever after to the end of his days.*" I hoped for the same, too.

I wasn't sure where or how my quest through all these fantasy worlds would end—or even whether my wanderings would end at all. Already outed, perhaps I would always be lured by this "vast game" that Tolkien himself found "fatally attractive." But I bought my plane ticket anyway. I crammed a blue backpack with clothes, notebooks, a video camera, my laptop computer, my three *Lord of the Rings* soundtrack CDs, and my twelve Special Extended Edition DVDs of the movie trilogy, and headed into the unknown again. Perhaps, at least, I'd find an ending for my book.

OCCUPATION: STUNT HOBBIT

"There's one degree of separation between anyone in New Zealand and people who have worked on a Peter Jackson film," Paul Donovan told me.

While standing in the Air New Zealand check-in line, I'd struck up a conversation with Paul and his partner, Kelly Bargh, who were flying home to Wellington after a three-week holiday. Kelly was a botanist at New Zealand's national museum, Te Papa. Paul worked in banking as a computer programmer. They played video games, loved movies, and competed in pub music-trivia contests. In other words, self-avowed geeks. I told them about my project and within moments, we started yammering about the trilogy.

It turned out Paul's best friend was a cousin of Fran Walsh, Peter Jackson's wife and coproducer; Paul himself once wore a mask as an extra in an early Jackson film called *Meet the Feebles*. Kelly knew folks who built miniatures at Weta Workshop, Wellington's Academy Award–winning special effects company. Her friend had been a "stunt hobbit" for a canoe-paddling scene on the Hutt River, not far from the city.

"I was up for a role as a stunt hobbit too," Kelly told me. "I used to kayak that river all the time. I was almost as tall as a hobbit. I was smaller then!" Her dream was snubbed when she couldn't get the time off from work.

Kelly, Paul, and I kept blabbing in our blissful fandom bubble. We shared a taxi from Wellington International Airport into town (they insisted on paying). They offered to meet me for a drink later in the week. True hobbit hospitality. It would be good to know someone in Middle-earth.

Speaking to Paul and Kelly, I understood why Kiwis were rightfully proud of their wunderkind, Peter Jackson. His eighteen-month, three-movie, $280-million, back-to-back *Rings* shoot was the most massive film production ever attempted anywhere. Amazingly, Jackson, an obscure Kiwi director best known for helming horror movies, had pulled it off, filming *Rings* in a country that had had no experience making blockbusters. New Zealand didn't even have a suitable soundproof stage. To make the trilogy, seemingly everyone pitched in. Paul's "one degree of separation" claim was plausible: In a nation of four million, 22,000 people had been employed by the production.

Once the *Rings* movies had hit the screen and started to break box-office records, New Zealand capitalized. At the peak of movie-driven tourism, a national PR campaign posited the nation as "Home of Middle-earth." Air New Zealand called itself "Airline to Middle-earth," and emblazoned a fleet of 747s with images of the films' stars. Yes, other movies—*Sideways, Field of Dreams, Napoleon Dynamite*—had enticed a wave of pilgrimages to their filming locations. But in terms of enduring tourist influx, no film had impacted the consciousness of the world, nor transformed its own citizens, like the *Rings* series. From 2002 (the year following the release of part one, *The Fellowship*) to 2006, Middle-earth-bound visitors rose from 1.7 to 2.4 million, an increase of 40 percent. Close to twenty tour companies had specialized in *Rings* tourism.

The trilogy was a "fantastic awareness-building opportunity," said Jane Dent, Tourism New Zealand's general manager for international PR, as we chatted on my first day in Wellington in a high-rise office building overlooking the city. Shock waves were still being felt in the tourism industries. Foreigners were still flocking here because the films had inspired them. "We had three three-hour commercials shown globally for three years," Dent noted. Even if hard-core tourists didn't travel to New Zealand expressly to see *Rings* sites as much anymore, the trilogy had put New Zealand on the tourist map. In a tiny country, a fantasy movie had created a lucrative reality.

WHO WANTS TO BE AN ELF?

My outer geek—the one I usually presented to the world—was circumspect. But ever since I had seen the trilogy, my inner geek had been desperate to meet Peter Jackson. Once a film major in college, I'd wanted to be the next Steven Spielberg. That highly unrealistic fantasy didn't pan out. Still, I remained a movie nut, and I idolized Jackson, just five years my senior and living out my abandoned dreams. I was also fairly drooling to meet Richard Taylor, the head special-effects wizard at Weta, who had supervised the making of the trilogy's orc prosthetics, sprung-steel swords, and digital Gollums.

In anticipation of my trip, those reveries of Ethan-as-movie-extra on the *Rings* set returned. Before departing the States, I had sent e-mails to Jackson and Taylor's assistants. Alas, "Peter" and "Richard" had become bona fide stars. All those Oscars and "making-of" DVDs had even turned the lesser technicians, like supervising sound designers and miniature builders, into minor deities in any film geek's pantheon. Everyone was "busy." Assistants' replies to me were polite, but always along the lines of "due to the hectic nature of this stage of production, [the person you hoped to speak with] will not be giving interviews during this time." Gaining access to anyone except a receptionist proved as hard as entering the Black Gates of Mordor.

In lieu of behind-the-scenes peeks or a guided visit to the nerve center by Peter himself, I settled for a full-day Wellington Rover *Lord of the Rings* tour. This explains why I was standing in what is, or was, the House of Elrond, home of the elves. Rivendell.

"And if we go back to the plan here, we can see there was a stream and it ran down into a pool," Rendall Jack said, pointing his finger at the laminated set-design plan in his hand and then to woody area around him in Kaitoke Regional Park. "And these two dots were these two trees behind me. So the stream actually came down the hill here"—he waved his hands—"between these trees and into a big pool in this area down here."

Rendall Jack was our guide. He drove the Wellington Rover van that shuttled me and seven others—two Brits, one Australian, one Swede, one American, and two Finns—through the drizzle from Wellington northward to the Hutt Valley (aka, the River Anduin, where Kelly almost achieved hobbit stardom), Harcourt Park (Gardens of Isengard), then back to the city and the Miramar Peninsula, home to "Wellywood," Wellington's modest film-production facilities. Rendall led us from one location to the next, telling us juicy tales from the shooting and narrating scenes from the movie. Good fanboys and -girls, we dutifully took pictures and video footage, cruising past Peter Jackson's house, a café called The Chocolate Fish where cast members had tea, the beach at Lyall Bay where stars learned to surf. We glimpsed Stone Street Studios, where many *Rings* interiors and back-lot exteriors had been shot. When we drove by Weta Work-shop, Rendall cried, "Look—there's Richard Taylor, up there in the window, the one with the glasses!" My heart leapt. So close, and yet so far. I imagined diving into the Dumpster for some scrap of Weta magic—a discarded sketch, a failed latex mask, even a dull blade of an X-ACTO knife.

We had spent a good portion of the morning in Kaitoke, that bucolic Elvish hideaway, about forty-five minutes north of Wellington. The park signage had pointed us to "Rivendell." Dead quiet, lush and unspoiled, it was easy to see why the location had been chosen. Of course, the Elvish structures, once built into the forested hills, had long since been dismantled. No legions of extras, trailers, or elaborate sets. I knew this. As a former college film major, and dedicated student of the *Rings* "making-of" documentaries, I had some idea of what I would and wouldn't be seeing. Still, I was discouraged. For example, later, when we had stopped at the location for the Helm's Deep fortress, site of the epic siege featured in *The Two Towers,* there was only an empty quarry, with piles of gray gravel and cement-making equipment. It made no sense, but I was suddenly regretful for not crashing the set during the film shoots years earlier. I had wanted to see Viggo (Aragorn) Mortensen swinging his sword, and the hordes of nasty Uruk-hai charging the Styrofoam walls. Not Wellington Rover's fault, but I had foolishly expected some-thing more. Not this . . . middling Middle-earth. I had to settle for the real.

Back in Kaitoke, near where the cast and crew craft-services tents once stood, we paused for tea—or as Rendall said, reverting to hobbit-speak, "Second breakfast. Actually, it's getting close to elevenses." He talked about a favorite fan who'd come on a tour, hopped behind a tree here in Rivendell, and emerged wearing a shimmering blue gown, a headdress, a pendant, and pointy ears. The Finnish couple spoke softly to each other and it sounded suspiciously like Elvish.

"So, who wants to be an elf?" Rendall abruptly asked. He produced latex elf ears and an Elvish sword, a replica of Bilbo's sword, Sting, to be precise, and a tiny leather cape. He wanted us to pose with the props.

I knew Sting had been given to Bilbo by the elves. Bilbo then gave it to Frodo. *So*, I reasoned, *it made no sense that an elf would have it now.* But I shut up and played along with everyone else. One by one, in the location where hunky Orlando Bloom once posed for publicity photos, the group donned the ears and cape and drew the sword, pretending to be Legolas on the hunt. I tried not to think of how many unwashed fan freaks had worn those ears since they'd last been sterilized. I was the only bearded elf to ever walk Middle-earth.

Rendall told anecdotes and jokes all day. Nothing in his delivery suggested he had done this a hundred times before. His enthusiasm was impressive. Later, he said to me, in private, "It's about making sure people have a good time." Our group seemed to be.

In particular, Howard and Georgette Sugars, the British couple. They had traveled to New Zealand because of the movies. Or, at least, Howard had. "This is why I'm here," he said. "I'm a massive fan." He had seen the movies a dozen times, and played the *Lord of the Rings* video games (and Grand Theft Auto). When he bought *The Two Towers* DVD boxed set, he picked the one packaged with a Gollum statue. "I haven't taken it out of the box yet," he told me. "It'll be worth a lot someday." As for where Georgette fell on the *Rings* neophyte-to-freak continuum, I wasn't sure. She hardly let out a peep all day. But she seemed pleased to be in Middle-earth with Howard. After all, this was their honeymoon.

The author in elf ears and drawing a replica of Bilbo's sword, Sting, at Kaitoke Regional Park, near Wellington, New Zealand.

"For me it's just pure escapism," Howard said. "I'd love to live in Middle-earth. That would suit me just fine."

We finished the day at Mount Victoria (site of the Outer Shire), a hilly, forested park in the heart of Wellington. Rendall led our group to the path where Frodo warned his hobbit pals to "Get off the road! Quick!" before they encountered the Ringwraiths and raced through the woods to Buckleberry Ferry. Rendall made us pose again. I joined Howard and Georgette; the three of us stood at the top of a hill and made like a Black Rider on horseback, in the exact place where Jackson filmed the scene in October of 1999. Silhouetted against the sky, I think we looked fairly evil.*

"I had a fantastic day," said the young Australian woman as we headed back to the van. She let out a sigh. "How can you go back to reality? I like to dream."

I SPOILED THAT SCENE, DIDN'T I?

"This is Ethan Gilsdorf, reporting live from Middle-earth," I announced to the camera. "We're off to find the elves! Where are those bloody elves?"

It was now a couple days later. I had set off on my own in a rented red Hyundai. I drove madly, nervously. (New Zealand is left-side-drive country.) On fast-forward. Armed with my movie location book, I took to side roads. I stopped at scenic overlooks, pulled out my video camera, and made little dramas of my journey, starring me, directed by me, my heroic quest. Me me me.

I had promised to return the car, unscathed, to the Auckland airport in four days. My route was to be free-form. I had no precise plan or hotel bookings. From the Hutt Valley and Kaitoke, I motored several hours further north, up mountain passes, through pastureland, along gorges, and into the night,

---

* In the photo, the three of us stood in a row: Georgette played the horse's head, Howard the rider. Bent over at the back of the line, I played the horse's ass.

The author's Kinder Surprise Fellowship figurines: Sam and Frodo in the area of "Mordor" in New Zealand, near Mount Ruapehu.

getting lost and nearly running out of gas. In Ohakune, I stayed in a motel called The Hobbit. The next day I explored Mount Ruapehu and the Turoa Ski Field, where parts of Ithilien and Mordor were filmed. I hauled out my *Lord of the Rings* Kinder Surprise toy figurines—yes, the very ones I'd purchased in Paris and brought to Boston—and reenacted movie scenes, helping a plastic and expressionless Sam and Frodo scale a little Mount Doom. It was utterly ridiculous, but kept me entertained as I crossed the North Island.

At one point, I ran into another tour group. I eavesdropped as the guide explained how a particular sequence had been filmed. "Well, I spoiled that scene, didn't I?" he said. "Ha ha ha." He saw me scribbling in my notebook. "So, you're a fan, eh?"

"Uh, well. Yes." I smiled. I don't think he saw the handful of figurines as I tried to stuff them into my pocket.

"Well . . . O . . . K." And he led his group far away from me.

On the third day, I sped across Tongariro National Park's barren wastes (Mordor again), blasting the *Rings* soundtrack on the car stereo. Trumpets and kettle drums celebrated my triumphant arrival. DUM . . . DUH-DUH-DUM . . . DUH-DA-DA! From Route 1 to 49, 4 to 47, I watched the landscape morph. Fields and forests became mosses and ferns; palms shifted into pines; tongues and tufts of grass mixed with purplish scree. Magnolias bloomed at the foot of a snowcapped volcano. Species were familiar yet strange. It all juxtaposed incongruously, as if an alien Hawaii had been joined to an evolutionarily twisted Switzerland, encompassed in a land slightly larger than the UK, but with about one-fifteenth the population. New Zealand was a pristine place that could role-play a parallel world. Just ignore the sheep.

I arrived at the Whakapapa Ski Field just as the sun was setting. Weary skiers left the slopes. A fog slid in across dark jags of rock. I had the eerie setting to myself. It was here that Frodo and Sam had met Gollum, and he led them through the harsh ravines of Emyn Muil to the Black Gates. The volcanic rubble, backlit by a yellowish glow, felt supernatural. I stumbled about in the snow, sneakers wet, my feet oblivious to the cold, reciting lines to the wind. "My precious . . . my precciousssss . . ." "An impassable labyrinth of razor-sharp rocks!" "Share the load . . . the load." I stopped. Sat in the snow. I had to take a breath. Perhaps it was the high altitude, but my heart raced. Silly, silly man.

I spent that night at the Chateau Tongariro, a luxury hotel set in the shadow of Mount Ngauruhoe (an active volcano that had served as Mount Doom). Most of the evening, I slumped in the lobby lounge, drinking beer and musing about movie tourism. Everywhere a *Rings* tour group stopped, it seemed, tourists wanted to "relive the magic," find the exact location of a film scene and pose for the camera. But the landscape wasn't simply a simulacrum of Middle-earth. It had become a place where visitors could feel a little closer to what Jackson's film crew had achieved. Some on movie pilgrimages had never even seen *Rings* and knew nothing of its heroic narrative. Yet oddly, they were drawn to the Herculean effort of the filmmaking itself.

Others were celebrity seekers, hoping to sleep in the same room Orlando Bloom had once occupied. That impulse to be part of a greater story—be it Frodo's or Peter Jackson's quest—struck me as the same reason gamers play D&D, a LARP, or an MMORPG. Only the heroic narrative was different. Tourists who followed in their favorite celebrity's footsteps seemed just as obsessed as the gamers who stayed up till midnight to buy expansion packs to their favorite game. Maybe more so.

"Wouldn't it be fantastic if the Pillars of the Kings were still here?" a guide might say, referring to the massive Argonath statues that had been digitally added to the landscape. Tourists were asked to superimpose, in their imaginations, the structures, armies, and cities. After my second beer, it occurred to me that perhaps Tolkien would have wanted me to see New Zealand this way, without the Elvish sets, gorgeous actors, and computer-generated Balrogs. The experience was like reading his novels. No pictures. Middle-earth was part language, but mostly desire.

After my third beer, I learned this fantastic piece of trivia: My bartender grew up in the Boston suburb of Billerica.

NOTHING BAD EVER HAPPENED HERE

On the fourth day, I arrived in Hobbiton.

"Welcome to Middle-earth," said Lesley Hurst as the tour bus chugged up the hill. Hobbiton—or, more accurately, Hobbiton Movie Set and Farm Tours—was a private farm in Matamata, a town about two hours southeast of Auckland. It remained the only *Rings* location where actual relics from filming could be seen. Once inside the compound (protected by fences because fans liked to sneak in after hours), I felt I'd entered The Shire. Gentle, sheep-dotted hills stretched endlessly. Rain soaked the vivid green, well-manicured grass. "Look out for hobbit droppings!" Hurst warned, pointing at sheep turds everywhere.

Our group disembarked. A five-year veteran guide, Hurst led a group of about twenty-five tourists through the 10-acre "green

The Hobbiton Movie Set and Farm Tours, in Matamata, New Zealand, showing facades of the former hobbit holes. Bag End is at the top of the hill.

set," the largest ever used for a movie. By heart, she recited long passages of movie dialogue, matching them to the exact location where characters had spoken them. We walked to the "Party Tree," where Bilbo announced, "I regret to announce—this is The End. I am going now. I bid you all a very fond farewell," before putting on his magic ring and disappearing. She showed us a foam piece of faux stone, before warning us, "I'm going to destroy all your dreams."

Built into the hillsides were the main attraction—the plain white facades marking seventeen of the movie's original thirty-seven hobbit holes. We ascended the hill. At the very top was Bag End, where Bilbo and Frodo lived. I went inside. Sadly, it was a plain square room, not a proper vaulted and circular hobbit hole. No desks covered with maps. No mugs of ale or plates of cheese. No walking sticks by the door. No one was home.

"I just want to be a hobbit," said an American named Will Hershey, as we walked back to the bus. "It's a nice little place here. The Shire had a nice atmosphere. Nothing bad ever happened here. It's very much back to rural, the way it was." For $58 NZD (about $33 USD), you could taste the way it was. Or would never be. I thought of Daniel Gauthier, the Frodo I'd met at Dragon*Con, and imagined that he would have liked this. Hobbiton was his idyllic agrarian community—an anachronistic utopia—where nothing ever happened, except when wizards showed up with promises of gold and dragon-slaying adventures. Of course, Hobbiton was not only a return to preindustrial innocence. It was also a valuable commodity that its owners tried to keep as bucolic as possible. Twenty-five thousand annual visitors from (at last count) eighty-one countries came with high expectations. A stop in Matamata had been "itinerized" into package tours, many from Asia, where fans had particularly emotional connections to *The Lord of the Rings*. As one tour operator told me, those fans would describe events and characters with tears streaming down their faces.

"We have a responsibility to provide that ambiance, that illusion to our visitors," said Henry Horne, Hobbiton's marketing manager. He sat in The Shire's Rest, the café/gift shop that sold espresso, Hobbiton mugs and postcards, and officially sanctioned *Rings* jewelry, like the replica One Ring that Horne wore on a chain around his neck. Like a dutiful student of Marketing 101, his speech was laden with buzzwords: "unique product," "high return on investment," "service provider." "For us, it's about authenticity," Horne added. Which was a curious thing to say, considering Hobbiton didn't actually exist. Except it did.

After visiting Hobbiton, I headed into Matamata and found a motel. I chatted with the owner, who wished another movie would be shot in her town soon. She could use more business. I spoke to dozens of people on my trek: taxi drivers, movie extras, tourism directors, film location specialists, tour company owners and guides, journalist-spies, gift-shop clerks, foreign TV crews, and average tourists whose dream it had been to see Middle-earth. No one saw a downside to the phenomenon.

Of all those I met connected to *Rings* tourism, Vic James offered the most over-the-top film fan experience. His company, Red Carpet Tours, led twelve-day excursions each month to all the major locations, from the top of New Zealand to the bottom. "The people who come are real fans," said the cherubic James. "They don't just see the films once. They see them fourteen times." His packages arrange high-end accommodations, coach transport (he was the driver), and Q&As with folks involved in the trilogy, like the stunt double for Gimli the dwarf and Daniel Reeve, the artist and calligrapher who drew the movie trilogy's maps and other decorative ephemera. James estimated 1,000 guests had booked his tour since 2002; fifty had taken it twice. The price? $5,500 NZD (about $3,000 USD). I couldn't think of any other movie series, not even *Star Wars,* that could have supported this level of fan devotion. I asked James about the ring on his finger—a certain, familiar gold ring inscribed with Elvish script. "Yes, that," he said with a chuckle. "I'm married to my job."

James was smart at marketing. "The Quest is about to begin," announced his full-color, 120-page prospectus. "You can feel it in the earth. You can smell it in the air." He put his clients in quest-like situations. On the hike to Mount Sunday, site of the Edoras location, they waded across three ice-cold streams. "The Fellowship really firms up here," he told me. Vic and his wife, Raewyn, call themselves the Middle-earth parents to a lot of people. Many left New Zealand with a fresh perspective, ruminating poignant quotes from the movie, like Gandalf's words: "All we have to decide is what to do with the time that is given to us."

"People reevaluate their lives on these trips," James said. "'Maybe I should get off the rat race,' they think." They dream of emigrating to New Zealand. Some actually do.

A DESPERATE FANTASY

Queenstown, in the South Island, is ringed by mountains known as the Southern Alps. These include a range called The Remarkables, dusted with powdered sugar–like snow and half socked in with fog. Planes run the gauntlet to land here, their wingtips practically grazing the sides of the narrow valley. The heart attack is worth it.

Known as the adventure capital of the world, this town of 10,000 attracts one million tourists a year. On the glacial-blue Lake Wakatipu and the surrounding waterways, down back roads and along mountain ledges, off towers and man-made bridges, adventuresome souls take jet boats and ride the rapids, rent Jeeps and mountain bikes, paraglide and downhill-ski and leap from ridiculous heights while tethered to bungees. Most activities were too hard-core for this hobbit, but I did hike the big hill that loomed over town, Bob's Peak, which gave a quintessentially wide panorama over Queenstown, the lake, and the peaks beyond.

I had booked a three-day, South Island whirlwind, but by now, *Lord of the Rings* tourism had exhausted me. The film location quest had given my trip focus, but I felt I was chasing a desperate fantasy. I wanted to see the "real" Middle-earth, except the more time I drove and hiked here, the more that world dissipated, like mist on the mountains that encircled the airstrip. The more I reflected on why I had fetishized the New Zealand landscape, the more it seemed like fakery. If I ever lived here—a longtime fantasy—I'd get bored, I said to myself. Middle-earth would seem mundane. I'd yearn for escape. That complaint lodged, I was also feeling a contradictory tug. I was falling in love with the real New Zealand, and feeling the emotional content of the landscape outside of its association with the trilogy. Especially here in Queenstown, dreams of poetic grandeur were hard to suppress. I had to resist strapping on a backpack and heading into the wilds.*

But I stuck with the program. I booked a tour with Nomad Safaris, one of the first companies to offer tours by Land Rover into the backcountry. Nomad Safaris was owned by a Brit, David Gatward-Ferguson. A big Tolkien fan, he had found the Frodo quest "quite appealing" since his youth as a disenfranchised English student. We chatted over tea as he explained that, to him, New Zealand had always looked like how he'd pictured Middle-earth. When he heard the film trilogy was in the works, he made certain to find work as an extra. He played a wild man and an Uruk-hai in 85-degree heat, and got paid $100 for each 4:00 A.M.-to-10:00 P.M. day. "I would have done it for free," he said.

In 2005, at the height of the *Rings*-driven surge, Gatward-Ferguson's business had increased by 500 percent. He built his company into a fleet of twenty four-wheel-drive vehicles, a staff of thirty employees, and a gift shop selling *Rings* tchotchkes, miniatures, and $1,200 swords. His tours were superior to others in the area, he said, and he envisioned being able to keep offering *Rings* tours for some time. I asked him about other tour companies. He did mention a competitor's "all-out geek tour" that let tourists wear and play with $15,000 (NZD) worth of weapons, costumes, and "top-secret" items used in the films. They toured thirty-five locations, including sites accessible only by helicopter. Unfortunately, I found out about it too late. Besides, the one-day $1,500 price tag put it a little out of reach.

Nomad Safaris was more reasonable. Despite my growing feeling that Middle-earth was nothing but a patchwork of locations cleverly framed so as not to show houses, cars, power lines,

---

* To further muddle the fantasy–reality divide, a South Island RV park operator had petitioned New Zealand's Geographic Board to label an unnamed stretch of the Waiau River the "Anduin," the river the Fellowship floated downstream in their Elvish boats. Unfortunately, the request was denied.

or any evidence of the modern world, the Land Rover expedition rejuvenated me. A young guide named Brent Clements drove myself, an Aussie, and a Brazilian couple to the sites of the trilogy's more-majestic scenes—remote areas near Glenorchy and beyond, like the Dart Valley (Isengard), and the beech forests of Mount Aspiring National Park (Lothlorien, and the woods where Boromir gets skewered by arrows). The license plate on our Land Rover read P1PP1N.

"People save for years to come here," Brent said as we bounced on gravel roads and charged across streams, spraying the truck with water and adding some excitement to the trip. "It puts a little pressure on me because they've been looking forward to it for so long. It's their dream." He did a great job inspiring adventure in our small group, even lifting my jaded spirits. Instead of saying "We're off to see the Dart Valley—you know, where they filmed Isengard," he'd simply announce, "Next, Isengard!" He told us *Wakatipu* meant "hollow of the giant," and wove in a Maori creation story of the giant who carved the mountains and rivers. Tolkien had created a folklore even more universal. "Some passengers don't understand English well," Brent told me. "But they understand *The Lord of the Rings*."

INSTANTLY AND INEXTRICABLY FILLED WITH ENVY

The next day, I drove to Arrowtown to check out the location of one of my favorite scenes from the first movie. There, at the Ford of Bruinen (on the real-life Arrow River), elf maiden Arwen called forth a magical flood in the form of horses that swept away the Ringwraiths. Geek alert. Wouldn't we all love to be saved by Liv Tyler? Sigh.

I also wanted to pay Ian Brodie a visit. Based in a small resort town called Wanaka, about an hour from Queenstown over the switchback Crown Range Road, Brodie was the author of the *Lord of the Rings Location Guidebook*. I'd pretty much destroyed my copy by now, I'd flipped through it so often. The guide had sold 400,000 copies, making him New Zealand's top-selling nonfiction author. He still ran the New Zealand Fighter Pilots Museum he'd helped found, which is where I met him one afternoon.

On Brodie's desk, Air New Zealand model jets sat next to a statue of Gandalf rearing up on horseback. The fifty-two-year-old with a shock of white hair had been a huge Tolkien fan for ages, and he told me he owned first editions of the trilogy and a FRODO LIVES T-shirt from the 1970s. He consulted on flight simulator software and played video games like Duke Nukem, Half-Life, and Unreal. When tourists using his location book complained that, except at Hobbiton, there was nothing left to see, Brodie replied, "Before the movies came out, we used our imagination. You can still use your imagination." What he seemed to not say: Some things are best left to our own fugitive fantasy. Our own images. Our own "reality," not some filmmaker's.

Brodie had also managed to land a six-week stint as an extra on the *Return of the King* Wellywood set. He and his son Travis played in several scenes: he as a merchant from Gondor, his son as an orc. They got to mingle with the likes of Aragorn and had the run of Stone Street Studios. "As a fan, you gotta pinch yourself," Brodie said with a raspy laugh. Somehow, he had scored a foam chunk of the Mines of Moria set, which he showed me, and a section of the rounded door frame at Bag End. I was instantly and inextricably filled with envy.

Yet, there was one drawback to his Cinderella story. In the course of writing the location book, Brodie had been forced to watch the films dozens of times. "Now I'm imagining the films when I read the books," he said. While he agreed with "90 percent" of how the films were visualized, he admitted, "Now we're stuck with Peter Jackson's version of Middle-earth." The net effect: Brodie wasn't getting the same enjoyment from the novels. He'd read *Rings* thirty-five to forty times, he said, but he hadn't cracked open the books since the release of the last film in 2003.

Brodie showed me around the fighter plane museum just as it was closing. A Hawker Hurricane Mk IIA, a de Havilland DH-82A Tiger Moth, and other planes loomed in the darkness. Amid these real relics of a real World War II—as close to a pure good-vs.-evil, world-ending conflict humankind had ever witnessed—Brodie still found his native land a fantastical place. "New Zealand is encapsulated in Middle-earth. Or Middle-earth is encapsulated in New Zealand." He couldn't decide. "But I'm a tech geek, too. I could never survive in Middle-earth."

THAT KIWI BASTARD STOLE MY LIFE

My second-to-last night in Middle-earth, I had drinks and dinner with Kelly and Paul. "How's your work coming?" they asked.

In truth, not so great. My quest seemed disheveled, aimless, meaningless. I had celebrated my forty-second birthday in Wanaka. Whereas my fortieth was spent sick on tequila, but happily surrounded by friends and my new love, my forty-second was spent in a hot tub, under the stars, with a cheap bottle of pinot noir, alone. I made a 2:00 A.M., wine-fortified phone call to the aforementioned girlfriend-in-limbo (plus, another ex). I had been eager to get back to Wellington, but since arriving the night before, I'd felt lost. I had not at all left my *Rings* obsession behind—not yet. Is that why I had come to New Zealand? I had been happy to be here, climbing my psychic version of Mount Doom. But I didn't know why. I had lost sight of my quest. I was too embarrassed to admit to Kelly and Paul that I'd wandered over to The Green Parrot, a low-key eatery where Viggo-Aragorn once chowed down on steak and fries, just to soak up the air of stale celebrity. And I was not going to tell my new friends that I'd fired off one last desperate fax to Peter Jackson's "people," pleading for fifteen minutes of his time. I had come to one conclusion: I accepted that Peter Jackson had become the filmmaker I had always wanted to be. *That kiwi bastard stole my life.* So be it. I vowed to give up stalking the streets of Miramar in hopes of "running into" him. ("You'll never find a celebrity coming out of there," a surly teenager warned me, pointing to a sound stage. "Never happens." Thanks kid.) My unhealthy PJ obsession was officially over.* OK, I loitered around Weta one more time. I spied on some carpenters on their cigarette break, but I swear, I dove into no Dumpsters. Instead, I went into the Weta Cave, the gift shop selling expensive movie souvenirs, and talked to Dan, who ran the shop. I watched the behind-the-scenes video of Weta magic, asked Dan about the swords, Elvish cloaks, and sculptures on display, and bought a copy of *Cinefex* magazine, autographed by Richard Taylor. Enough.

How was my work coming?

"Pretty good, I guess," I lied to Paul and Kelly.

When I'd first arrived in Wellington, I'd spoken with Judith McCann, CEO of Film New Zealand, the office that marketed the country as a film location. She was frustrated that all my questions kept returning to *The Lord of the Rings*. McCann reeled off other high-profile films shot in New Zealand: *The Piano, Whale Rider, The Last Samurai.* "We're so beyond *Lord of the Rings* by now," she sighed. "We've moved on." I was ready to move on, too, and accept what was really here. And yet my ears pricked up when I heard McCann mention the next Tolkien-based production in the pipeline. "Yes, we've got two *Hobbits* coming," she said, reluctantly.

The movies, produced by Peter Jackson and directed by Guillermo (*Pan's Labyrinth*) Del Toro, were slated to be filmed in 2010. The first installment would likely be released in 2011—a decade after *The Fellowship of the Ring* had hit the big screen. Like Uruk-hai storming Helm's Deep, the next wave of *Rings* frenzy would soon be mustering to bang its spears on the gates to Middle-earth. I wondered if I'd be there with my battering ram, also clamoring to get in. Or if I'd try to land a walk-on role as a journalist/orc named Ethoriac.

---

* Jackson's next movie, *The Lovely Bones*, was in post-production while I wandered Miramar. The subject? A girl's rape and murder, told from the point of view of the dead victim. Perhaps PJ had graduated from conventional fantasy and horror.

Fantasy can, of course, be carried to excess. It can be ill done. It can be put to evil uses. It may even delude the minds out of which it came. But of what human thing in the world is that not true? Men have conceived not only of elves, but they have imagined gods, and worshipped them, even worshipped those most deformed by their authors' own evil. But they have made false gods out of other materials: their notions, their banners, their monies; even their sciences and their social and economic theories have demanded human sacrifices. Abusus non tollit usum.* Fantasy remains a human right: we make in our measure and in our derivative mode, because we are made: and not only made, but made in the image and likeness of a Maker.

—J. R. R. Tolkien, "On Fairy-Stories" (1964)

---

* Latin: "Abuse does not take away use."

Get Off the Road

During my last two days in Middle-earth, thankfully, a few fruitful encounters finally fell into place.

One was with the aforementioned calligrapher Daniel Reeve, who met me at a downtown Wellington café on a sunny morning. He let me paw through his portfolio of Middle-earth maps and bound books full of Elvish script he'd done for the movies (as well as a few pages of Bilbo and Frodo's "calligraphy practice," done in the hands of actors Ian Holm and Elijah Wood). I thought of my D&D days, drawing dungeons and maps again, and was impressed (if not a little green) that Reeve had found a way to make a living at it. Also, I managed to get an audience with Gino Acevedo, head of Weta Workshop's prosthetics and makeup department, who gave me a fleeting, behind-the-scenes peek as we walked past cubicles of artists to his lair. As he showed me a Gollum model on his shelf, one of the seven rubber Gandalf noses, and the latex pieces that transformed Holm into the "old Bilbo," I tried not to pee my pants. We talked about our favorite fantasy movies. I glanced at a box under his desk labeled "Frodo hair." I'd made it to the inner sanctum.

I also had a conversation with Peter Lyon, Weta's swordsmith, who forged the real swords and stunt blades for battle scenes in

Rings. It did not surprise me when he said he used to be into D&D, was a combat instructor for an SCA-like group called the Wellington Medieval Guild, and jousted with a troupe called Order of the Boar. The jousting, in particular, had improved his confidence, helped him face fears, and built his character.

My chat with Lyon gave me pause. I wondered how much my character had been tested over the years. At once, I knew it had been. Perhaps I had grown up fast . . . too fast. Helping care for a parent at age twelve will do that to you. But my experience built confidence. I had faced fears. I had a strong foundation. I wasn't so childish after all. And I could forgive myself for sometimes needing to be juvenile as an adult. If that meant playing games, so be it. I deserved a break. Take that, girlfriend!

Before my chat with Lyon, after peering into a glass case full of Oscars, I was waiting in the lobby. Then, I saw him: Richard Taylor, exiting from the bowels of Weta.

"Hi," I blurted.

"Hello," Richard said with a smile. He looked harried.

I managed a "Bye!" as he crossed in front of the seven-foot orc brooding in the corner, and left for the evening.

My final morning, I had coffee with Erica Challis, a writer for TheOneRing.net who I had spoken with back when I'd written that story that included Mark Egginton and Oxford. Challis had scooped some juicy news and rumors during the trilogy shoots. Her involvement in that tempest of fan activity felt like "standing on the pivot point of a world phenomenon," she told me. Challis had been part of something bigger than herself—a sentiment I'd heard again and again from people involved in making the movies. Via TheOneRing.net, she had also found a husband, a Californian. When I met her in Wellington, a child was on the way. Geek love had struck again.*

---

* I asked Challis if she and her husband knew the baby's gender, and if they had already picked out a name. "It's a boy," she replied. "And we're not naming him Aragorn."

Challis and I chatted about the need for fantasy. Perhaps society's lack of a coming-of-age ritual explained the appeal. "We have a driver's license, and a drinking age," she noted. But not much else. The fantasy genre filled this void, framing the hero's journey in right and wrong, good and evil, a blueprint for behavior. "It's an attractive vision of the world, in the way we wish instinctively it should be," she said.

Perhaps to get one's driver's license, one should have to fight an orc. Perhaps to bring a baby into this world, one should first have to scale Mount Doom (just to weed out the wussy parents). Perhaps before we died, we should all write in bound leather books with quill pens in long, slow calligraphy the stories of our lives to pass on what we knew to those who'd live after us. Some structure seemed better than all my stumbling about.

GATHERING STRENGTH TO FACE THE REAL WORLD

I'm normally good at keeping track of my possessions. But all through New Zealand, I had sprinkled behind me a trail of lost things. I left my satchel (with my computer and passport, among other treasures) at a rest stop and wasted three hours retracing my route to retrieve it. Near the volcano of Ruapehu (aka, Mordor), bushwhacking through the brush to try to find an obscure filming location, my notebook had fallen out of my back pocket. I went back and found it dangling from a tree branch.

The third time I left something behind, it wasn't exactly by mistake.

A few hours before my flight home, I went back to Mount Victoria. I'd wanted to reenact the hobbits' "Get off the road" scene. I was alone on the wooded path. The macrocarpa pines towered above me. I set up my computer and found and played a video file of the scene.

"I think we should get off the road," Frodo cried to Pippin, Merry, and Sam. "Get off the road! Quick!" They hopped into the hollow under a tree trunk as the Black Rider sniffed and snorted evilly above them.

I dumped out my Kinder Surprise figurines, grabbed the four hobbits, and planted them in the pine needles. I got out my video camera and began shooting, darting back and forth between the movie playing on my MacBook and the plastic, motionless hobbits. I looked up at the real world. There was a crook in a tree branch, the exact one visible in the movie clip. Cool and all . . . but . . .

I put the camera down.

I'd accomplished much of what I'd set out to do in New Zealand. The truth was, I didn't want to make my little movies. I didn't want to wear Frodo hair, elf ears, or hold a prop sword. I wanted to *be* a hobbit, and *be* an elf, and *be* part of a heroic story. Not dress the part, *be* the part, 24/7. Total immersion. That's why at Pennsic, I found the disconnect between puffy-shirted minstrels eating fried chicken and drinking Pepsi too jarring. I wanted to live in a *real* medieval town, or Rivendell, where I'd have a starring role and could accomplish great deeds. None of this was going to happen in New Zealand, or Middle-earth. It was folly.

Goofing around with the figurines had been fun, until it began to feel pathetic. What was I doing, a forty-two-year-old, single, and childless man, traveling on his own, sleeping in youth hostels, and playing with toys? All this fruitless grasping to be closer to "movie magic" was depressing. Each time I watched the trilogy—which I had been doing in hotel rooms, late at night, in bed—its power diminished. Seeing the movie locations and the behind-the-scenes secrets of the special effects dispelled the incantation even further.

I thought about what Erica Challis had told me. She had heard stories of people in oppressive societies who read Tolkien. The books gave them hope in hopeless times. "Fantasy is a genre people can read and retreat [to] and gather strength to face the real world," she said. Refuge from oppression, personal or political, lay in the fairy world and the possibility of imagination. Fantasy kept the spirit alive and kicking.

I gathered my strength. It was time to leave Mount Victoria and Middle-earth behind. I packed up and headed down the path. Then, I heard a voice.

This is what you're going to do, Ethan. You're going to leave them here.

Huh?

Yes, you. Turn around, Ethan. Retrace your steps. Follow the path. Dig.

I spun around, found a stick, and began digging a hole on the path. I picked the location where I guessed the actors (Elijah Wood, Sean Astin, Billy Boyd, and Dominic Monaghan) had once stood playing fictional characters (Frodo, Sam, Pippin, and Merry) of made-up beings (hobbits), for a movie adaptation (Peter Jackson's version) of a fantasy book (*Rings*), filmed in a real country (New Zealand) that the author (Tolkien) had never visited, which now stood in for this imaginary world (Middle-earth). *You are digging a hole in a hillside in New Zealand,* the voice continued. It was hard to turn it off. *You are doing something symbolic. This is what it feels like to have an epiphany.* I was role-playing a person who had epiphanies like this. I felt like an avatar of myself in World of Warcraft, having a major life moment. Me and not me.

I put the figurines in the hole. *You are burying these figurines.* I covered them in earth, tamped down the spot, and scattered it with pine needles to cover my tracks. Then, I grabbed my bag and marched quickly off the hill.

My trip had demystified the power of Middle-earth. Some force in me had felt some urge to put childish things behind me, and travel closer to adulthood, whatever that meant. Plus, I had an ending for my book. If anyone wanted to exhume *Le Seigneur des Anneaux* Kinder Surprise chocolate egg Fellowship, all they had to do was bring a shovel to Mount Victoria, find the path, make a guess, and start digging.

Wildly popular, virtual worlds are marketers' playground

By mingling aspects of video gaming, social networking and communicating, virtual worlds have appeal for both genders and are an intriguing opportunity for those marketing to kids and teens, according to eMarketer's latest report, "Kids and Teens Online: Virtual Worlds Open New Universe." . . .

What makes virtual worlds appealing to young people? Virtual worlds are about connecting and communicating—the two recurring themes for online youth. Virtual worlds also allow kids to tap into their creativity, indulge their desire for self-expression and exercise their proclivity for exploration.

The good news for marketers is that most virtual worlds are capable of offering detailed information about how their users interact with brands and advertising.

"The bad news," says Debra Aho Williamson, senior analyst and author of the report, "is that it is difficult to know what all this virtual interaction really means. What value is there in a person's avatar drinking a Pepsi? Or wearing a shirt bought from a virtual store? What if a person's virtual activities have no bearing on their real-world activities?"

—from a press release from eMarketer (2007)

Being a Hero Ain't What It Used to Be

There and back again. I was home. Quest completed.

What had I learned, other than the obvious—that being an online gamer or a D&D freak wasn't a horrible fate? One, fantasy escapist entertainment had a purpose: distraction, amusement, an excuse to dress up, write a plot, or hang with the guys or gals. For some, fantasy built character or taught good behavior. For Sir Gareth or Levi Hunt, their role-playing formed the cornerstone of a belief system, a philosophy; or, like sports or the military, a life structure. For others, like Mark Egginton, it was pure escape. Although games brought people together, addicts like Rajeev used games to drop out, tune out, and fail in life. In Phyllis Priestly's case, WoW played a role in hard times, filling a void, while also opening her eyes to a new version of herself. Some dwellers of imaginary realms had been traumatized. In Nissa Ludwig's case, fantasy was a lifesaver. I wasn't sure that even those who claimed "pure escape" were aware of what games, books, and movies did for them. But I was happy to see my prejudices against fantasy freaks and gamers—and my inner geek—ripped to shreds.

Most of the list that I'd scribbled in bed, during the Oxford-Tolkien leg of my quest, still held true. Perhaps we did have too much leisure time, compared to ancient or feudal days; too many choices, too many temptations. An online love or identity was beyond reach of most people twenty years ago. We do want to feel part of a larger narrative, which is to say, we fear death, and want to be remembered. We desire immortality. Of course, few of us can slay real dragons, or even topple the captains of industry on our climb to the top. And it's not socially acceptable to duel that surly night-shift manager with a staple gun at twenty paces. The "hands-on" problem-solving approach that fantasy stories promote gets us into a crapload of trouble, IRL. As much as we'd like to sometimes, aside from criminals and sociopaths, we really can't settle our disputes with death matches.

You could train for days playing violent games, or whacking foes with wooden sticks, but neither was an accurate predictor of follow-through in battle. I don't think fantasy escapism reflects a crisis in heroism. Our culture has many ways to be heroic. But being heroic—getting the bad guy—is easier in a LARP or D&D than in real life. For these reasons, the explosion of video games is not hard to understand. They can appeal to the downtrodden or disenfranchised—more than just teenage boys who are bitter or frustrated that life is a puzzle. Civilization and other strategy games give players world-building, god-like power. But even the most Neanderthal, gun-toting, FPS game delivers heroism's baser pleasures: They make the disempowered feel powerful. Lost in a strip-malled wasteland, the protagonist of Grand Theft Auto may be no quest-driven Ulysses, but for the average suburban couch potato, a little, pixelated* "me" stealing cars and blowing away crackheads, or building a medieval fiefdom, is a rush that sure beats another night of *Family Guy* reruns. Besides, the real world is mostly a known—and scary—quantity. It's hard for real-life travelers to blaze new trails through uncharted lands. Fantasy games let us uncover mystery and discover new realms.

Sociologist Norbert Elias, author of *The Civilizing Process,* suggests that in our increasingly structured society, we must exert proper control over our emotions. In the "civilizing process" described by Elias, people don't get to flex our primal emotional muscles. So we have created acceptable arenas to blow off primal steam and experience adrenaline and danger—even if real death has been removed. Elias called it "controlled decontrolling" of emotions. It's acceptable to bellow battle cries at football games, or hoot during rock concerts, or get drunk and crazy at Mardi Gras. Among the right group of friends, it's also acceptable to hoot after killing a cave troll.

The minutiae of our modern, mundane troubles—politics, race, jobs, communication, relationships, family—are hard enough to tackle. The world is flawed. Dissatisfied with ATMs and speed limits, mediated experiences and the suburban blahscape, who wouldn't prefer trying his or her luck with a broadsword against a horde of orcs rather than paying the Visa bill or looking for parking? The even grander troubles we want to unravel—like good versus evil—seem only solvable in our imaginations. If, outside the movie theater, the real terrorists slip through our fingers, at least in our imaginations, we can take revenge.

Of course, vanquishing the "bad guys" would be a fantasy come true if the enemy of your choice—an abusive father, abortion rights advocates, Rush Limbaugh—had raspy voices, glow-

---

* Sign of the times: the nineteenth-century term "pixilated," literally "pixie-led" or led astray by fairies, has given way to "pixelated," or to be divided into pixels.

ing red eyes, and blood-stained helmets. Reality offers no such sharp divisions. But delving into these black-and-white worlds can make our own conflicts, personal or political, seem more manageable. Call it regression to childhood, but these infinite hero stories played out in games, books, movies, and even kids' schoolyard antics involve villains, heroes, and monsters for good reason: so we can face and overcome our fears in a good-guy, bad-guy, clear-cut world. Fantasy's apocalyptic, end-of-civilization scenarios, by comparison, make our troubles seem simpler. A romantic breakup might appear to be a piece of cake next to saving the world—but it's easier to win an imaginary war or storm a digital castle than it is to conquer real heartbreak.

The attraction to these heroic experiences and imaginary worlds is, ultimately, a hopeful gesture: that we could live otherwise, by an honor code, by taking bold action and slaying our demons in hand-to-hand combat, not in the mental space above our therapists' heads. That nothing "real" comes of our virtual triumphs is beside the point. We like to complain about how hard it is to be modern, to live amid the myriad distractions and demands of a pluralistic and PC-oriented civilization. Tolkien and other authors fed on postwar weariness and fear of industrialization. Hence, it can be a relief to control the fate of an imaginary character rather than make decisions about our puny, insignificant selves. We should be forgiven for our personal need to clamber out of our minds and into some other imaginary place. Besides, I think pretending to be a hero in a game is preferable to worshipping a hero IRL.

MIDDLE-EARTH HAD NO GLOBAL WARMING

To paraphrase the writer and futurist David Brin, many might prefer if we had queens and kings, rode horses, and encountered magic and so-called "wonder." If alchemy and mystery, not logic, politics, or media, ruled the lands. If nature was pristine. This is why fantasy takes place in an imaginary, medieval realm, not the sci-fi world fast-forwarded 500 years. In fantasy, modern science and democracy have yet to be invented—and won't be. Middle-earth had no global warming; its cloud of doom was not our fault, either. In that world, suffering and annihilation can be blamed on pure evil. Nor did we help create that evil through misguided foreign policy or neglect of our responsibilities abroad. Nostalgic and backward-looking, the realm of fantasy escapist entertainment remains static and predictable. Thankfully, so-called "progress" stops. *Rings* and Warcraft offer this world again. So do other games, movies, and books.

Clearly, Dungeons & Dragons was not the first manifestation of immersive fantasy. Nor was Tolkien the first teller of heroic tales. Glowing computer screens induce trance-like mental states that hearken back to nightly fires and cave art. As we march forward into the twenty-first century, glued to our LCD screens, Americans seem more nostalgic than ever for this lost, preindustrial age, rich with fairy-tale wonder and possibility—falsely nostalgic, as it turns out. We never had it to begin with.

But nowadays, being a hero ain't what it used to be. We have entered a more complex age. We've lost the sense of self-sacrifice and faith that the epic poem's ethical value system championed. The brute-force approach to problem-solving hasn't always been a positive development for humanity. The Vietnam War chased from the battlefield once and for all any vestiges of the "good fight." According to Gerard Jones, author of *Killing Monsters: Why Children Need Fantasy, Super Heroes and Make-Believe Violence,* those cops-and-robbers thrillers and cowboys-and-Indians scenarios of decades past just don't fit in our increasingly multiethnic, culturally relativistic, journalistically and media-examined world. Politics, race, and empathy with the enemy all get in the way.

As for the "escapism" tag, I don't think it's often justified. Watching gaming groups huddling around tables, it became clear to me the whole enterprise is not simply a war between suitcases full of intricately painted armies arranged on foam landscapes. True, some gamers just dig painting the miniatures, and some do play for hours to the detriment of other facets of their lives. But something else is going on here. Socializing is inseparable from the game itself, as are the bigger topics raised during games, such as politics, history, art, love, treachery, loyalty, and perseverance. A swords-and-sorcery or futuristic realm has conflict, and when there's a conflict being acted out, just like in all great literature, we learn useful stuff about the human condition. Just don't kill anyone, OK? We all need to keep that fantasy–reality divide clear in our heads.

There's nothing particularly escapist about a fantasy novel like Tolkien's, either, if by escape we mean retreating from the world or shirking responsibility. Unfolding the intertwined fates of imaginary races in the face of evil domination, *Rings* is infused with a relentlessly grave and foreboding tone. Tolkien's prose may be absurdly anachronistic, but his heroes are burdened and world-weary, just like you and me. They make impressive sacrifices to do the right thing (i.e., to stop the apocalypse). They are beleaguered by moral dilemmas about free will, personal sacrifice, and the common good. It is a story born of the twentieth century's sorrows.

OTHER TEMPTATIONS

What is the future of these fantasy games, worlds, adventures, exploits, and escapades? Will any of us be able to recognize what game designers, special-effects wizards, programmers, and inventors will come up with five years from now? Twenty-five? Are there any dangers?

We have come far already—far enough, it sometimes seemed to me during the more curmudgeonly and skeptical moments of my quest. What had begun as the innocent dreams of quirky Oxford dons telling stories, then pot-smoking college kids grooving to Led Zeppelin lyrics, evoking some place "over the hills and far away," has since mutated. All is not pure goblin-blood black and shimmering-wizard white. Commerce poisons; power corrupts. The unregulated, boomtown economy of online games like WoW and Second Life—no police, no legal system, no taxes— has created problems. Lawlessness breeds fraudsters, harassment, and other crimes. Perhaps these fantasy worlds deserve to be ethically complicated; the murky behavior they inspire only proves that human nature is human nature, no matter the fantastic backdrop.

As we grapple with the consequences, pundits and experts line up for battle on either side of the question, to tell us these fantasies are quite helpful, or utterly doomed. Some posit that today's pop-culture junk food is more cognitively nutritious than the crapola of yore. Role-playing video games, virtual environments on the Internet, and even *The Simpsons* require greater mental prowess and a sophisticated grasp of narrative than *Six Million Dollar Man, Gilligan's Island,* and the other dreck I was raised on. That this so-called "interactive entertainment" makes us more savvy is undoubtedly true. But are we any smarter? More able to engage with and solve real-world problems? More hopeful?

As long as thirty-five-year-old American men are spending eight hours a day playing Warcraft, or South Korean kids are being sent, cold turkey, to outdoorsy boot camps to wean them off their online addictions, there is some cause for concern. Like with D&D "It's the devil's work!" fear-mongering in the 1980s, it's easy to overreact. Yes, spouses and parents have reason to worry about a mass phenomenon's effect on their loved ones. A teen or geriatric can get hooked on Warcraft or EverQuest. The game can supercede friends, families, and jobs. But other temptations can as well—drugs, alcohol, the Internet, religion, porn, or double-fudge brownie ice cream. Addictive personalities are vulnerable to all manner of self-erasing activities.

Some fantasy entertainment seems more susceptible for abuse. And it can be argued (although I'm wary to make the case) that, say, the experience of folks actually bopping each other with foam swords, or attending Renaissance fairs, or weaving tapestries, or designing dungeons on graph paper, *must* be better than sitting in front of digitally driven amusements for hours on end. At least with the Nintendo Wii, you have to get up and move, and you tend to play with your friends. I might argue that reading forces one to flex the imagination: The image-making occurs in the mind, not on the screen. As early computer games became more sophisticated, the chunky 2-D outlines of spaceships and characters were replaced by flawless 3-D renderings. The more "real" the image, the less for the imagination to do. Paradoxically, we embrace movie and gaming technology to bring us richly textured, often digitally rendered, neo-medieval worlds. As special-effects designers and video-game developers apply their talents to rendering everything as realistic as possible, our tolerance for low-grade special effects lowers. We now crave increasingly believable artificial experiences. When *The Hobbit* movies hit theaters, for example, fantasy fans can count on its computer-generated eye candy to have leapfrogged, once again, to new heights of immersive verisimilitude. (Similarly evolved will be the sophistication of tie-ins to consumer products.)

Along the digital way, perhaps our imaginations do lose out. As Gary Gygax said in a 2006 interview, "The analogy I make is that pen-and-paper role-playing is live theater and computer games are television." An old grognard, his prejudices were clear. But I don't know what goes on inside the minds of gamers and geeks—and I'm hesitant to rank the reader of *Rings* higher or lower than someone dressed up like Frodo or someone who offs snow- and stone-trolls in *Lord of the Rings* Online. I do know this: The online gamer's social mind is now being trained in different, fascinating, and not necessarily damaging ways, and the formations of online guilds, friendships, and community is something that neither Tolkien nor Gygax could have predicted.

Heroes of the future? Visitors to the U.S. Army's Virtual Army Experience try out virtual killing, for free.

On the negative side, I'm not entirely comfortable with how "gaming" is being used. For example, an army recruiting tool called the Virtual Army Experience, a sort of simulator where players sit in real army vehicles and shoot realistic guns at huge video screens and kill people, makes war seem too much like fun. Especially when kids as young as thirteen are being allowed to play and the army is snagging their personal information along the way. Similarly, game-like graphics added to news broadcasts further blur the already flimsy news–entertainment divide.*

---

* During its 2008 election coverage, CNN "holograms" beamed digital versions of interviewees far, far away into the studio, a page taken right out of the scene in *Star Wars* when Princess Leia retrieves Obi Wan's message from R2-D2. "Help me, Obama-Wan Kenobi. You're my only hope . . ."

I worry about how online culture is muddling that fantasy-reality divide. Researching this book, I came across hundreds of examples of marriages brought down by Second Life affairs and virtual sex, or how little girls dressed their dolls and designed dream houses not in their bedrooms with Barbie, but at barbie girls.com. Would the coming generations find Second Life shopping centers and nightclubs just as satisfying as the real thing, and never leave their homes? (Perhaps parents would be relieved not to have to drive their teens to the mall.) The sense of "here and now" keeps eroding. What is "place"? What is a physical "thing?" The research firm eMarketer predicts that by 2011, some 20 million children and teenagers—53 percent—will interface with virtual worlds, up from 8.2 million in 2007. Generations will be raised on these games. Will they be able to tell what is "real" on the screen, and what is a real tree, a real river, a real mountain, a real kiss, real sex, a real relationship? Is there potential for widespread social illiteracy about "real" flesh-and-blood people who, it turns out, are not "characters" in a game? Not to mention those little avatars tramping across acres and acres of digital playground; I wonder if someday, we'll forget how to use our feet for walking and to feel our body's responses to wind, rain, and gravity.

But enough from Mr. Gloom and Doom. For every person who argues that fantasy turns us into cowards, infantilizes us, or prevents us from being able to take actual risks, I would meet two more who said the opposite. LARPs train role players to take action. WoW is cathartic, engaging players with life. The SCA models good behavior. Any time gamers or fantasy communities band together in the real world for a cause, like the Harry Potter Alliance, good things happen.

Some computer games have clear therapeutic benefits. They help disabled people connect and communicate. MMORPGs and virtual worlds help Nissa Ludwig, and others like burn victims, manage pain. Therapeutic virtual-reality simulators like Virtual Iraq help returning vets combat post-traumatic stress disorder. Soldiers wear goggles and watch a digital environment that re-creates elements of the harrowing episode. Props, smells, sounds, and vibrations—a call to prayer in Arabic, diesel fumes, body odor of a fellow soldier—increase the verisimilitude, as the soldier with PTSD recounts what happened. Repeated over time, the individual eventually becomes less immobilized by terror. (Other applications include Virtual Airplane, Virtual Heights, and Virtual Vietnam.) The army uses a mock-Iraq village, called Medina Wasl, for role-playing simulations, much like a LARP site, and hopefully to save lives.

On the "toss-up" side are the many new developments in game technology. The latest twist is games like Tom Clancy's EndWar, a World War III real-time strategy game whose major innovation is a voice-activated system that enables players to speak commands into their headsets, which the game understands and translates into action. Cool, or scary? Likewise with a company I visited called Vivox, which provides online games, virtual worlds, and other online communities such as EveOnline with voice-chat technology. The audio technology is designed not only to make voices of other avatars louder and softer depending on how close your avatar stands from them, but other tricks can also change a player's voice. If you play a burly dwarf, your voice can sound like a burly dwarf. A twelve-year-old boy can play an orc and sound like an orc. But what if the boy chooses to sound like a thirty-five-year-old man or woman and interacts with people he never sees IRL? Or the thirty-five-year-old chooses to sound like a boy? Or a girl? That seems to open the door to thornier problems of identity and behavior.

One thing is clear: More and more experiences are being adapted to immersive games with participatory narratives. Pro sports "fantasy" leagues are making other fantasy possibilities more acceptable. Game developers are mining settings and plots from every genre and mode of leisure. Audiences (or potential audiences) want elaborate stories that offer more than killing monsters. This is where the definition of "heroic fantasy" will be changing. New games using sport and entertainment narratives mean heroes won't just be sword-wielding ones. In Football Superstars, your avatar plays soccer and works its way up from grassroots leagues to pro superstardom. You interact with other players worldwide, and between matches, you wander a virtual town and hang out in restaurants and pubs. A game like Rock Band won't likely have dwarves playing heavy-metal bass, but it will become a powerful tool for social networking. And it wouldn't surprise me to see it adding more narrative aspects— as lead singer, your band rockets up the charts and signs a deal; you fire your drummer; you implode and go into rehab; then you reunite with your band and stage your comeback tour. Not exactly an Icelandic saga, but a heroic narrative the kids can relate to.

I LIKE WHERE MY HEAD GOES

It seems as a culture, we have two options: We can be terrified of fantasy games, books, and movies and continue to marginalize them and their players. Or we can understand them, and see that fantasy in all its stripes has its proper place alongside other amusements. Meanwhile, as Warcraft reaches 15 or 20 million players, as it likely will, I predict a real-world backlash. People crave face-to-face contact. Old-school gaming, of the Diet Coke and Doritos variety, will always have its audience. Folks need to get their hands dirty and busy, making costumes, putting on makeup, swinging swords, all in the real world. Digital worlds only satisfy some of the gamers some of the time. Events like Dragon*Con, Pennsic, and Forest of Doors might become even more popular, not to mention other hybrid in-person games that

Megan Gardner, director of the Guard Up! fantasy Wizards and Warriors LARP summer camp for kids, in her unicorn costume.

no one has dreamed of yet. As game designer Tom Wham told me in Lake Geneva, "Board games are here to stay, because people like to gather around a table and be social."

I was heartened by a woman in the Boston area, Megan Gardner, who had started to teach "sport sword" medieval-style combat with foam weapons at her martial arts facility, Guard Up! She was also into LARPing. In 2008, she ran a first-in-the-nation overnight fantasy LARP for kids called Wizards & Warriors Residential Summer Camp. Campers stayed in costume for the entire week, solved puzzles, went on quests, and learned about honor, courage, and compassion. Gardner was indoctrinating a whole new generation of gaming geeks—only these geeks were running around outside, and they were learning how to kick ass with swords. Another positive force: A hard-core gamer named Bill Walton created a Web site, theescapist.com, to dispel misconceptions about RPGs. His organization, called the Young Person's Adventure League, tries to persuade kids to keep the tradition of RPGs alive in the coming generations.

One must not discount the power of the written word. Text and free-form role-playing will always offer something that a computer game or movie cannot—the ability to create, participate, and add to the story. I was reminded of what Nissa Ludwig told me, in describing her slow conversion from text-based games like Dragon Realms—literary experiences—to graphical ones. "I fought graphics games forever. If you gave me text, my imagination was better than anything that could be programmed. I grew up in a text world. I'm more comfortable there. I've always been in a family of readers and storytellers. Your mind is an amazing tool to take a book and make it so much more. My imagination is better than the graphics. It's going to be a long time before the graphics catch up with my imagination. They're getting there, but they're not there yet. The dragons in my mind are better than any you can put in a game. Doing all the reading is hard work for people. I read because I like where my head goes."

I think what I missed most about my D&D phase was where my head went—that anything-can-happen imaginary space. As Frank Mentzer, the Lake Geneva Gaming Convention Dungeon Master told me, D&D isn't all about "the win." The game itself was the purpose. He grew up in the Midwestern land of Vince Lombardi, who said, "Winning isn't everything—it's the only thing." "What D&D showed people," Mentzer said, "is that happiness is the journey, not the destination. It's not who wins the game, it's what you do along the way. And the whole game became the 'what you do along the way.'"

So, my fellow freaks and geeks, if we must escape, let us escape for a reason—not just to be entertained by a vast game, but because of where our heads go. Let's escape to do something along the way. Perhaps to find a truth. Michel Guyot wanted to know how they built castles in the thirteenth century, so he built Guédelon. When he gets there, to that imaginary place in the future—which his crew makes real each day, stone by stone— that home-world won't be "perfectly rendered." Just as mine is not. But its imperfections will make it real.

[Saving throw] represents the chance for the figure concerned to avoid (or at least partially avoid) the cruel results of fate. . . . By means of skill, luck, magical protections, quirks of fate and the aid of supernatural powers, the character making his or her saving throw takes none or only part of the indicated results. . . . So a character manages to avoid the full blast of the fireball, or averts his or her gaze from the basilisk or medusa, or the poisonous stinger of the giant scorpion misses or fails to somehow inject its venom. Whatever the rationale, the character is saved to go on. Of course, some saves result in the death of the character anyway, as partial damage causes him or her to meet death. But at least the character had some hope, and he or she fought to the very end. Stories will be told of it at the inn, and songs sung of the battle when warriors gather around the campfire.

—from *Advanced Dungeons & Dragons
Dungeon Masters Guide* (1979)

Saving Throws

OK, I lied. My quest still felt incomplete.

Like the blue cooler, one last place called to me. One final pilgrimage to the "ur-text" of my fantasy life. I had a desire to see the original, seminal Tolkien manuscripts. I was surprised to learn they were not located in some musty archive in Oxford, nor in some London law firm vault. They weren't squirreled away in an eccentric collector's villa at the end of an archipelago of Greek islands, either. They were in a library archive at a small Catholic university in, of all places . . . drum roll . . . Milwaukee. The last place I'd expected to find them.

Yep. Marquette University, in Wisconsin, the heart of war-gaming country, and an hour from Lake Geneva, where Dungeons & Dragons had been invented. Matt Blessing, the head of the Department of Special Collections and University Archives, was kind enough to meet me. His department's Web site explained that Marquette's J. R. R. Tolkien Collection includes "holograph renderings (manuscripts in the hand of the author), various sets of typescripts with corrections by Tolkien, and page proofs or galley sheets, also with corrections in the hand of the author" of his major works, *The Hobbit* and *The Lord of the Rings,* plus two lesser works. The archives contain dozens of Tolkien's original drawings and sketches, his notes on linguistics and philology, and his charts of story timelines and character locations.*

---

* *Rings* has a particularly complex plot, which cuts back and forth in a very cinematic fashion among multiple characters in several locations. Very postmodern, actually.

The Marquette collection also holds thousands of other items of Tolkienalia produced by the scholarly and fandom community—press clippings, articles, dissertations, studies of Elvish languages, poems and songs, calendars, games and puzzles, and teaching materials—relating to Tolkien's life and fantasy writings. Blessing told me that in the 1950s, Marquette's library director had an ambitious plan to beef up the university's archives. A London rare book dealer was hired to approach Tolkien. They made a deal. In 1957, the papers began to arrive at Marquette: 1,586 pages of *The Hobbit* manuscripts, 9,250 pages of *Rings* manuscripts.

I began to salivate.

"For a passionate Tolkien reader, it's almost a pilgrimage to see the manuscripts," Blessing said. During the *Rings* movie hype of 2001–2004, he'd received as many as seventy-five requests per week to see the collection. But it was only open to legitimate researchers.

"Might I see a few pages of . . . you know . . . the—?" I asked nervously.

"The manuscripts? Sure."

We donned white gloves while Blessing's assistant Susan went to a back room to retrieve a few folders. Blessing set them down on a long, empty wooden table. He slowly leafed through a kind of "greatest hits" folder of highlights. I tried not to drool on them.

Tolkien wrote with a fountain pen. He edited with pencil. Up to eighteen drafts existed for some chapters. The calligraphy was gorgeous, as were Tolkien's sketches, such as a page from the ancient Book of Mazarbul (the book that the Fellowship finds in the dungeons of Moria), drawn to appear burned and torn. For Tolkien, the drawings must have been like props in a LARP, or a bit of set dressing to better role-play his fantasy as he composed various scenes.

Blessing showed me a few more pages, then said he had a meeting to go to. Time was up. My heart sank.

"Listen, just see Susan. Fill out a request. She'll get you what you want."

"What I . . . want?"

"Anything." Then he left.

I felt like a kid who'd sweet-talked his way into Willy Wonka's chocolate mother ship.

"Consider yourself lucky," Susan said, as she went to retrieve more folders for me. "They don't let people see originals very often." She directed most scholars to the microfilm.

I was alone with the Professor. For two hours, I requested folder after folder. I turned page after page. I saw the sheet where Tolkien crossed out an early title idea, *The Magic Ring,* and wrote above it, *The Lord of the Rings.* I scrutinized the ancient Elvish script, the language of Mordor, etched on his design of the One Ring. I saw that Tolkien had used whatever scrap of paper was at hand—an Oxford exam book, a faculty club menu, an Air Warden's report. I could picture the old professor grading a final exam, becoming disheartened by some student's analysis of *Beowulf* he'd probably read a hundred times before, and letting his mind wander one more time to Middle-earth to imagine what went on there. *Scribble, scribble.* I saw, in Tolkien's own hand, that scene on the Bridge of Khazad-dûm, where Gandalf confronts the Balrog, falls, and cries out to the Fellowship, "Fly, you fools!" And, finally, the page I had hoped to find: Tolkien's elegant picture of the decorated gate, the Doors of Durin, that led to the Mines of Moria, with the Elvish script above, "Speak, friend, and enter." A kind of invitation, all over again, to enter these worlds.

I flashed back to my freshman year in high school, and the race with my friend Mike to see who would finish *Rings* first. To my senior year British Lit paper that, much to Mrs. Whaley's horror, compared Tolkien's literary voice in *The Hobbit* to *Rings.*

Tolkien's Lord of the Rings *manuscript page, showing an early design for the Doors of Durin that led to the Mines of Moria. The Elvish script above the gate reads "Speak, friend, and enter."*

To the D&D dungeons and maps I loved to make. To the camaraderie of Friday gaming nights.

I realized in that moment that I hadn't necessarily been escaping. Like Tolkien, I had been creating—drawing pictures, making movies, telling stories—I suppose most of my life. Which, I thought, wasn't such a horrible way to spend all my long years after all. Perhaps I hadn't gone so far astray. As Tolkien himself wrote, "Not all those who wander are lost."

SAVING THROW

Back from Marquette, I remembered I still had my own archives to raid. The blue Coleman cooler sat in the corner of my office. I opened it once again.

After some deep digging through graph-paper purgatory and dust-mote hell, I unearthed a photocopy of a photocopy of an article from 1982, published in my old New Hampshire hometown newspaper. A reporter from the *Transcript* had been intrigued by D&D and what some strange local boys had been up to on Friday nights. The images that accompany the story, entitled DUNGEONS AND DRAGONS SWEEPS KAUFMAN [sic] HOME, are smeared and overexposed as a memory one wants to remember but can't. Still, it's not hard to make out Bill K. behind his Dungeon Master's screen, and clockwise to his left, JP, Bill S., Mike, and me, all sitting at the round table strewn with papers and pencils and dice. John is sitting on a couch in the background. The article says my character is named Yigi-Sci the Cold, whom I don't recall at all. Like so many episodes of my adolescence—gone. But everyone's clothing from my sophomore year is, strangely, just as I remember: Bill K.'s flannel shirt, JP's white cable-knit sweater, and my button-down collar poking up from the neck of my sweater. I can just make out my face and my helmet of hair the way I painstakingly combed it. My eyes are pointed slyly to the right, uncomfortably, as if I'm eyeing my escape. The reporter isn't fastidious about attributions, but one of us, discussing the appeal of D&D, is quoted as saying, "It takes you away from the real world." I wonder if that was me.

It's not a horrible article, but the reporter doesn't come close to capturing what we were actually trying to do—what my friend JP called the "crystal castles" we created for each other, as we listened to Electric Light Orchestra, Bob Seger, and Paul McCartney and Wings, eyes ragged, jacked up on cola and cheese doodles—castles that no one but us understood. "If they won't write the kinds of books we want to read, we shall have to write them ourselves," Tolkien wrote to his buddy C. S. Lewis. In their anachronistic tales set in self-made places, they both lost and found themselves, and sated their dissatisfied ids and broken egos. Like Tolkien and Lewis, JP and I and the rest of the gang told riddles in the dark—in person, every Friday night, in someone's living room. No hiding behind aliases and computer screens, in lonely bedrooms behind closed doors. Playing D&D, we became bards, storytellers, and entertainers. We played roles—fighter, cleric, magic-user, thief—and we played face-to-face, and made a better place for us. We helped each other through, as "The Gary Gygax Song" said, that "labyrinth of bein' a teenage boy."

Unlike Tolkien and Lewis, no Great War defined my life—no ordinary war, anyway. But my childhood had tested my physical and emotional strength and cunning. My twelve-year-old self was faced with obstacles I should not have been asked to face. It took derring-do to dress my mother, to endure her strange remarks, and to tie her shoes. No one recognized my heroics, or my mother's. I don't say that out of self-pity. As an adult, it's a blessing of self-realization to finally understand we are all beset with misfortune, and often we can't choose what misfortune will follow us. That's life.

D&D has a rule called a "saving throw." Just before a poison from an arrow or paralyzing sting from a giant scorpion takes effect, you roll the dice, a "saving throw." The DM consults a chart to see if your character can weather the toxin. Did my mom make her saving throw? Partly. Perhaps her wisdom, intelligence, charisma, and dexterity had been diminished. But in my rule book, her strength and constitution were all 18s. That she survived the aneurysm at all was magic.

Of course, no chart could have predicted my mother's fate in 1978. Those gem-like dice—d20, d12, d6—tumbled like tiny Magic 8-Balls in a murky blue fluid but did not foretell our fortunes. They only calculated the damage. Monster and damsel, dragon and innocent, my mom lived for almost two decades after the aneurysm, but she did not escape her tragic narrative. In my mother's final years, surrendering to lung failure, she wheezed like a dragon whose scales had been pierced by an arrow. She died before I learned the right healing spell, whether it was "Cure Serious Wounds" or "Remove Paralysis," to mend her. Nor did I ever find a Rod of Resurrection to raise her from the dead, as if bestowing an extra life were as easy as slipping two more quarters into a video game. My +2 long sword never worked in the real world.

I couldn't save my mother. And if I couldn't smite the Kitchen Dragon and the Momster, by play-acting in a safer D&D world at least I could defeat creatures like them, or creatures even more wicked, and delve into the forces of evil that cursed Sara Gilsdorf's life. But it turned out that I never had to defeat my mother—only my fears about loving someone who couldn't love me back the way I'd wanted, or needed. As a teen, I didn't let myself get too close. As an adult, I got a little closer. I still found it hard to embrace the idea she might love me. I felt guilty I didn't—couldn't—try harder. It took a decade after she died to finally make peace with myself. (This was helped by another quest: a 75-mile, Boston-to-New Hampshire wintertime pilgrimage walk to her gravesite.) Since all these grimmer days, I've found a better set of rules to love her by, if only in that fantasy-land of the afterlife.*

THE EXPLOITS OF THAT PARALLEL ETHAN

Curiously, I was drawn to two age groups on my quest: twelve-year-olds, and forty-year-olds. Some subconscious force seemed at work. I often thought, when this younger generation of D&D and Warcraft and Harry Potter fans grows up, will they be permanently trapped in an eternal childhood? I doubt it. As for my own big fear—my own failure to face adulthood, at age 42-plus—I no longer believed that I was still stuck in my twelve-year-old brain. I had grown up, and quickly, just not in the ways I'd expected. I may be the same familiar blend of scared and fool-hardy, immature and sensitive, married to real life and always dreaming of the next better thing. But I'm OK with that. I am this way because I had to be—in order to straddle two worlds.

Perhaps because of the calamity the world has shown me—be it Iraq, global warming, or my personal history—I am compelled to believe in a hidden realm, be it Middle-, Upper- or Lower-earth. But this I know: I don't want to regress to childhood or play cops and robbers again. I don't want to return to some false state of innocence, nor my adolescence. I know I don't want to play Dungeons & Dragons regularly again. I don't want to become a World of Warcraft addict, either. I can't say for sure I'll never read *Lord of the Rings* again, or see the movies. I probably would. Nor am I certain I'd never go back to that spot on Mount Victoria to dig up the figurines. Middle-earth would always be with me, as would the landscapes of New Zealand—its volcanic peaks of Mordor, dim forests of Rivendell, undulating sheep-and-hobbit country of The Shire. Yet I know something had shifted inside me, like a magic portal closing.

---

* JP helped me see this. He remembered the post-aneurysm Sara as "smart and fast" with "tons of friends who . . . were loyal to her and loved her." She was different, "an adult who was not entirely an adult," unpredictable and even fun. Not like other parents. "I liked her," he said.

Early on in my quest, playing games again, I felt too self-conscious to be open to those open-ended realms. I resisted. I told myself I was regressing, or backsliding, into a former self. That I had closed that blue cooler for good. But I am who I am. I can't turn my back on myself. I am the sum of all my many selves—myself at age twelve, age sixteen, age twenty-four, and age forty-two. All of the statistics and die rolls and adventures that made me who I am: a geek. I resolved to adopt Dragon*Con's credo and embrace all of my parts. Putting myself through this quest, my relationship to geekhood moved from detached and skeptical to accepting and celebrating. I used to be a scared kid stashed in a basement rolling dice; now I'd wear that purple shirt with pride in a fool's parade down Main Street. (Don't quote me on that.) I had gathered strength to continue facing the real world. As one old grognard told me, "Life is just a game. If you know the rules, you can get through OK."

I will always struggle with some dissatisfaction with reality. Simple pursuits—folding laundry, mowing the lawn, watching *American Idol*—can seem paralyzingly dull when compared to the exploits of that parallel Ethan in a faraway land. But that's real life. I would always be a fantasy freak, even if I wouldn't always indulge it. I know the reasons why I used to escape. I now understood I didn't *need* to escape again. But that didn't mean I shouldn't, from time to time. As Steve Chenault told me in Lake Geneva, "Maybe it's more important when you're an adult to stop a little bit and have fun, than when you're a kid. What's that commercial? 'Life comes at you fast.' Stuff happens."

But for most of us, it's not mind-numbing escapism we seek. It's a second chance. For most of my adult life, I had wanted a do-over of my childhood. I now knew no do-overs existed. All I could do was march forward into the unknown ahead, live life as a quest or adventure, in the hopes of leveling up, gaining experience, and bettering myself. Perhaps storytelling would create that better kingdom. Perhaps a world might be fashioned—in my mind, anyway—where my mother might make her saving throw and live again, whole and complete. A new story to make up for past suffering. A new realm where we all might have a second chance. Is this not the gift of imagination?

HUNTING WOMEN AND ELF

As for things between my girlfriend and me, our relationship inhabited a half-real, half-fantasy world for almost two more years. I feinted, she dodged. I hit back, she parried. We each wore an invisible ring, or the Ring of Power, when it suited us. I once charged onto her lawn on my horse, in shining armor— figuratively—believing that's who I had wanted to be, or who she had wanted me to be. Sometimes she role-played that damsel in distress. But I didn't want to live in a fantasy relationship any- more.

On a quintessential New England October afternoon, she and I took a walk along an old carriage path and ended up in the middle of the woods. Red and orange maple leaves veiled the forest floor as far as the eye could see. Slivers of blue sky shone through the branches. We stood among the trees and looked at each other.

Among many things she said that afternoon was how she'd always appreciated that I was a kid at heart. "Your Peter Pan qualities. That's why I love you."

Sweet. But wasn't my supposed hesitation to grow up, or her perception of my inability to grow up, the original wellspring of our trouble? Perhaps she meant, *I get it now.* Or that, at times, she could be a little girl herself.

We walked, my arm around her. Were we lovers? Not quite. Would be we lovers again? We didn't know. We both had our Balrogs glowering inside. Nothing felt resolved. We both kept walking.

I did not know where the road would take me, but I had hope. I know now there's no shame in gaming, in role-playing, or in fantasy. I think of my young nephews, Jack and Henry, and how someday I might teach them to play Dungeons & Dragons (assuming their parents are not horrified by a certain geek uncle). I can inspire them to discover magic, wonder, and heroism for themselves. Should I ever have children of my own, I would teach them the same. Or perhaps it worked the other way around: I would be the student, and the children would teach me.

The author storming a castle near his home in Somerville, Massachusetts.

Whomever I might end up with, she doesn't have to be a *Lord of the Rings* freak. But it might help. Surely, this woman has to be easier to find than an elf in the suburbs of Bos—

Wait! What's that I hear? I see something. An elf? An orc? Or some solution to my real-world heartbreak, lurking behind a tree.

"Fear not," I say, strapping my +2 long sword around my waist. I throw my cape over my shoulder. "I'll be right back." And I bound off into the woods and keep running, beyond the next bend of the stream that twists through stands of beeches and maples, and on to some place beyond my sight.

Acknowledgments

Dozens of people in many states, countries, and parallel worlds helped shape this book. Without the help of the individuals acknowledged here, *Fantasy Freaks and Gaming Geeks* would have been a vastly diminished book. Wait—it would have been an impossibility. My apologies in advance for any glaring omissions.

First, I would like to thank Sorche Fairbank, my agent. She recognized the kernel of this story, nurtured its first sprouting, and through her insightful and relentless feedback, helped this baby grow into a beast. She then helped tame the beast. Above all, she kept the faith. I could not have asked for a more dedicated, challenging, and savvy champion. Thank you. (PS: Your 2:00 A.M. ideas are always welcome.)

Keith Wallman, my editor, took a huge chance on a certain procrastinating, doubt-filled, self-taught journalist with a penchant for endless niggling. I am thankful for his wise advice, gentle nudgings, meticulous edits, endless patience, and constant enthusiasm. All writers should be so fortunate to work with him. Also at Globe Pequot Press, I want to thank Jennifer Taber for her attention to every detail, and the art and design team, particularly Bret Kerr and Sheryl Kober, for their fine work; and John Spalding, Bob Sembiante and Geoff Cox for their marketing and publicity efforts. Copy editor Melissa Hayes polished my prose to a high sheen.

My family has given me boundless encouragement and guidance. My father Bill Gilsdorf and stepmother Susan Joiner could not have been more open to this project, or, for that matter, to all of my life's insane projects. Thank you for your loving support. (The money I owe you is in the mail—I promise.)

Thanks to my sister Jessica Gilsdorf, wannabe geek, for egging on my fantasies, and for always being there. Adam Gilsdorf and Joan Glutting have been helpful (and terrified for me) in so many ways. Jess and Adam, thank you for allowing me to tell the tip of our story's iceberg (warning: more to come). I also extend my gratitude to Alice MacKinnon.

I owe so much to Isabelle Sulek, who supported and cared for me for so long. Thank you.

Fellow scribes Kevin Kennedy and Ted Weesner spent many hours slogging through early drafts of this manuscript, raising red flags, and making brilliant suggestions. I could not ask for better comrades, confidants, readers, or drinking buddies. (Dudes: You're next.)

Numerous friends, colleagues, and therapists cheered me, vetted the many ideas raised in this book, provided leads and writerly advice, bought me drinks, left food on my doorstep, watched *Lord of the Rings* with me, and tolerated my whining, excuses, and tardy emails for months. Among them: Lauren Davis, Hisham Matar, Jess Payne, Ravit Reichman, Sage Guyton, Elly Truitt, Litty Mathew, Heather Stimmler-Hall, Bridget Samburg, Laura Harrison, Hathalee Higgs, Sari Boren, Julie Batten, David and Holly Kelleher, and Jenny Cutraro. Pagan Kennedy offered invaluable insider tips on book publicity and the business of being an author. Jennifer Dorsen kindly looked the other way when my rent check was late. Kim Howe let me borrow her car, among other generous gestures. My gratitude also extends to Amy Thibeault, Rhett Richard, and the crew at True Grounds (Somerville's best café), where much of this was written. A special thanks to Page Carter for always listening.

I am also grateful to the Vermont Studio Center, Vermont Arts Council, The Millay Colony for the Arts, the Hall Farm Center, and the Somerville Arts Council / Massachusetts Cultural Council for residencies and financial support of my career, and this book. Chris Castellani, Whitney Scharer, and Sonya Larson at Grub Street, Inc., gave me a writing community in Boston. My many teachers—Greg Jones, Ellen Donkin, and Paul Jenkins among them—ignored my initial hapless writing efforts and offered their encouragement. My students have been inspiring and energizing.

The editors of the various publications that have sustained me deserve recognition. First, John Koch and Joe Yonan at the *Boston Globe,* and Mark Eversman of *Paris Notes,* took a chance on a clueless writer who had no idea how to write a feature story. Other editors generously assigned me articles that became chapters (or parts of chapters) in this book: Jeremy Keehn, K. C. Summers, Stephen Humphries, Francis McGovern, Barbara Ireland, Steve Reddicliffe, Daniel Born, and Kathleen McGowan. At the *Globe,* the following people helped to support my livelihood: Steve Greenlee, Wendy Fox, Anne Fitzgerald, Paul Makishima, Scott Heller, Leighton Klein, Veronica Chao, Jim Concannon, Debbie Jacobs, Marjorie Pritchard, Doug Warren, and Thomasine Berg. Thank you all.

The dozens of fantasy gamers and fans that I interviewed for this book are too numerous to mention by name, but I want to call attention to a few who answered endless questions, put me up for the night, gave me rides, facilitated visits and interviews, provided contacts, and were otherwise extra-generous with their time and expertise in countless ways: Matt Blessing at the Marquette University Department of Special Collections and University Archives; Judith Priestman at Oxford University's Bodleian Library; David Randrup; Mark Egginton; Jen and Matt Ender and Camp Crook'd Cat; the Society for Creative Anachronism's Joyce Oswald and Lynn Shaftic-Averill; Cassy Gordon at Dragon*Con; Steve Chenault at Troll Lord Games; Ian Collier and the Tolkien Society; Andrea Schneider at 38 Studios; everyone at the Forest of Doors, especially Charles Kelley, Lauren Massengill, Christopher Tang, Nick Perretta, and Chris and Rachel Jones; Juan Carlos and Victor Piñeiro Escoriaza; Nissa Ludwig; Jeff Curie; David Vierling; Paul and Joe DeGeorge; Trent Kielley; Mike Scott and Elyse Boucher; Ri Streeter, Peter Lyon, and Gino Acevedo at Weta Workshop; Daniel Reeve; Adriena Daunt at Tourism New

Zealand; Kristin Thompson; Paul Donovan and Kelly Bargh; and Brian Mullane. Questions fielded by David Brin, Gerard Jones, Michael Drout, and John Suler formed the spine of my initial investigation in fantasy escapist entertainment.

I would also like to recognize all of those who gave me or helped me gain free permission (or accepted a greatly-reduced fee) so I might reprint art, text, song lyrics, and images for this book: Dave Nelson (www.davenelson.com); Tami Chappell; Nathan Backous; Mike Scott; Sean "Dragons" Stalzer and The Syndicate; Jane and Dick Kaufmann; Delphine Bourselot and Guédelon; Damian Hess; Alan De Smet; Chris and Rachel Jones; Marty Allen; Katie Page at Porter Novelli; Adam Merksy at Turbine, Inc.; Ron Hussey at Houghton Mifflin Harcourt; Helen McFarland and Rohini Janda at HarperCollins UK; Cathleen Blackburn at Manches LLP and the Tolkien Estate; and Kacy Dishon at Blizzard Entertainment.

It all goes back to JP Glutting, who turned me into a fantasy freak, and for that I am eternally (and mostly) grateful. Discussions with him about our D&D past and his early comments on the manuscript helped chart the course of this book. May you keep rolling natural 20s, good friend. To Mike Wellington, Bill Kaufmann, John Giles, Eric Moore, Eric Hagman, and the rest of the old gang, I say, Grab your vorpal swords—twenty-five years may have passed, but many dungeons remain to be conquered.

Finally, a shout-out to Wendy Harrington: You gave me and this book a kick in the pants when I needed it most. Thank you, you big pain.

Glossary of Terms and Abbreviations

AD&D, or Advanced Dungeons & Dragons: A more complex version of D&D popular in the late 1970s and 1980s.

Aspera: In the LARP called Forest of Doors, a member of a race of water-breathing people who live in a land called Undersea.

Avatar: An on-screen electronic representation of a player in a computer game.

Baggins, Bilbo: The hobbit protagonist of *The Hobbit,* and uncle to Frodo Baggins.

Baggins, Frodo: The hobbit protagonist of *The Lord of the Rings,* who inherits the One Ring from Bilbo and destroys it during his quest to Mount Doom.

Balrog: A menacing, demonic fictional creature, vaguely humanoid and shrouded in fire and darkness, from J. R. R. Tolkien's Middle-earth.

Basilisk: A mythical reptile with a deadly gaze; according to the D&D *Monster Manual,* "it is able to turn to stone any fleshly creature which meets its glance."

Boffer LARP: A live-action role-playing game with combat, usually involving padded weapons.

Character: The fictional persona in a video or role-playing game, controlled by a player.

Con: Short for "convention"—an event where gamers and fans gather to play games, attend seminars, purchase products, etc.

Dungeons & Dragons, or D&D: A tabletop fantasy role-playing game (RPG) created by Gary Gygax and Dave Arneson, involving paper, dice, and rule books. Guided by a referee, participants play characters and use improvisational storytelling to create imaginary adventures in a swords-and-sorcery setting.

Dungeon Master, or DM: The person in a D&D game charged with preparing each game session and describing its imaginary world; a combination of theater director, referee, world-builder, and God. Also known as the "game master." "To DM" is to run a game.

d20: A twenty-sided die, in the form of an icosahedron. Gaming dice have a variety of sides: four, six, eight, twelve, and twenty.

Experience points, or XP: A numeric figure that quantifies a character's progress through a role-playing game. After a certain number of experience points, a character reaches the next level in the game.

Fantasy: A genre of literature, gaming, and pop-culture entertainment that uses magic in its story; typically set in a neo-medieval milieu.

First-person shooter, or FPS: A video-game genre featuring a view of the action through the eyes of a single protagonist; the goal is often to move through a scenario and shoot enemies.

Filk: A musical genre that encompasses songs about novels and characters, computers, technology, pop culture and the culture of fandom itself.

Forest of Doors, or FoD: A combat-oriented live-action role-playing game in the Atlanta, Georgia, area, set in a mysterious frontier between eight "Homeworlds."

Game master, or GM: See "Dungeon Master."

Gandalf: A powerful wizard and leader of the Fellowship in *The Lord of the Rings.*

Gank: To wantonly attack or kill fellow players, without warning, in an online game.

Gelatinous cube: A D&D monster. A 10 foot by 10 foot cube that scours the passageways of dungeons and paralyzes its victims.

Gold farming: Activity in an MMO in which players "farm," or exploit game mechanics, to acquire powerful items or level up characters, and then sell those items or characters to other players.

Gollum: Fictional character from Tolkien's novels. Once a hobbit, the pathetic Gollum possessed the One Ring and it drove him mad.

Griefing: Harassment or other antisocial behavior in an online game intended to cause grief to other players. A "griefer" engages in griefing.

Grinding: Activity in an MMO in which players engage in repetitive game-play, such as killing monsters strictly for experience points, in order to level up characters.

Grognard: Slang for wargamer. Typically an experienced gamer who prefers the older version of a game or rules.

Gygax, E. Gary: (1938–2008) The co-creator of Dungeons & Dragons and a pioneer of the tabletop role-playing game genre.

Halberd: A pole weapon with an axlike blade and spike mounted on a long shaft.

Hit points: In an RPG, the amount of damage a character or creature can take, or the amount of life force a character has left. The damage caused by weapons and spells is also measured in hit points.

Hobbit: Tolkien's fictional race of human-like creatures; they are short and fun-loving, with large ears and hairy feet. *The Hobbit* is Tolkien's 1937 children's fantasy book.

In-game: Used to describe actions that take place within a game world.

In-period: When an item, word, food product, etc. matches a particular game or reenactment society's world. See "Period."

IRL: In real life—versus activities that occur "in-game."

LARP, or live-action role-playing game: A type of RPG wherein players physically act out their characters' actions and dress in costume.

Lembas: In Tolkien's world, hearty bread made by the Elves used for sustenance on long journeys. One small bite is enough to fill the stomach of a grown man.

Level: A number that represents a character's power and experience, akin to a rank. To "level up" is to increase a character's power by achieving a higher level.

The Lord of the Rings, or _Rings_: The epic fantasy masterwork novel by J. R. R. Tolkien, published in 1954–55, set in his imaginary world of Middle-earth.

Lowbie: A low-level and often weak character in a game, often played by an experienced player (vs. "newbie").

Massively Multiplayer Online Game, or MMO, MMPOG, MMOG: A video game played on the Internet, often simultaneously by thousands of players; its milieu and action takes place in an imaginary world.

Massively Multiplayer Online Role-Playing Game, or MMORPG: An MMO with a role-playing element. Users play characters that can interact with one another in a virtual world.

Middle-earth: Tolkien's imaginary world, and the setting for _The Lord of the Rings_ and his other fantasy works.

Muggle: A common or ignorant person; in the _Harry Potter_ books, a person without magical powers.

Mundane: Literally, "of this earthly world rather than a heavenly or spiritual one." In the SCA or games, someone or something outside of the game or reenactment world. A person's mundane name is his or her real-world name.

Multi-User Dungeon, or MUD: An online game set in a virtual world that uses no graphics; text describes the action and setting.

Newb, newbie, noob, or noobie: Someone new to an activity or subculture.

Orc: The humanoid creatures of J. R. R. Tolkien's creation who serve as evil foot soldiers in Middle-earth.

Out-of-game: Used to describe actions that take place outside a game world.

Out of period, or OOP: When an item, word, food product, etc. would not exist in a particular game or reenactment society's world. Computers would be "OOP" in medieval Europe.

Period: The confined time period of a game or reenactment society's world. Someone who attempts medieval European "period" cooking would follow relevant recipes and avoid ingredients such as tomatoes that were unavailable prior to the sixteenth century.

Player vs. environment, or PvE: An online game-play mode where characters primarily fight other creatures, compete against the computer-controlled game world, and are prohibited from fighting each other.

Player vs. player, or PvP: An online game-play mode where characters are allowed to fight each other.

Raid: In a game such as World of Warcraft, a group battle involving several players, who fight together against a common foe.

Role-playing game, or RPG: A game involving players who take on the roles of characters and, in an improvised fashion, create a collaborative, in-game narrative.

Saving throw: In D&D and other role-playing games, a roll of dice in a game that gives a character the chance to avoid the effects of a spell or poison and survive.

SCAdian: A member of the Society for Creative Anachronism.

Science fiction, or SF: A genre of literature, gaming, and pop-culture entertainment that often involves science or technology and speculation about the future; sometimes called "sci-fi."

Society for Creative Anachronism, or SCA: An organization dedicated to researching and re-creating the arts and skills of pre-seventeenth-century Europe.

Subculture: A group of people whose identifying activities differentiate them from the larger culture; hence, "gaming subculture," or "punk subculture."

Tabletop game: A game, such as a card game, board game, miniature war game, or D&D, played face-to-face with simple items such as paper, dice, and rule books.

Tactical Studies Rules, or TSR: Gary Gygax's former Lake Geneva, Wisconsin, game company that created and published D&D.

Tauren: A race of nomadic creatures in World of Warcraft. They are humanoid, bovine in appearance, with hooves and horns.

Tolkien, J. R. R.: (1892–1973) The English philologist and professor recognized as the father of fantasy; he wrote *The Hobbit* and *The Lord of the Rings.*

'Toon: Short for cartoon, or a player's digital avatar in a video game.

Trebuchet: A machine used in medieval siege warfare for hurling large stones or other missiles, usually with a sling, arm, and counterweight for power.

Wizards of the Coast, or WotC: Seattle-based publisher of trading card and tabletop role-playing games, many with fantasy settings, including Magic: The Gathering and Dungeons & Dragons, and Avalon Hill war games.

World of Warcraft, or WoW: A fantasy MMORPG played by some 11.5 million people worldwide, and set in the fictional game world of Azeroth; created by Blizzard Entertainment of Irvine, California.

Photo Credits

Page vi: Courtesy of the author.

Page x: Courtesy of the author.

Page xiii: Courtesy of the author.

Page 3: Courtesy of Jane Kaufmann.

Page 10: Courtesy of the author.

Page 13: Courtesy of the author.

Page 19: Courtesy of the author.

Page 36: Courtesy of HarperCollins Publishers Ltd, © John Wyatt.

Page 44: Courtesy of the author.

Page 54: Courtesy of the author.

Page 66: Photograph of Gary Gygax © Alan De Smet.

Page 93: Courtesy of Rachel Jones and Chris Jones.

Page 102: Courtesy of Tami L. Chappell.

Page 107: Courtesy of Tami L. Chappell.

Page 113: Courtesy of Mike L. Scott.

Page 120: Courtesy of Mike L. Scott.

Page 127: Courtesy of Guédelon, © Guédelon.

Page 135: Courtesy of Guédelon, © Christian Duchemin.

Page 147: Courtesy of Nathan Backous.

Page 169: Courtesy of the author.

Page 173: Courtesy of the author.

Page 176: Courtesy of D. Randrup.

Page 197: LOTRO Screenshots © 2009 Saul Zaentz Co. All rights reserved.
™ Saul Zaentz Co. under license to Turbine, Inc.

Page 198: Courtesy of Blizzard Entertainment, Inc. World of Warcraft and Blizzard Entertainment are trademarks or registered trademarks of Blizzard Entertainment, Inc. in the U.S. and/or other countries.

Page 209: Courtesy of Sean Stalzer and The Syndicate (www.LLTS.org).

Page 213: LOTRO Screenshots © 2009 Saul Zaentz Co. All rights reserved.
™ Saul Zaentz Co. under license to Turbine, Inc.

Page 222: Courtesy of Dave Nelson, © 2008 www.davenelson.com and © 2008 DragonCon/ACE, Inc. All rights reserved.

Page 233: Courtesy of Dave Nelson, © 2008 www.davenelson.com and © 2008 DragonCon/ACE, Inc. All rights reserved.

Page 248: Courtesy of the author.

Page 250: Courtesy of the author.

Page 253: Courtesy of the author.

Page 277: Courtesy of the U.S. Army.

Page 281: Courtesy of the author.

Page 288: Courtesy of HarperCollins Publishers Ltd and Marquette University Libraries, J.R.R. Tolkien Collection, 3/3/10; © J.R.R. Tolkien.

Page 295: Courtesy of Ted Weesner.

Permissions

Portions of this book originally appeared, in vastly different form, in the following publications: *Boston Globe, Boston Globe Magazine, Washington Post, The Christian Science Monitor,* the *Common Review,* the *Walrus, Psychology Today,* and LiteraryTraveler.com. The author is grateful to the editors of these publications for their help in shaping the stories, and for assigning them in the first place.

Excerpt from *The Letters of J.R.R. Tolkien,* edited by Humphrey Carpenter with the assistance of Christopher Tolkien. Copyright © 1981 by George Allen & Unwin (Publishers) Ltd. Reprinted by permission of Houghton Mifflin Harcourt Publishing Company and HarperCollins Publishers Ltd. All rights reserved.

Wizards of the Coast and Dungeons and Dragons are trademarks of Wizards of the Coast, LLC. *Dungeons & Dragons Basic Rules Set 1, Advanced Dungeons & Dragons Monster Manual* 4th Edition, *Into the Shadowhaunt,* a 4th edition Module, *Advanced Dungeons & Dragons Dungeon Masters Guide,* and *Dungeons & Dragons Rulebook Basic Set* are © Wizards of the Coast, LLC. Excerpts used with Permission.

Quotations from *The Hero with a Thousand Faces* by Joseph Campbell, copyright © 1949, 1976, 2008; reprinted by permission of Joseph Campbell Foundation (jfc.org).

Excerpt from "On Fairy-Stories" and from *Tree and Leaf* by J.R.R. Tolkien. Copyright © 1964 by George Allen & Unwin Ltd. Copyright © Renewed 1992 by John F. R. Tolkien and Christopher R. Tolkien, and Priscilla M.A.R. Tolkien. Copyright © 1988 by The Tolkien Trust. Reprinted by permission of Houghton Mifflin Harcourt Publishing Company and Harper Collins Publishers Ltd. All rights reserved.

Excerpts from *The Lord of the Rings* by J.R.R. Tolkien, edited by Christopher Tolkien. Copyright © 1954, 1955, 1965, 1966 by J.R.R. Tolkien. Copyright © Renewed 1982, 1983 by Christopher R. Tolkien, Michael H.R. Tolkien, John F.R. Tolkien, and Priscilla M.A.R. Tolkien. Copyright © Renewed 1993, 1994 by Christopher R. Tolkien, John F.R. Tolkien, and Priscilla M.A.R. Tolkien. Reprinted by permission of Houghton Mifflin Harcourt Publishing Company and Harper Collins Publishers Ltd. All rights reserved.

Except from www.hordelings.com posting courtesy of Peter Nelson.

Excerpt from Forest of Doors Web site http://www.forestofdoors.com and *Forest of Doors* First Edition rulebook courtesy of Adrian McCleer, Charles Kelley, Mike Boaz, and Christopher Tang.

Except from "The 10 Real Reason Why Geeks Make Better Lovers" by Regina Lynn. Article originally appeared on Wired.com.

Excerpts from http://merouda.blogspot.com copyright © 2008, Elyse Carole Boucher.

Excerpt from www.yankeesiege.com courtesy of Steven Seigars.

Song lyrics for "Penny Arcade Theme" from the album *Nerdcore Rising,* © 2005 by Damian Hess, published by Nerdcore Fervor Conglomerated (ASCAP).

Song lyrics for "The Weapon," "Voldemort Can't Stop the Rock," and "Save Ginny Weasley" courtesy of Paul and Joe DeGeorge. Dumbledore lyrics "D.Bowla" and "U Down w/ OOTP?" reprinted with permission of the artist.

Song lyrics for "The Gary Gygax Song" written and performed by Uncle Monsterface.

Excerpt from valgards.livejournal.com courtesy of Dr. Michael Cramer. Used with permission.

Excerpt from World of Warcraft Game Guide courtesy of Blizzard Entertainment, Inc. World of Warcraft and Blizzard Entertainment are trademarks or registered trademarks of Blizzard Entertainment, Inc. in the U.S. and/or other countries.

Excerpts from Dragon*Con program schedule and "convention policies" © 2008 Dragon-Con/ACE, Inc.

Index

About the Author

Photo courtesy of Wendy Harrington

After playing Dungeons & Dragons religiously in the 1970s and 1980s, Ethan Gilsdorf went on to be a movie projectionist, cemetery groundskeeper, and bookstore manager before settling into the life of a poet, teacher, and journalist. In the U.S. and in Paris, he's worked as a freelance correspondent, guidebook writer, and film and restaurant reviewer. Now based in Somerville, Massachusetts, his travel, arts, and pop culture stories appear regularly in the *New York Times, Boston Globe,* and *Christian Science Monitor,* and have been published in other magazines and newspapers including *National Geographic Traveler, Psychology Today,* and the *Washington Post.* He has also been a guest on talk radio as a fantasy and escapism expert. He does not own elf ears, but he has kept all his old D&D gear, and has been known to host a *Lord of the Rings* party or two. Follow Ethan's adventures at www.ethangilsdorf.com.